HOUSE
Unauthorized

OTHER TITLES IN THE SMART POP SERIES

HOUSE
Unauthorized

Vasculitis, Clinic Duty,
and Bad Bedside Manner

edited by
LEAH WILSON

BENBELLA BOOKS, INC.
Dallas, Texas

BenBella Books, Inc.
6440 N. Central Expressway, Suite 503
Dallas, TX 75206
www.benbellabooks.com
Send feedback to feedback@benbellabooks.com

Printed in the United States of America
10 9 8 7 6 5 4 3 2 1

Library of Congress Cataloging-in-Publication Data

House unauthorized : Vasculitis, clinic duty, and bad bedside manner / edited by Leah Wilson.
   p. cm.
 ISBN 1-933771-23-2
 1. House, M. D. I. Wilson, Leah.

 PN1992.77.H63H68 2007
 791.45'72--dc22

                  2007030714

Proofreading by Emily Chauvier and Stacia Seaman
Cover design by Allison Bard
Text design and composition by Laura Watkins
Printed by Bang Printing
Cover photo © Corbis Images

Distributed by Independent Publishers Group
To order call (800) 888-4741
www.ipgbook.com

For special sales contact Robyn White at robyn@benbellabooks.com

CONTENTS

HOUSE'S BRAIN: THE PSYCHOLOGY OF GREGORY HOUSE

WILSON, CUDDY, AND THE COTTAGES: OTHER CHARACTERS OF INTEREST

TUESDAYS AT 9/8 CENTRAL
House, the Show

A show like House M.D. *doesn't just come forth fully formed; it's the end result of months or more of work by writers, directors, producers, designers, and a long list of other folks who labor behind the scenes. Glenn McDonald treats us to his imaginative version of one part of the process, and along the way highlights exactly what it is about* House *that really makes it* House.

HOUSE, T.B.A.

GLENN MCDONALD

a s is typical with network television pilots, the initial concept for Fox's enormously popular medical drama *House* underwent many permutations before finally making it to the small screen. Attentive viewers will recall that when the pilot first debuted, the full title was *House M.D.* This was intended to better convey the show's essential structure as a medical procedural, as opposed to, say, a forensic procedural, police procedural, military procedural, legal procedural, military-legal procedural, historical procedural, or any of the other countless procedurals that now constitute 95 percent of television network drama.

What is not commonly known, however, is that for much of its incubation period, House wasn't a medical drama at all. Well before the pilot episode was even filmed, the concept for *House* had gone through several substantial, even radical changes. In fact, the very profession of the title character was in flux from the first pitch meetings. Only after a long and difficult process of rewriting did Gregory House find his home at Princeton-Plainsboro Teaching Hospital.

What follows is a collection of script excerpts from earlier versions of the *House* pilot.

"HOUSE, HEATING AND PLUMBING CONTRACTOR"
PILOT EPISODE
DRAFT #4b

INT. RESIDENTIAL BATHROOM — DAY

GREGORY HOUSE, Heating and Plumbing Contractor, addresses three of his apprentice workers in a cramped suburban bathroom. Listening attentively are ERIC FOREMAN, attractive and ambitious; ALLI- SON CAMERON, attractive and earnest; and ROBERT CHASE, attractive and arrogant. After INTRO CRED- ITS, we CUT to the scene, in media res. . . .

> HOUSE
> . . . so remember, that which does not kill you only gives you third-degree burns on your face and hands. Now, then, let's turn our attention to this charming ceramic washbasin. It appears to present as a leaky faucet. What else do we know?

CAMERON and FOREMAN share a frustrated look.

> FOREMAN
> It *is* a leaky faucet.

> HOUSE
> To the dim and inattentive layman, yes. But we're all trade school graduates here, I think, right? Cameron, what do you see?

> CAMERON
> I see a faucet. It's leaking.

4

                    HOUSE
No, goddammit. You're not thinking!

HOUSE brings out a whiteboard on an easel and
writes: "LEAKY FAUCET".

                    HOUSE
Let's start over: Chase, how would you
describe the humidity in here? Dry?

                    CHASE
No, it's rather damp, actually. A bit
moldy, perhaps.

                    HOUSE
Precisely.

HOUSE writes "HUMID" on the whiteboard.

                HOUSE (cont'd.)
Foreman, what about the barometric pressure?

                    FOREMAN
How the hell should I know?

                    HOUSE
Excellent rejoinder. You're right, it's
completely irrelevant. Just keeping you
on your toes. Cameron, what do you notice
about the accoutrements in this bathroom?

                    CAMERON
Well, there are a lot of bath toys.

                    HOUSE
Bath toys! Right!

HOUSE writes "BATH TOYS" on the whiteboard.

                    HOUSE (cont'd.)
What kind of bath toys?

                    CAMERON
Rubber duckies.

                    CHASE
Elmo washcloth.

                    FOREMAN
Bubble bath.

HOUSE writes the new items on the whiteboard.

                    HOUSE
What kind of bubble bath?

                    FOREMAN
Uh, Scooby Doo. Scooby Doo bubble bath.

                    HOUSE
Thank you. Specificity is critical in
diagnostics! The smallest detail can
spell the difference between life and
death for your patient!

                    CAMERON
You mean, your plumbing fixture.

                    HOUSE
Don't interrupt. We can deduce from the
evidence gathered so far that a small
child uses this bathroom regularly, probably 3 to 3 1/2 years old, quite verbal,
prone to tantrums, green eyes, left-hand-

ed, likely will grow up to be a Cubs or Reds fan.

                    CAMERON
                  (to FOREMAN)
How can he possibly know . . . .

                    FOREMAN
                  (to CAMERON)
Let him go, he's on a roll.

                    HOUSE
Furthermore, the dampness and slight odor of industrial resin suggests that this leak is merely symptomatic of a more fundamental problem. Note the brand of lighting fixtures. Manufactured in China. Shijiazhuang Province, if I'm not mistaken. We also know that this house is more than three miles from the interstate, but less than five miles. Now then, considering that the CD collection in the other room is primarily country music, and that Democrats hold a slight advantage in the state Senate, we can safely come to our conclusion.

HOUSE hands flashlight to FOREMAN.

                    HOUSE (cont'd.)
Foreman, look down there into the crawlspace, notice the piping between the heat exchanger and the backflow valve. Copper-nickel alloy, installed in 1972. No, no . . . 1973. Susceptible to corrosion when adjacent to a trap seal or stack vent.

                    FOREMAN
He's right!

                    HOUSE
    Replace it.

HOUSE pops two Vicodin and starts to leave.

                    CAMERON
    But what about the leaky faucet?

HOUSE steps over and turns the sink knob.

                    HOUSE
    You just have to twist it really tight.

As we can plainly see in this early draft, many of the narrative elements of *House* as a procedural drama were already in place. Yet House's diagnostic genius seems somehow misplaced in this milieu.

    In the following script sample, we can observe the writers starting to draw a bead on House's persona as a lovable misanthrope. Note the audacity with which the title character is kept deliberately off-screen.

"HOUSE, TELEMARKETER"
PILOT EPISODE
DRAFT #5a

INT. KITCHEN — DAY

A sunny suburban household. KITTY PRESTON, a 30-something homemaker, washes the dishes. The phone rings.

                    KITTY
    Hello?

                    HOUSE
    Mrs. Preston?

                    KITTY
    Yes, speaking.

8

                    HOUSE
This is Gregory House, calling on behalf
of Geico. Look, I've got a whole
spiel written down here on how you can
save up to 15 percent on your car insurance, but let's cut to the chase, shall
we?

                    KITTY
Pardon me?

                    HOUSE
You're, what, forty-something, I imagine?
Good looks slowly succumbing to weight
gain and wrinkles. Gravity having its way
with your anatomy. Ass getting fat.

                    KITTY
Who the hell is this?

                    HOUSE
I told you that already. Memory starting
to go, too, huh? Pity, that. Middle age
is ravaging, I can sympathize. But the
point is, with age you should at least be
enjoying a relatively stable financial
situation. Better than when you were in
college, blowing all your cash on alcohol
and experimenting with alternative
lifestyles. You remember: the shallow
politics, the raves, spiking the punch
with Ecstasy. . . .

                    KITTY
What?

                    HOUSE
Methylenedioxymethamphetamine. Stimulates
secretion of serotonin and dopamine in

the brain, inducing a general sense of openness, empathy, energy, euphoria, and well-being. Makes you want to dance to bad techno music and make out with your roommate.

> KITTY
> I don't know who you are or what kind of game you're playing. . . .

> HOUSE
> Look, sister, I haven't got all day. You want to switch over your car insurance or what? I promise I won't tell anyone about your roommate.

> KITTY
> Go to hell!

KITTY hangs up the phone.

The phone rings again. KITTY picks up.

> HOUSE
> My point is still valid.

Clearly, the character of Gregory House is coming into sharper focus. This draft of the script was rejected by producers, however, when the concept of telemarketer-as-protagonist tested poorly with audiences.

Next we have a diversion into yet another profession, one with which House would seem well-paired. Note here the introduction of the authority figure, Cuddy, who would survive into the final incarnation of the show.

"HOUSE, TENURED PROFESSOR OF ENGLISH"
PILOT EPISODE
DRAFT #3a

INT. CLASSROOM — DAY

PROFESSOR GREGORY HOUSE arrives for his first class teaching at the prestigious WILSHIRE ACADE-MY. The head administrator of the college, DEAN LISA CUDDY, has hired HOUSE, knowing him to be a brilliant, if eccentric, scholar. Aware of his abrasive personality, she insists on monitoring his first few classes.

HOUSE enters, pulls down an overhead projection screen, and pops a handful of pills.

> HOUSE
> Greetings, humbly endeavoring young stu-dents. In the interest of saving time and avoiding your breathtakingly boring under-graduate questions, let's set a few ground rules. My name is Professor Gregory House. You may call me "Professor," "Professor House" or—preferably—"Exalted One." I am a Harvard-educated author and scholar, published in more places that you can comfortably imagine, with a dual specialty of criti-cal theory and postmodern American liter-ature. Most importantly, I am fully tenured. For those only dimly aware of the marvelous institution of tenure, this means I can say any damn thing I please and get away with it, all in the name of academic freedom. In fact, it's virtually impossible for me to get fired, isn't that right, Dean Cuddy?

CUDDY
(whispering fiercely)
Watch it, House!

HOUSE
I'm sorry, where are my manners? Class, this is Dean Lisa Cuddy, administrator, overseer, and final arbiter of your education and my paycheck. If you think she's cute now, you should have seen her a few years ago. Speaking of which, you may have heard rumors that Dean Cuddy and I have been intimate in the past. I want to be very clear. For the record, I can neither confirm nor deny whether I have, in fact, tapped that fine ass.

CUDDY
Professor House! A word with you privately, please?

HOUSE
(to the class, cocking his head)
Did you hear something just then? A kind of squeaking sound? Moving on. I will not be keeping attendance records. I will not be grading your papers—that's what teaching assistants are for. They will also be preparing your syllabi and reading lists. I am, however, contractually obliged to hold office hours for individual consultations, and I encourage you all to forget that fact instantly; right now. If for some reason you do wish to consult with me, please remember that I am a drug addict, armed with a cane. Oak. Hardwood. Density of about point-seven-five grams per cubic centimeter.

CUDDY

Professor House! Now!

HOUSE

There's that sound again. . . . Finally, I will be holding forth—voluminously, inspirationally—every Tuesday and Thursday in this room from 11:00 to 11:50 A.M. Attend or don't, as you wish. As the semester progresses, I will allow for limited discussion, at which point I will be able to discern who amongst you is actually deserving of the education your parents are underwriting. I will follow up with you individually, and if you pay attention and do as I say, you will have your choice of fully funded Ph.D. scholarship programs when you graduate. The rest of you will get "C"s, provided you do not bother me. Any questions? Good. I brought a DVD for today, "General Hospital." Luke and Laura's wedding. Behold and weep.

HOUSE pops the DVD in, and turns to leave.

CUDDY

House!

HOUSE

Ah, yes. Dean Cuddy. I've been meaning to speak with you. When do I get my first sabbatical?

Note the biographical details that are beginning to coalesce: House's disregard of professional behavioral norms, the suggestion of an intimate past between House and Cuddy, and House's affection for daytime TV dramas.

In the next excerpt, we see a certain creative desperation setting in among the show creators. Frustrated with their inability to find a proper environment for House, the writers attempt to co-opt the success of other shows targeting a similar demographic.

"HOUSE, PRISONER WHO REALLY WANTS TO BREAK OUT!" [WORKING TITLE] PILOT EPISODE DRAFT #3b

EXT. PRISON YARD — DAY

GREGORY HOUSE, convicted Vicodin trafficker, is lifting weights with other inmates of Cell Block D. His best friend and cellmate, JAMES "J-BLOOD" WILSON, is finishing up a prison tattoo on House's stomach. It reads: CURMUDGEON LIFE. They are playing a game to pass the time, trying to guess the crimes and backgrounds of the other prisoners.

                    HOUSE
          How about that guy?

                    WILSON
          Hmm. He's built; got some serious scar-
          ring. Shaved head, spiderweb tattoo. I'd
          say Aryan Nation.

                    HOUSE
          Nice. Very literal. Very one-dimensional.
          Why do I even bother talking to you? Note
          the limp; the way he keeps looking over
          his shoulder. He's skirting the Crips
          territory, too. Suicidal or narcissistic.
          That slight twitch in the upper left
          quadriceps. Anaerobic. Lactic acid build-

up, most likely. Let me think. Allowing
for differentials, I'd say . . .
pseudopsychopathic personality disorder;
secondary paranoic/narcissistic traits;
he's in for aggravated assault and armed
robbery; gang is the Nazi Lowriders.

                WILSON
How do you DO that?

                HOUSE
Actually, he's my cousin.

Obviously, the idea was a non-starter, although it's interesting to note these early details suggesting that House's real ambitions point toward the medical field. Unfortunately, this avenue of development—later to prove so very successful—was not immediately pursued. Instead, the producers were forced by network executives to place the character of House into a more sports-oriented environment designed to attract the desirable 18–35 male audience.

"HOUSE, M.L.B."
PILOT EPISODE
DRAFT #6a

EXT. MAJOR LEAGUE BASEBALL DIAMOND — DAY

GREGORY HOUSE, #19, stands at first base having
just drawn a base-on-balls from the opposing
pitcher. HOUSE is a brilliant, if eccentric,
major-league shortstop with a reputation for
unpredictability. He takes a short lead off the
bag while chatting with the OPPOSING FIRST BASE-
MAN. Oddly, he is using a cane.

                HOUSE
Your pitcher is grossly overweight. Have
you noticed that? Why is it that pitchers

get away with being fatties? Well, pitchers and first basemen, come to think of
it.

> OPPOSING FIRST BASEMAN
> Go screw yourself.

> HOUSE
> No time for that right now. In case you
> haven't noticed, we're in the middle of a
> game here.

The PITCHER throws to first, attempting a pick-
off play. HOUSE retreats to the bag, easily
beating the tag.

> HOUSE
> Nice tag, Shirley. Does your husband play
> in this league?

> OPPOSING FIRST BASEMAN
> Kiss my ass.

> HOUSE
> You seem to have a bit of a fixation with
> me. Don't worry, it's nothing to be
> ashamed of. I am an uncommonly handsome
> man. I've noticed that macho, athletic
> types tend to sublimate their sexual
> desires by using aggressive language. So
> what are you into? Rough sex? Casual sex?

> OPPOSING FIRST BASEMAN
> Please shut up!

> HOUSE
> Rough, casual sex?

THE BATTER hits a screaming line-drive to first

base. The OPPOSING FIRST BASEMAN, distracted, flubs the play and the ball bounces past him into the outfield.

                    HOUSE
              (limping to second base)
    Oopsy. Well, gotta run! Keep practicing,
    you'll get better!

CUT TO:

EXT. DUGOUT — DAY

HOUSE is holding forth to the other players and managers in his favorite spot — in front of a whiteboard. The team manager, SKIPPER CUDDY, looks on irritably.

                    HOUSE
    . . . so we've got a two-one count, run-
    ners on first and third, southpaw on the
    mound, lefty at the plate, infield play-
    ing deep. What do you see?

                    PLAYER #1
    Double steal?

                    HOUSE
    Not with Rodriguez at first. He's got no
    speed in the late innings.

                    PLAYER #2
    Suicide squeeze?

                    HOUSE
    Lefty at the plate! Pay attention!

                    PLAYER #3
    Hit-and-run?

> HOUSE
> Not with those elevated sodium levels—
> he's been eating sunflower seeds all day.
> Could be ischemic bowel. Or acute viral
> gastroenteritis.

> PLAYER #1
> Hereditary angioedema?

> PLAYER #2
> Small cell vasculitis?

> HOUSE
> Order an EGD and colonoscopy. And bring
> the infield in.

> SKIPPER CUDDY
> What the hell are you people talking
> about?

Clearly, the writers had finally found the proper direction for their title character. A medical consultant was brought on board, and *House* quickly found its bearings as a medical procedural. There were till a few road bumps—a pilot draft for *House: Equine Veterinarian* made the rounds, but, predictably, found very little traction.

As improbable as it seems, this sort of lengthy development process is not at all uncommon in Hollywood. Many are the Burbank storage rooms littered with unsuccessful early drafts of what would later become legendary television programs, including forgotten gems such as *Gary's Anatomy*, *Desperate Housepainters*, *CSI: Akron*, and *23*. The creative development of a television pilot script is an endlessly fascinating pageant, but as House ably demonstrates, in the end it is character that counts. And America loves nothing better than a hyper-articulate, pill-popping, emotionally damaged misanthrope.

GLENN MCDONALD writes about the busy intersections among film, TV, technology, games, and pop culture for various Web sites and magazines. He is the author of *Deal Me In!: Online Cardrooms, Big-Time Tournaments & the New Poker*, and a contributing writer to the National Public Radio program *Wait, Wait . . . Don't Tell Me*. His humor essays have been described as "grammatically consistent" and "remarkably frequent." He lives in a series of fortified underground bunkers, or virtually at glenn-mcdonald.com.

Doctor shows these days are a dime a dozen. You can expect a certain level of quality from them, but rarely anything more. House, though, is the exception— right? Not really, Steven Rubio says . . . or at least not most of the time.

"THAT WAS A TEN"

Why House Is More Ordinary Than House

STEVEN RUBIO

He's a Jerk

There's no accounting for taste.

A group called the Parents Television Council announced in its annual "Faith in a Box" analysis of religion on television that Fox was "by far the most anti-religious network" when it comes to prime-time broadcasting (Gildemeister). Some of their reasons were unsurprising. They seemed to be particularly angry at *Family Guy* and *The Simpsons*. But they also cited an episode of another Fox series, *House*, where, as they explained, "House tells a religious patient that the patient is either psychotic or a scam artist for believing that God speaks to him."

The PTC quite accurately describes the titular character as follows:

> Dr. House is a genius but also an eccentric and a borderline misanthropist. He's has [sic] been in severe pain for years and has become addicted to Vicodin. In addition, his pain has made him cantankerous and resentful. His social manners are questionable and House shows almost zero tolerance to those

21

patients who complain about trivial issues, lie to skip work, or claim to have a disease not recognized as such by traditional medicine. House is a scientist more interested in diseases than in people . . . (PTC).

The PTC apparently thinks this makes *House* a bad show, while I'd argue it is the main thing that makes *House* worth watching.

On *House*, we have one of the great characters in television, acted by Hugh Laurie at the top of his game. And it's not just Laurie: without House's snarky behavior, this would be just another doctor show, no matter how good Hugh Laurie is. House is a terrific character who wouldn't be nearly as terrific if he didn't have to suffer from self-analysis and he suffers because he is flawed, not in the curable way of an Andy Sipowicz, but in a fundamentally misanthropic way that is fairly unique for popular television.

Laurie is capable of taking a character with no apparent signs of empathy or kindness and getting the audience to understand, through his acting, that there is something more underneath the surface. Yet it often seems as if the people making *House* don't know what they've got. It is a bit silly to complain that Hugh Laurie's employers don't appreciate their star when Laurie is the focus of much of the show's promotion. Fox is perfectly willing to let Laurie represent *House* in the public eye. But such confidence in the star isn't always as clear when you look at actual episodes from the series. *House* generally relies on its formula, only breaking away about once a season for a Very Special Episode that they can use to get Laurie nominated for an Emmy. Watch enough episodes and you can practically set your clock in advance and predict what will happen and when. The result, as often as not, insults the viewer, undercutting the best thing they've got (Laurie and the character of House), as if they don't believe their good fortune.

Take a highly regarded early season three episode, "Lines in the Sand" (3-4). The patient *du jour* is a ten-year-old autistic boy. The episode, unsurprisingly, follows the standard formula (unusual, hard-to-diagnose disease; several red herring diagnoses; a trip breaking-and-entering to the patient's home looking for clues; and an aha moment for House a few minutes before the end of the episode where he solves the mystery; all mixed with interplay designed to show what a jerk House is). But "Lines in the Sand" rises above the normal *House* episode largely by being better than most at the little things which make *House* a fine series, in particular his interactions with colleagues and patients (one hesitates to use the word "friend" to describe any of them, even House's purported best pal Wilson). *House* often walks a thin line between subtlety and a more obvious pounding on the viewer's head. Exquisite moments arise when the subtle approach takes precedence. It is then that Hugh Laurie is allowed to convey depths in the character of House that aren't apparent on the surface. *House* fails when they lose sight of that subtlety. And that is when the audience is insulted.

House makes an unusually deep connection with the patient in "Lines in the Sand," because, as he points out at one point, he envies the autistic child:

> This kid doesn't have to pretend to be interested in your back pain or your excretions or your grandma's itchy place. Imagine how liberating it would be to live a life free of all the mind-numbing social niceties. I don't pity this kid, I envy him.

Unlike House, we in the audience feel pity for the autistic kid, but we do have an object for our envy: House himself. We, too, can imagine being liberated from social niceties. House generally acts as if he is already liberated in that regard, and one of the pleasures of watching *House* is seeing its main character stomp on those niceties.

Wilson makes a different connection to House's behavior. Mirroring the online guessing of many fans, Wilson wonders if perhaps House has Asperger's Syndrome, a mild version of autism that features "difficulty establishing friendships and playing with peers" and "trouble accepting conventional social rules." Hospital administrator Dr. Cuddy gets directly to the point, replying, "House doesn't have Asperger's. The diagnosis is much simpler. He's a jerk." She apparently convinces Wilson, as he later lectures House:

You're not autistic. You don't even have Asperger's. You wish you did. It would exempt you from the rules. Give you freedom. Absolve you of responsibility. Let you date seventeen-year-olds. But, most important, it would mean that you're not just a jerk.

In these moments, *House* approaches excellence. The show's formula helps illuminate the main character. Note that Wilson's speech is not intended to turn his friend into a better person (although he does make the attempt at other times in the series), but instead describes House in the same terms Cuddy had used earlier: he is a jerk. (This is a good thing because it rejects the usual "let's learn a lesson" approach to television in favor of character-driven writing.)

There are advantages to having House remain a jerk, the biggest one being that it separates *House* from the pack of medical shows on TV. There must be a balance, though, between his jerky side and his potential salvation. Some of us are just happy to have an energetic curmudgeon on our televisions, but without the possibility of a "New House," the show would stagnate. In "Lines in the Sand," the balance is struck at the end of the episode, when the autistic boy gives his treasured PlayStation Portable to House (House regularly plays video games, while the boy often seemed able to connect solely to his PSP). Hugh Laurie plays the scene just right; we see the tiniest breakdown in his defenses as he accepts the gift (and young Braeden Lemasters is also muted and effective as the boy).

If the creators of *House* truly trusted their audience, the episode would end with the boy and his family leaving the hospital, with perhaps a last shot of House's face. But, as is too often the case, our intelligence is not trusted. First, as the boy and his family are preparing to leave, House says to Wilson that on a scale of one to ten, having your child saved from death is a ten, but the parents are "clocking at a very tepid 6.5" because while they love their son, they will be returning to a very difficult life as parents of an autistic boy. The family begins to leave, the boy gives House his PSP, they exchange looks, the family walks out of the hospital . . . and Wilson pipes up with, "That was a ten."

An entire attitude toward the audience can be summed up in those four words. A show that trusted its audience wouldn't need Wilson's comment to drop like an anvil onto our collective head. When Wilson explains what has just occurred, we are once again left to wonder if the show's masterminds realize that Hugh Laurie can convey the necessary emotions without superfluous explanatory dialogue.

Nor are they done. As Wilson speaks, Ben Harper's voice swells on the soundtrack, singing "Waiting on an Angel":

> Waiting on an angel
> One to carry me home
> Hope you come to see me soon
> Cause I don't want to go alone

There is nothing wrong with Harper's song, but there is everything wrong with its use at that moment. As with Wilson's four words, Harper's lyrics draw a simplistic picture for the people in the audience too stupid to understand the dynamics of the scene simply as it was played by Laurie, Lemasters, and Robert Sean Leonard as Wilson.

This hand-holding would not seem necessary, but then *House* is a very popular show, so we have to assume the producers know what they are doing. The show is extremely formulaic, but perhaps there is a method to the lack of madness. They may have properly assessed the need for some kind of normalcy, crushing as it might be, to balance out the effect of having a jerk at the center of the show, and so they give us a standard medical drama to cover up the jerkiness.

If this is the case, then the handling of the rather delicate relationship between House and Ali, a seventeen-year-old female patient, is excellent. Ali, who appeared in two episodes (including "Lines in the Sand," 3-4), was a young girl with a serious crush on House. He flirted with her harmlessly . . . but then, is "harmless" ever the proper word for such a relationship? The resolution came when House diagnosed her with an odd disease (there are no other kinds of disease on *House*) that makes her lose her inhibitions. Both sides were being played here: fans of the antisocial, Asperger's House could enjoy his tempting walk on the wild side as he contemplated his underage admirer, while those who would disapprove of such behavior could be satisfied because 1) nothing happened, and 2) the girl was just suffering from an odd disease, anyway.

Comfort

House must constantly seek out a balance between the odd character at its core and the relatively ordinary formula designed, one assumes, to be acceptable to a large audience. It's the kind of tightrope walk that wouldn't seem to make anyone happy. The audience for a standard medical drama might accept a jerk as a secondary character, but making him the center of attention risks alienating that audience. Meanwhile, those who appreciate the existence of a character like House precisely because he's odd and alienating are unlikely to find the formula of the doctor show worth their time. From that perspective, *House* is a truly remarkable show, for managing to take a character who, in other circumstances, would have guaranteed a short run for the series and at best a subsequent cult status, and create alongside that character a program popular enough to become part of the mainstream. In terms of that continued popularity, it would seem to be the right move to attempt to balance the character of House with blandness, the narrative equivalent of "social niceties," so that no matter how far out House-the-character goes, *House*-the-series will always remain safely nearby.

I don't want to give the impression that the formula always triumphs over the prickly sensibilities of the main character. For instance, one particular aspect of House that is fairly unusual for a character on an American television series is his relationship with God, which may be why the Parents Television Council is so concerned. In "Three Stories" (1-21), the patient standing in for House was "technically dead for over a minute." Wilson, who along with House's "ducklings" had joined the lecture audience, asked House if his near-death experiences were "real." House responded that the patient saw "white light" visions, but "they're all just chemical reactions that take place when the brain shuts down." Dr. Foreman was surprised, asking "You choose to believe that?" House offered up an answer that helps define his character and draws attention to how he differs from the standard television hero: "There's no conclusive science," he replies. "My choice has no practical relevance to my life. I choose the outcome I find more comforting." Dr. Cameron couldn't seem to accept that House would get comfort from believing "this is it." But House told her, "I find it more comforting to believe that this isn't simply a test."

House is, at best, agnostic, and given a choice, prefers the concrete here and now to speculation about the beyond. Science gives him comfort. It is a brave stance to take on a popular American television series in the first decade of the twenty-first century. In some ways, it puts House farther outside the mainstream than does his general jerkiness. And it most certainly offers a balance to the more traditional structure under which the show operates.

Also, thus far, *House* has not succumbed to the kind of lazy good will that would smother its cranky hero. The Christmas episode that sent season three into a break was proof of that, as it was one of the most messed-up Christmas episodes ever. House spent most of "Merry Little Christmas" (3-10) going through withdrawal, as no one would supply him with Vicodin any longer. Near the end of the episode, he managed to get some Oxycontin, took way too much, drank it down with alcohol, and passed out on his living room floor. "Best friend" Wilson found him, got pissed off, and just walked out the door. Meanwhile, a cop was doing everything he could to put House in jail for narcotics abuse. And this was the Christmas episode.

Wilson stopped by House's office on Christmas Eve and offered to spend some time with him, saying he thought perhaps House would rather spend Christmas Eve with people than with drugs. Hugh Laurie got a look on his face: there is contempt on the surface but underneath we can tell he got the message. Then he gave a short, mirthless laugh, and walked past Wilson and out of the room, Oxy bottle in hand. At times like this, no one could accuse the writers of milking Christmas as an opportunity for touching moments or making House lovable. Indeed, it almost seemed that House's poor outlook was affecting those around him. It is hard to believe that anyone was made more comfortable, including the audience.

Breaking the Formula

On at least two occasions, the creators have written emotional depth into House's character without relying on cheap tricks (or, for that matter, just assuming Laurie's acting chops will take care of business). Not coincidentally, these occasions have occurred when the show has gone beyond the formula.

Generally when a television series offers up a Very Special Episode, that episode stinks. Usually the VSE involves some "important" hard-hitting storyline that "proves" how bad drugs are, or something similar. But occasionally, the VSE involves a break from whatever traditions the series has established, a one-shot step back from the norm. Such was the case in the season two finale, "No Reason" (2-24). As the episode began, House was shot by the angry husband of a former patient. The remainder of the episode couldn't have been more different from the *House* Formula; there was time-shifting and even a hard-to-define character-shifting, it was almost psychedelic. It might have played as pretentious, but with the show's plots having fallen into predictable patterns, this momentary change from those patterns was welcomed.

It was revealed that everything in the episode except the very beginning and the very end took place in House's mind over the course of a couple of minutes. In the process, House figured out how to cure his leg problems. But figuring out how to fix his leg wasn't really the important thing. What was important was that he passed that knowledge to the person who could help him. House seemed to have finally realized that he was purposely preventing himself from being happy, that he had built his life around being a super-smart jerk. It was about time, to be sure, but to the extent he loses his snarkiness, the series will suffer (another reason the subsequent Christmas episode was good news).

"No Reason" showed that the series could break the formula, expand on the titular character, and still retain the edginess that makes House (both character and show) worth watching. The aforementioned "Three Stories," perhaps the most acclaimed of all *House* episodes, was even better evidence that the only thing keeping *House* from greatness is the reliance on the formulaic.

In this, the penultimate episode of season one, House was called upon to give a lecture. He established the parameters for a medical puzzle: three patients complaining about pain in their legs. He then queried the students as they walked through each of the three cases, much as House and his assistants do in a standard *House* episode, but with the twist that there were three patients rather than one, and House was teaching students

28

using past case studies rather than working through a current problem with the other doctors. The episode snaked through the various cases, jumping around in time, using Carmen Electra to good advantage. Paris Barclay, the always-dependable director, and David Shore, who wrote the Emmy-winning screenplay, did an excellent job of keeping things simultaneously clear and complex. As House's lecture progressed, we gradually realized that one of the patients he was describing was in fact himself . . . he was telling the story of how he ended up with chronic pain in his leg (and the Vicodin addiction that goes with it).

As in "No Reason," this episode stepped outside the formula, and was the better for it. The artfully intricate narrative rewarded the viewer's intelligence instead of insulting it and we learned more about House's character than in most other episodes combined.

The Smarter Audience

In 2005, as House was finishing its first season, Steven Johnson's book *Everything Bad Is Good for You: How Today's Popular Culture Is Actually Making Us Smarter* was released. In it, Johnson argued that people today expect more from their popular entertainment, and for the most part, their expectations are being filled. "Viewers . . . no longer require . . . training wheels, because twenty-five years of increasingly complex television has honed their analytic skills" (77). The medical dramas on television today are more complex than those of earlier eras; compare something like *ER* to *Ben Casey*. Large casts and multiple intertwining narrative threads, along with an assumption that viewers can cope with the complexity, lead to "smarter" television. When I complain about an audience being insulted by the unnecessary addition of superfluous dialogue or banal soundtrack lyrics, it is to this I am referring. We no longer need the superfluous (if we ever did). When *House* eschews the superfluous, as in "Three Stories," it is as good as anything on television. When it wallows in formula, when it essentially acts as if the changes Johnson describes have not occurred, it is just another show. More often, you get episodes like "Lines in the Sand," where excellence is compromised by "dumbing down."

I would argue that the complexity at the heart of *House* lies not in the plots, which are repetitive, or in the interactions of the cast (the show isn't called *Teaching Hospital*, it's named after one and only one character). Instead, the complexity lies in that one character without whom there is no series. Gregory House is irascible, and there have been cranky doctors in television's past. He is misanthropic, and we see these types on occasion as well, although more often they are either guest stars in a single episode, or secondary continuing characters, not the primary, titular character. He is a drug addict, and the only time those drugs really cause a problem is when House is cut off from his supply (the drug isn't the problem, the addiction isn't the problem, it's just a supply matter, although his recent troubles trying to pee may foreshadow other problems). At this point, we're looking at a pretty unusual central character for television. Irascible, okay. Misanthropic, a bit of a problem, but can be worked with. Drug addict? Oops. Toss in a rationalist's disdain for religious belief and you have a pretty dangerous character, at least in the context of prime-time American broadcast television. Is it any wonder that Shore does everything he can to normalize his show, that he covers the complex House with a mundane *House*? How else can he sneak this godless druggie past the public?

Ultimately, House succeeds in walking its thin line. Hugh Laurie is excellent and the main character is fascinating; thus far, these positives outweigh the draggy repetition that constitutes most of the plots. *House* follows a formula, and mixes that formula with just enough quality to entice an audience. One can only hope that Shore and company finally accept that the smarter audience is ready for more than just enticement.

Science gives STEVEN RUBIO comfort. Unfortunately, he is an English teacher, not a scientist. His never-ending Weblog, "Steven Rubio's Online Life," is now in its sixth year and can be found at begonias.typepad.com/srubio. This is his fifth appearance in a Smart Pop book.

REFERENCES

Gildemeister, Christopher. "Faith in a Box: Entertainment Television & Religion 2005-2006." *parentstv.org*. Retrieved 30 Mar. 2007. <http://www.parentstv.org/PTC/publications/reports/religionstudy06/main.asp>

Johnson, Steven. *Everything Bad Is Good for You: How Today's Popular Culture Is Actually Making Us Smarter*. New York: Riverhead, 2005.

PTC Family TV Guide Show Page. "House." Retrieved 30 Mar. 2007. <http://www.parentstv.org/ptc/shows/main.asp?shwid=1937>

They say you always hurt the ones you love. The writers of House *take that literally: the explanation for Princeton-Plainsboro patients' mysterious ailments can almost always be traced back to their families. It's a strange pattern for a show without any overt family focus. Jill Winters puzzles out the meaning behind the disturbing trend.*

DYSFUNCTIONAL FAMILY IN RESIDENCE

Disturbing Group Dynamics in House M.D.

JILL WINTERS

here are two core elements of fascination that anchor each episode of *House*. A bizarre, hard-to-diagnose illness is one. The brilliant but antisocial Dr. Gregory House is the other. Week after week, we step into the fictional Princeton-Plainsboro Teaching Hospital (PPTH). We meet different patients—and the concerned relatives by their side. We see the head of Diagnostic Medicine, Dr. House, and the team of specialists by *his* side. But *House* is a deceiving show and nothing should be taken at face value.

The curious maladies that House's patients suffer always appear to be something other than what they are. House appears not to care about his patients—as more than science projects, really—yet he reveals, through sheer persistence, that he often cares the most. *House* is a show built on giving us a picture and then inverting it. Family enters the stage to lend support, but usually ends up being the cause (whether direct or indirect) of a patient's distress. In fact, despite the myriad representations of family in *House*, very few—if any—are flattering. Too often to be an accident, *House* strips "family" of its generally positive associations—that of stability, safety, and protection—and instead reveals it to be an ignorant,

33

negligent, or even perverse mess of toxic destruction.

But to what end?

The series premiere opened on elementary school teacher, Rebecca Adler. While teaching, she suddenly lost control of her speech and then collapsed. Fast forward to the PPTH, where Dr. House and his team were discussing her case. As Drs. Foreman, Cameron, and Chase ruled out the illnesses that were "highly unlikely," House casually pointed out, "She's twenty-nine years old—whatever is wrong with her is highly unlikely" (1-1).

While I was watching, I couldn't help thinking that perhaps the *most* unlikely aspect of Rebecca's plight was the fact that no one came to visit her at the hospital. A sweet, young school teacher with no concerned family members at her bedside? An off-handed remark was made that her students were her family. Here *House* began setting the tone for what would be its inherent disrespect for the institution of family—albeit very subtly. While Rebecca's family was not depicted negatively, it was glaringly not depicted at all. Family as a support system was simply absent.

The tapeworm that had traveled to Rebecca's brain had been a random fluke. However, as the series progressed, the medical anomalies became less random, and more preset—or at least *bound* to happen. Whether due to heredity or personal history, the source of a patient's trouble can almost always be traced in some way to his or her family. Of course, there's little we can do about our genetics. But family behavior—or more specifically, the wrong choices that family members make—is a different matter, and one that seems to be a main concern of the show. Embedded in the continuing text of *House* is the implication that one's family is the primary source of one's pain. The medical diagnoses vary, but it is in the *details* of a patient's family that we see this theme carried out consistently.

A homeless woman lost consciousness and, after an array of strange symptoms, Dr. House diagnosed her with both cancer and rabies. One could argue those afflictions were the least of her problems. It turned out that she'd become homeless after her husband and son were killed in a car wreck—a car *she* had been driving.

A woman who suffered mysterious seizures and mental confusion ended up killing her baby. Ultimately, Dr. House figured out that she had celiac disease, a hereditary condition that went untreated and eventually caused a kind of psychosis. Now add to that the disturbing details: her husband had turned a blind eye to his wife's increasingly bizarre behavior. Self-indulgently, he drowned himself in the proverbial bottle, and by the time she finally snapped, he rebuffed her with disgust.

A teenage girl exhibited aggressive behavior. Dr. House wound up with a shocking diagnosis: testicular cancer. She was actually a *he*—a boy born with "male pseudo-hermaphroditism." If only that had been the biggest revelation . . . but alas, there was something else. Apparently the girl's father had been having sex with her, unaware of her true sex— and she'd encouraged it in order to control him.

If you want to look for the subtexts in episodes like these, you could assign them rather quickly. Mother as destroyer. Husband as schmuck. Father as abuser. However—thematically—*House* goes beyond this. Disturbing family details are more than cheap tricks and shock value. They are focused, deliberate. Family becomes a metaphor for the coterie of people we surround ourselves with—our closest allies—often to our own peril.

Young interracial couple Tracy and Jeremy both began suffering the same symptoms—throat swelling, abdominal pain, and more. As always, it was a rapid-fire yet arduous process for the PPTH team to figure out what was wrong. Dr. House's final diagnosis was something Tracy and Jeremy never could have predicted. Hereditary angioedema, a rare genetic disease that they *both* had. It turned out that the two were actually related. Unbeknownst to them, Jeremy's father had had an affair with his next-door neighbor, Tracy's mother, years ago. Tracy and Jeremy were lifelong friends before becoming romantically involved, never suspecting they had the same father.

According to Jeremy, his father had flown into a rage when he discovered his son was dating Tracy; he went on racist rants, claiming he was against the relationship because the girl was black, and even broke his son's arm in one of his tirades. The man committed suicide, never telling Jeremy and Tracy that they were half-siblings or that he was suffering from the rare genetic disease he'd passed on to them.

This is an abundantly anti-father episode. We have father as adulterer, abuser, hypocrite, and bigot. We have father as bearer of "bad genes." We have father as ultimate villain *and* ultimate coward.

The show makes sure to idealize the love and optimism of its young couple at the beginning—so it can provide the sharpest of contrasts by the end. We learn that escaping their destructive family situations was not enough for Tracy and Jeremy to get their happy ending; rather, their love had been poisoned from the start. Through no fault of their own, their romantic dreams were destroyed. Their sibling relationship disgusted them. By the end of the episode, "family" had become this perverted thing, a tool of misery, a concept that is horrifying instead of comforting.

Not that *House*'s anti-family theme is always played out with such malevolence. A patient's parents do not have to be demonized. Often they are just clueless and incompetent. Take the teenager with a head injury, night terrors, and leg twitches. It turned out that his mother had never been vaccinated for measles and hence, when he was exposed to the virus, it was able to "mutate" and travel to his brain. Or the boy suffering from acute asthma—because his mother wouldn't let him use an inhaler, citing her philosophical opposition to medicine as the reason. (A scathing rebuke from Dr. House changed that.)

The list goes on. A boy with radiation poisoning—which he got from a junkyard souvenir his father had given. A boy with leprosy—which he caught from his dad. A boy infected by raccoon roundworms—which he contracted from the sandbox in his own backyard. That particular episode was *House* at its sly best. What could be a more wholesome symbol of home and family than a child's sandbox? Yet that became the very thing that was infested and dangerous.

Often the implication that runs through these episodes is: Even well-meaning parents do more harm than good. Though sometimes, as *House* points out, parents have agendas that are in direct conflict with the best interest of their kids. Case in point—Abigail, a teenage dwarf, was rushed to the hospital with a collapsed lung. After thorough treatment, House discovered a tumor on her pituitary gland. To everyone's surprise, Abigail *was* not a dwarf at all. People had always assumed she was because her mother, Maddy, was a dwarf. In actuality, Abigail's growth had been stunted by the pressure the tumor was putting on her pituitary, and with surgery and a dose of growth hormone, she would grow to a normal height.

Instead of her mother being elated by the news, she was displeased.

Maddy had raised Abigail to believe that being "normal" was far less noble than being a dwarf. It had been a way to give her daughter *as well as herself* an active sense of pride. So now that Dr. House was opening the door for Abigail to become "like everyone else," how could Maddy encourage that? Wouldn't that be like admitting normality is somehow preferable to abnormality?

Sadly, Maddy was actually prepared to deny her daughter the opportunity to reverse her situation. As usual, only a verbal beat-down from House got through to the stubborn parent. Dr. House chastised Maddy for her shortsightedness, instructing her to put the quality of her daughter's life first, to think beyond her ego, and most crudely: to grant Abigail "a ticket out of the freak show" (3-10).

Typical House, gratuitously rude and insensitive—yet effective.

Of course, Dr. House is no stranger to fighting with anyone in his path, especially a patient's parents. In one episode, he went as far as to petition a judge to deny a mother and father the right to make decisions on their daughter's behalf. Here little Alice's parents, who were obviously still bitter from their divorce, spent most of their time by Alice's bedside bickering and sniping at each other—even *after* Dr. Cameron told them that the stress of it was making their daughter's condition worse.

And in fact, spousal discord is a common subset of the anti-family theme that runs throughout *House*. A wife poisoning her husband. A cheating husband contracting herpes. A wife undergoing fertility treatments yet secretly sabotaging them with birth control pills. A pregnant woman doubting seriously that her husband has fathered her baby. The episodes that are the most darkly comical are the ones in which the misanthropic Dr. House has to break the news to the clueless spouse. Take the man who had turned orange from too much beta-carotene. As House bluntly informed him, his wife was clearly sleeping with someone else—otherwise she would have *noticed* that her husband was orange and he wouldn't have needed House to point it out for him.

In the world of *House*, it's abundantly clear that heredity sucks, parents are selfish, and spouses hurt each other. And certainly, the toxic-family theme is not restricted to the patients at the hospital. The main characters have their own unpleasant family baggage. House has a terrible relationship with his father, whom he pretty much hates, and yet whom he is *like*. A former Marine, House's dad was always a hard case. In one episode we learn that growing up, House suffered some extreme punishments from his militaristic father, and that the man was critical and "brutally honest" to the point of being hurtful—just as House is now. In fact, according to Dr. Wilson, House was actually a jerk long before the infarction that crippled his leg and left him in constant pain. (We can surmise that it is no coincidence; clearly he takes after his dad.)

Dr. House's team of specialists has its own wealth of family woes. Dr. Eric Foreman has an ailing mother and a brother who is perpetually in jail. Dr. Robert Chase had a contentious relationship with his father— until his father died and disinherited him. Dr. Allison Cameron's family past is shrouded in mystery. All we do know is that she won't talk much about herself and when she was barely twenty-one, she married a man who was on his deathbed.

As for spousal deceit, even affable Dr. James Wilson isn't immune. Not exactly a prize of fidelity himself, he was already on his third marriage when he discovered that his wife was cheating on him. And House's ex, Stacy, cheated on her current husband, Mark—*with* House.

If you think of *House*'s anti-family theme in concentric circles, you can see it working its way inward. The outermost circle contains the stories of the patients that come into the hospital. The next circle follows the family histories of the main characters. And the most central circle is for the core group themselves—House and his team, who make up their own dysfunctional little family.

Well—when it comes to diagnostic medicine, they are quite function-al. But it is in spite of their collectivity, not because of it.

In the PPTH "family," House is the patriarch, Lisa Cuddy the mother figure, protégés Foreman, Chase, and Cameron the "kids," and Dr. Wilson the uncle. (Like a brother to House, Wilson has known him the longest and is the only one who can get along with him.)

Interestingly, each one's role in this metaphorical family closely paral-lels his/her role in "real life." Just as House is crusty, sarcastic, and diffi-cult with his staff, so is he in private. Cuddy, who, like an aloof mother, is more overseer than nurturer to the staff, has been trying unsuccessful-ly to get pregnant. She even remarked to Wilson that she must be miss-ing the mothering gene.

Cameron is the good daughter in the PPTH family, the one who over-compensates for unaffectionate parents by always being nice. Just as she was the selfless soul who married a dying man, she carries that same martyrdom with her at work. When Foreman knowingly stole her idea for an article, Cameron ended up apologizing to *him*—for getting so angry, insisting that above all she did not want to ruin their friendship. (Pathetically, Foreman had to point out to her that they were *not* friends, they were colleagues.) Solicitous to a fault, it is as though Cameron has learned being "good" as the way to ensure others' approval. In one episode, Dr. House was told he would have to let one of the team go. Dr. Cameron approached him before he could make his choice, to offer herself up. What was supposed to look like "taking the high road" was actually a testament to her low confidence. Already anticipating that *she* would be the one fired, she wanted to make things easier by simply leaving.

Like an unloved daughter, Cameron does not bother to compete directly with "brothers," Foreman and Chase. Rather, she paves her own path as the sweet and kind one. At one point, she was complimenting House and he derisively told her that he didn't need her praise. She replied, "I was just trying to be nice," and he candidly pointed out, "You don't always need to do that."

The parallels go on. Just as Foreman coolly rejects his felonious, drug-addicted brother, he is generally unmoved by his closest colleagues. Unlike House, Foreman is not gratuitously insulting. However, *like* House, he is direct, unapologetic, and for the most part, unsympathetic to the messes people make of their own lives. Like a first-born son who most emulates the father, Foreman is a highly competitive achiever, determined to one day not only match his father, but also to surpass him. Foreman regularly stands up to House, goes toe-to-toe with him and won't back down (until he has to because House ends up being right).

This dynamic partly accounts for why Dr. Foreman and Dr. Chase are more like competitive brothers than colleagues. Chase is like the younger son who desperately craves his father's approval—mirroring exactly his role in real life. Just as Chase suffered a long rift with his father, he has had a particularly difficult relationship with House. (In fact, the death of Chase's father allowed House, symbolically, to supplant him.)

Chase rarely confronts House head-on, but tends toward a more soft-soaped approach. While he does contribute opinions, he also tries (futilely) to kiss up to House at the same time. And yet, as much as he idolizes House, Chase has gone behind his back at times—showing the complexity of Chase's *feelings* toward his boss. Seeped in a mix of resentment, respect, deference, and anger, Chase is deeply invested in and affected by his relationship with House. In a recent episode, Chase figured out what was wrong with a patient before House did, yet instead of thanking or praising him, House rebuffed him. (This was when House was going through withdrawal from his Vicodin addiction and became so belligerent that he actually punched Chase.)

Afterward, Chase bitterly remarked to Wilson that even when he does a good job, House won't give him any respect. Here you could see how profoundly hurt Chase was by House's demeanor. He was more like a wounded child than a disgruntled professional. His feelings were at the heart of the matter, not his career.

Yet, despite how cold and impervious Dr. House seems to be to his team, there are times when he comes through for all of them. He has helped Cuddy with her fertility efforts, he has been a friend to Wilson, he has let Foreman know how important he is to the team, he has shown reluctant kindness to Cameron, and despite being hard on Chase, House made a point to defend Chase on a mistake he made so that he could keep his job. But these kinds of warm, interpersonal moments are the exceptions, not the rule.

The thing about *House* is—despite having an ensemble cast—it is *not* a show about teamwork. It is a show that by its nature (even by the title itself) is antisocial.

If you get caught up in the few glimmering moments when House shows affection toward his colleagues or his patients, you will miss the more important point—which is that House does not truly need any of these people. You will miss the fact that Cameron, Foreman, and Chase do not bring out anything new or better in each other, but rather bounce off each other like balls in a lotto machine. That while House has shown some camaraderie toward Chase at times, he has also screwed up his confidence and—like any cold, critical parent—has given him issues that will far outlast the occasional pats on the back.

In its own crafty way, *House* is a show that lauds the individual. House

40

enjoys talking through the symptoms of each patient with his team and getting their feedback, he prefers it, but he doesn't truly *need* to do it. One might like to imagine that House needs Foreman, Cameron, and Chase, that he "couldn't do it without them" and whatever other warm, fuzzy axioms might apply. But the reality is, we have no evidence that they are integral. As individual doctors they might be valuable, but within the structural context of the show, they are not necessary. As viewers, we have every reason to believe that House *could* do it without him since week after week, it is *House* having the final epiphany about a patient's condition. (Only when Dr. House is suffering from drug withdrawal and is acting out of character does he miss his mark and break this pattern.)

In the world of *House M.D.*, people form groups and cling to some kind of notion of togetherness, but at the end of the day (or episode, as the case may be), are still a mass of individuals with their own agendas—their own sense of aloneness that resists change. And *House* consistently portrays family in a negative light because family is really just a symbol, a tool to support the show's larger theme, which is its disdain for the collective.

Marriages fail—or survive on dishonesty. Parents screw up constantly. Children bring disappointment. House remains lonely and miserable, despite having a coterie of colleagues that worship him and would embrace him as a friend in a second. Because that is who he is. The team has not and can not change him. Foreman, Cameron, and Chase have not changed over the course of three seasons in any personally significant way, either. There is no true sense of "group" in *House M.D.*, but only the *appearance* of it—whether it be among a family gathered at a patient's bedside, or among House and his team gathered in a conference room. In one episode House even quipped to his staff, "I thought I'd get your theories, mock them, then embrace my own—the usual" ("Merry Little Christmas," 3-10). The writers couldn't have summed the show up any better.

A Phi Beta Kappa, summa cum laude graduate of Boston College with a degree in history, JILL WINTERS has taught Women's Studies as well as numerous workshops for aspiring writers. She is the author of five novels, including *Lime Ricky*, *Just Peachy*, *Raspberry Crush*, and *Blushing Pink*. Her books have topped the Barnes & Noble Bestseller Lists and Book Sense's Top Ten, and her debut novel, *Plum Girl*, was a finalist for the Dorothy Parker Award of Excellence. Jill has also contributed essays to the anthologies *Flirting with Pride and Prejudice*, *Welcome to Wisteria Lane*, and *Coffee at Luke's*. You can visit her online at www.jillwinters.com.

There's a lot of deception in House. If you ever wished you could have a fool-proof guide that told you who was lying, who was telling the truth, and why, you're in luck—Craig Derksen has laid it all out for you . . . including the one thing you can always, always trust.

EVERYBODY LIES EXCEPT FOR THE CGI

A Practical Guide to Deception in House M.D.

CRAIG DERKSEN

"**e**verybody lies" is the catch phrase of *House M.D.* In fact, much of the vaunted diagnostic prowess of the main character Dr. Gregory House comes from his ability to see through deceptions. However, the lies that drive the show are not random, but rather a structured set of deceptions that never seem to be without cause. Just as some people have created guidelines for how to survive in a horror movie based on the patterns of the genre, we can formulate a list of guidelines to detect deception in *House M.D.*

Without further ado, I present the rules to deception in *House M.D.*

Some General Comments about the Diagnosis of Deceptions in Fiction

There are many conventions about deception in fiction, and like all fiction, *House M.D.* follows some of these conventions and disregards others. One of the most prominent of these conventions involves characters concocting overly elaborate stories to hide their deceptions. *House M.D.* has not indulged in this particular theatrical device. Some shows (most

43

situation comedies, for example) present us with elaborate webs of deception and attempt to entertain us with the uncomfortable feelings we experience as those webs are spun. Even though *House M.D.* is as much about deceptions and their consequences as *Friends* or *Three's Company*, its treatment of these deceptions is unlike the treatment of deception in these shows. The deceptions in *House M.D.* lack this sort of overwrought complexity. Interestingly, the lies in *House M.D.* are usually concealed by the most mundane, uninteresting stories. There are exceptions, like in the episode "Cursed" (1-13), where the patient's father went on a spiritual retreat but told his son that he was a fighter pilot. But even in this case, the fighter pilot story was mentioned only in passing and there was no attention drawn to it. Part of the reason for this is to make the lies more difficult to discover. If we smelled an elaborate story, we would expect a lie right away. The mundane stories, on the other hand, slide right past us without a moment's notice.

Often House takes note of these stories, but that is only because of his fictional ability to know *exactly* what an appropriate response is relative to a situation; stories that seem bland to us seem overly elaborate to him. House himself concocted an elaborate lie when he relayed his own medical history in "Three Stories" (1-21), replacing himself with Carmen Electra. But while we suspected that he was lying, the scope of the lie was unclear.

Identifying appropriate responses is a skill that not everyone possesses to the same degree.[1] But House's ability to detect appropriate responses, and his personal disregard of them, is practically supernatural. House's suspicions in the episode "Sports Medicine" (1-12), when Foreman showed up a few minutes late for work claiming that he had car trouble, is a perfect example of this.

While *House M.D.* does not spoon-feed us its deceptions, they are still detectable and non-random. *House M.D.* does not follow the tradition in television where mysteries are solved based on a mere pittance of under- or over-determined clues. It is often quite difficult to find

---

[1] I once had a friend who would respond to any insult with the harshest string of expletives that he could manage. With repeated instructions ("You can respond to 'stupid' with 'jerk' or 'idiot' but not '$&*#$%^&^,' okay?"), he eventually learned how to escalate insults proportionately.

deductive fiction that allows appropriate use of one's abilities. Even children get annoyed by the randomness of *Scooby-Doo, Where Are You?* and the Choose Your Own Adventure novels, or the obfuscation of the mystery by production failures, like when the acting in *Murder, She Wrote*, conceals important clues.

It is common to identify deceptions in fiction based on the conventions of the type of fiction in question, which tell us what counts as clues and how to interpret them. We all know that, in any given episode, *Murder, She Wrote's* Jessica Fletcher will solve the mystery based on some random prompting that allows her to see something that she had previously missed. *House M.D.* often appeals to this same convention, as well as the timing of it. When there are ten minutes left in the show and House goes to see someone, often a patient in the clinic, we can be pretty comfortable in assuming that something will happen with that person that will allow House to correctly diagnose that episode's illness.

There are two narrative conventions that contribute to the sort of event just discussed—the convention of the problems being wrapped up in the last ten minutes, and the convention of an incidental event revealing the key to solving the bigger problem. Many people are annoyed by the resolution-in-the-last-ten-minutes convention, but such annoyance is somewhat unjustified. Certainly such a convention is problematic in that it makes the arrival of the resolution expected rather than surprising. However, it is not like stopping the ticking bomb with only one second left on the timer. The amount of time left in the show is not a fact internal to the story; it is a fact external to the story. The last ten minutes can take from less than ten minutes to several days, weeks, months, or even years of fictional time. Internal to the show, House does not figure things out in the last ten minutes, he figures things out and that's what makes it the last ten minutes. What is there for a diagnostician to do when he's already diagnosed the disease? The fact that the major problems in *House M.D.* are resolved in our last ten minutes, not theirs, is a useful convention for us. When a character makes a claim in the last ten minutes, and sticks to it despite being badgered, we can usually trust that it is the truth.

On the other hand, the fact that the resolution to the show is prompted by an external cue unrelated to the problem is something that can be quite annoying if it is overdone. The sort of lightning bolt "eureka" inspiration portrayed in fiction does not correspond to the way that we figure things out in the real world. Rather, it's a fictional device included as a way to heighten drama. It is also one last attempt to help the audience figure out the episode's puzzle. A pregnant woman in the clinic allowed House to diagnose the epidemic among the newborns in the episode "Maternity" (1-4), Steve McQueen allowed House to diagnose the patient in "Hunting" (2-7), and a patient's use of breath spray allowed House to diagnose an infected jaw in "Love Hurts" (1-20).

Another convention of fictional deception that *House M.D.* utilizes is the movement toward more explicable and more subtle deceptions rather than obvious or unjustified deceptions. Actually detecting deception ourselves, rather than just marveling at another's ability to detect it, has become more central to fiction. The fact that poker tournaments have become a staple of television reveals how interested we have become in trying to detect liars on our own. (Obviously the makers of *House M.D.* are aware of this trend, based on their inclusion of poker scenes in the episodes "All In" [2-17] and "House vs. God" [2-19].)

House M.D. gives us the option of either figuring things out for ourselves or just waiting to see how they turn out. For those who like to just follow along and trust the smart character, they need simply trust House's claims about who is lying and what they are lying about. Those who are interested in taking a more personal hand in things can use House as guide and as a test of their own abilities to uncover deception. While it is possible that House is wrong at the end of the episode, it is unlikely. Certainly having Bryan Singer as executive producer of *House M.D.* can cause us to doubt our basic narrative assumptions; the man who brought us *The Usual Suspects* can hardly be trusted to follow the rules. However, the facts seem to confirm House's claims—although sometimes he helps them to do so, as when he injected the Munchausen patient in the episode "Deception" (2-9). There needs to be some external reason why we can trust House; I think that there is, and I will discuss it below. But the biggest problem with the "trust House" approach is that it doesn't tell us when *he* is lying, and House's deceptions make up a large portion of the deceptions in the show. Maybe supplementing House with a little Wilson, since Wilson seems to have House mostly figured out, is the best way to go . . . but the formula of whom to trust and when to trust them is as complex as figuring out the individual deceptions.

For those who just say "x is lying" and set up for the big "I told you so," I should mention that just identifying a character as a liar is woefully inadequate. With so much lying going on, identifying a liar is like shooting fish in a barrel. It is more important to diagnose the content of the lies relative to their motivation—namely, to discover things about the liar's psychology based on the lies that they tell.

Deceptions of People as Family Members

The characters in *House M.D.* seem to love lying to their families. Actually, that's not true; they seem to hate it, one and all, but that doesn't stop them from doing it. While nearly all of House's patients lie to their families, they each have their own particular pathology. Almost everyone in the show has something that they don't want their family knowing about. Illicit affairs, terminal diseases, and deviant behaviors are only a few of the things that the characters hide from their families. They have big secrets, and we get a guilty, voyeuristic pleasure from figuring out what they are hiding. We love to discover their particular flavor of lies as much as House does, although we might not be so abusive in the revealing of them.

Symptoms and Diagnosis

The recurring theme in characters' lies to their families is that they lie because they want their relationship with their family members to go a certain way. You can detect that a patient is lying to their family when their relationship with that family member is going the way they want it to. House himself lied to his parents so he wouldn't have to see them in the episode "Daddy's Boy" (2-5) and it was one of the few times he seemed to not enjoy telling fibs. Some characters lie so their families will be happy, like the "perfect wife" in "Need to Know" (2-11); some lie so they can grow old together, like the about-to-be-dumped liver donor in "Sleeping Dogs Lie" (2-18); and some lie so their parents won't make them work over spring break like the college student in "Daddy's Boy" (who was in turn lied to about the circumstances of his mother's death so he wouldn't drink and drive). Anytime a character in *House M.D.* offers an easy solution to a complex family situation, they are probably lying.

Deceptions of the Fire-Panted Patients

Almost all of the patients and their representatives in *House M.D.* lie to their doctors. The examples of this are too numerous to list, but a perfect example is the first season episode "Paternity" (1-2), when the parents of the patient refused to admit that their son was adopted. Those who don't lie are usually acting foolishly based on the lies or the perceived lies of others. The clinic patient in the episode "Humpty Dumpty" (2-3) is a great example of this: he was too worried about white oppression to listen to his doctors.

Maintenance of the patient/doctor relationship motivates many patient lies. Patients want doctors to think well about them in both medical and non-medical contexts. They are appropriately and inappropriately embarrassed by things they have done and have not done, and they don't want the doctors judging them in this regard. Judgment is a key element of *House M.D.*; House behaves like someone who judges more than most—he often talks about patients and makes fun of them—but he actually judges less. The patient in the first season episode "Control" (1-14) was too worried about being judged to allow embarrassing medical procedures, but seemed to appreciate House's treatment of her. Likewise, much of the second season episode "Acceptance" (2-1) was about the patient being judged because he was a murderer, but House doesn't seem to care.

The patients aren't only concerned with what the doctors think about their personal lives; they also want to impress the doctors with their medical knowledge. The patients research diseases on the Internet so that they can show their doctors just how smart they are. And if you can impress doctors with hard work, you can also impress them by lying to them in a way that simulates hard work. Internet research is also a way to second-guess the doctor, because we've all heard stories about the doctors making mistakes and sometimes they need patients checking up on them. This is not always a bad thing—as we learned in the episode "Three Stories" (1-21), House, as a patient, was the one who diagnosed himself with muscle death.

Symptoms and Diagnosis

A talking patient is usually a lying patient, and a silent patient is usually trying to hide something. Mute patients, like the father of the clinic patient in "Control," are an exception, except when they can talk but choose not to. Patients have lied to doctors in *House M.D.* in a wide variety of ways and there is no simple pattern that allows us to determine which patients are lying and what they are lying about. Part of the reason that we are so impressed by House's ability to detect liars is that there *seems* to be no discernable pattern to the deceptions of the patients. Nonetheless, there is a pattern; it just is not helpful because it is based on information that we usually lack, but House, with all of his diagnostic experience and savant-level human insight, seems to possess. Since the patients are concerned with their health and don't trust the doctors to do a good job, they will replace the judgment of the doctor with their own or with the judgment of other doctors. In order to get the doctor to treat them "correctly" they will offer internal observations that they think will be most likely to get what they perceive as the correct treatment. In other words, they will lie to the doctors in order to have the doctor make the correct diagnosis so that they can be healthy. This is not a perfect rule because some people want things other than good health from their doctor—the clinic patient in "Sex Kills" (2-14) would have rather been chemically castrated than healthy so he reported an uncontrollable attraction to cows—but it is generally a good rule.

Deceptions of People Doing "Doctor Things"

The doctors on *House M.D.* are merely human, and lie about all the normal things that non-doctor humans lie about, but they also have their own particular quirks as doctors; specifically, they lie to protect their careers. While all doctors seem to care about patients, in most cases they care about themselves more.

Unlike most medical shows, there are no nurses as major characters in *House M.D.* The medical professionals whose personalities we get to see are all doctors and administrators. Part of the reason for this might be that much of the show takes a poke at the skills of those performing medical procedures, and the creators of the show choose not to take such a poke at nurses; hence the need for House's lackeys to perform all the tests for themselves.

Symptoms and Diagnosis

The doctors in *House M.D.* lie as much as the patients do. While the patients lie to protect their health and their reputations, the doctors lie to protect their careers and the comfortable lives that they've built. While this may not apply so well to the caring Wilson and Cameron, the utilitarian Cuddy, and the curious House and Foreman, it does seem to apply to the other doctors in the show. Chase at his worst is probably the best example of a doctor who is concerned only with maintaining his comfortable life. Examples of doctors concerned more with their comfort than the lives of others are the bit part doctor that only operated on a tumor after House shrunk it down with ethanol in "The Socratic Method" (1-6) and the bit part doctor who needed to be blackmailed to do a transplant in "The Mistake" (2-8); both were more concerned with their success ratings than the patients in question.

Of course, these doctors are only established as typical in order to better define the major characters. Establishing that doctors who desire above all to protect their careers are the norm makes us more interested in characters who are willing to lie for better motives. We respect the willingness of the doctor/patient in "TB or Not TB" (2-4) to sacrifice not just his career but his life to gain awareness for his cause, even if House didn't. We respect Cuddy's big picture decisions—even House respected her rejection of the transplant in "Sex Kills"—because we respect what she is trying to preserve: not her career, but people's health. In this way Cuddy is contrasted with Vogler, the villainous businessman from the first season. They both seemed to be most concerned with the big picture, but Vogler just wanted to run the hospital as a business and didn't really care about the people involved. Cameron and Wilson are willing to lie to protect not only their patients, but also their patients' feelings. They are concerned with their patients as people and not just as patients. This sets them apart from most of the doctors in the show.

So what sets House apart? Does he care about patients? He cares about some personally if he meets them and they don't annoy him too much. More consistently, he cares about patients because they are *his* patients. The legal system is adversarial; this means that each side is represented by an advocate. House treats the medical system as adversarial. He will do *anything* to protect *his* patients. Let me reiterate that: he will do anything to protect his patients. House's best lies are lies intended to get medical care for his patients that they would otherwise be unable to get. House cares about the health of his patients and lies as often as necessary to help them.

Deceptions of the Show's Creators

The discussion above reveals one of the key principles of *House M.D.*: what people lie about reveals what they care about. The most interesting thing about this principle is what it means when it is applied to the making of the show. What does it tell us about the writers and the producers? What do they care about?

The people who make *House M.D.* lie to us in many ways; all fiction is, in a sense, deception. I'm not interested in that sort of deception. I'm interested in the more unusual deceptions that are part of *House M.D.* Sure, the characters lie, and those lies are decided and written by the people who make the show, but those lies are not the pure lies of the creators, they are lies filtered through the characters. The pure deceptions of the creators of the show are the deceptions of the world. When the world conspires to mislead the audience, then that is a lie of the show's creator.

Symptoms and Diagnosis

House M.D. is not a show that we enjoy because we're never sure what's going on. At the end of an episode, we think we have a good idea of what's really happened. In order to provide the audience with this level of certainty there must be some elements of the world that we can trust. *House M.D.* has two: the medical canon and the visual effects.

When I say we can trust the medical canon, I do not mean that all medical elements of the show are infallible. Many of the medical elements of the show are used to deceive the audience based on established weaknesses of the medical canon. For example when testing for diseases we don't actually test for the diseases, we test for markers that accompany the disease; this allows the creators of the show to hide diseases from us until the appropriately dramatic time because it's possible that a patient has a disease but lacks the markers. Similarly, tests have error rates; sometimes tests fail to detect a disease and sometimes they provide a false positive (both testing for markers and false positives are discussed explicitly in the episode "Role Model" [1-17], through a little speech about the Inuit looking for herons when fishing and a failed AIDS test). Using these medical facts to deceive the audience reveals something about the creators of the show.

There is some criticism of the medical facts of the show. Some of it is appropriate, but much of it reflects individual limitations and passions about medicine. Some say that there are obvious medical errors, while others fail to catch those "obvious" errors and cite different errors that the first group didn't catch. Medical science is a field where people feel strongly, but often disagree, and that makes it impossible to keep everyone happy. There is a myth that there is one medical canon that all reputable doctors know and support, but this is not the case. Medical science is such a large, complex, and diverse field that there cannot help but be disagreements.

It is quite clear that the people who make the show really care about maximizing its medical credibility. The show walks a fine line: they appear to take great care not to contradict or undermine what they believe is viewed as the existing medical canon, while choosing to avoid disagreements within that canon in favor of firmer ground. Since the series is fiction, those who make it can set up whatever medical rules they like, but they choose not to. Instead, they deceive us with the documented and undisputed limitations of current medical knowledge, and dazzle us with some actual medical knowledge. The deceptions are not just ones that are possible based on current medical knowledge; they are deceptions that are actually a *part* of medical knowledge. (Tycho Brahe, the scientist who introduced the idea of documenting margins for error, would be so proud.) Rather than squeezing in deceptions anywhere that medical science is undocumented, the creators make use of places where medical science has documented wiggle room in order to deceive us, because they care about the appearance of medical accuracy.

In this way, the creators of the show can maintain their credibility, and the credibility of known medical facts, despite all of the deceptions that they foist upon us. This allows us to actually know whose diagnosis is accurate at the end of an episode.

By establishing the medical canon as irrefutable, we also establish a standard that allows us to judge the character's medical abilities, something that is very important to the show. When House goes into the clinic and frightens away all the patients with a little speech about his Vicodin habit in the episode "Occam's Razor" (1-3), we are meant think that the patients are afraid of a great doctor for irrelevant reasons, and we cannot do this unless we think that House *is* a great doctor. This is true of many of the moments in the show: they are only effective if House is a great doctor. The sort of lies the creators of the series tell reveals to us how important our perception of House's medical skills is to them.

However, those of us who aren't medical professionals might require a little help in figuring out what is going on medically and confirming the diagnoses that we lack information on. For this we have the great equalizer—pretty pictures. Once they cut to computer-generated imagery, or CGI, that's basically a guarantee that what we see is actually happening. In the same way that murder mysteries re-cap by letting us see the murder happening, *House M.D.* (as a medical mystery) re-caps by letting us see the medicine happening. If we see a CGI tapeworm settle in someone's CGI brain we know they have a tapeworm even if we haven't been to medical school. Maybe the tapeworm isn't the cause of all of their problems, but we know that they have one. The CGI tells us, as a fact, what is going on, but does not tell us all of the implications of what we see; after all, something needs to be left for House to explain. When we see CGI iron bond with CGI medicine and punch CGI holes in CGI lungs we know that the medicine did something.

Interestingly, since the CGI leaves nothing to the perceptions of any of the characters, it would be a direct and obvious deception of the creators if such a scene were deceptive. In the episode "No Reason" (2-24), when House was having elaborate hallucinations, he apparently hallucinated CGI effects as well. However, it is not a big deal in this case; since House hallucinated all of the treatment and the diagnosis of the patient, it is appropriate that he hallucinated the CGI, since it established what was going on internal to the hallucination.

Generally, the CGI effects, like the medical canon, let us know that we are in the presence of medical greatness. They give us a stable basis on which to confirm House's diagnoses and to judge his medical prowess.

If only there was an equally reliable source of information outside of fiction.

CRAIG DERKSEN received a BA from the University of Manitoba and an MA and Ph.D. from the University of Maryland. He works in many areas of philosophy but his primary interest is the philosophy of popular art. His first exposure to Hugh Laurie was as the Prince Regent in *Black Adder the Third* (also as Prince Ludwig the Indestructible in *Black Adder II*). Craig sometimes wishes he was a House, but is only a Wilson.

A LIMP, A QUIP, AND A CANE
House, the Character

One of the most delightful things about watching House *is what an unapologetic bastard House is: he lies, he cheats, he steals; he mocks with abandon. That's nothing, Brit Karen Traviss says. You should see* her *country's protagonists.*

THE WAY OF THE BASTARD

KAREN TRAVISS

he's arrogant, rude to patients, and dismissive toward his colleagues. He's out of his skull on painkillers a lot of the time. The milk of human kindness doesn't flow in his veins. Dr. Greg House is a beastly, *beastly* man.

Hang on, though. Let's look at him through the eyes of a nation raised on really nasty anti-heroes—Britain. Even one of our iconic kids' TV characters, Dr. Who, has a long history of being a right Bastard—high body count, abandoned assistants, even a spot of genocide now and then. He's much more sympathetic in the latest series, but that Bastardness is still there, and remarked upon by the characters.

So, by that yardstick, is House *really* a bastard? Hell, no. He's pretty loveable, actually, at least in comparison.

U.S. TV doesn't seem to do complete anti-heroes. In many ways, this walking advert for Vicodin is more sinned against than sinning. (And we Brits don't get all the angst over Vicodin, by the way. But more on that later.)

One of the most striking things for a British TV viewer is that so few U.S. series have central characters who are also genuine Bastards. Even

Vic Mackey of the sublime *The Shield* isn't a proper full-on Bastard. Okay, so he beats ten shades of the brown stuff out of suspects, and murders fellow officers, and steals drug money, but his redeeming features—love of his kids, loyalty to his mates, the willingness to give deserving scumbags a good smacking, sheer physical *courage*—make him more of a loveable rogue. Provided you're not a gangsta, Vic would be a pretty good neighbor by our reckoning.

There's a school of thought over here in the U.K. that American TV shies away from showing good things happening to, or emanating from, bad people because there's some fundamental moral lesson required in every show. Some of my compatriots put that down to cultural immaturity—a kind of Panglossian social optimism—or a national lack of willingness to embrace the fact that shit happens and bad guys do win the lottery. They cite the strong religious component in the American psyche: sinners have to be punished, and they have to be *seen* to be punished, if not by the end of the episode then certainly by the end of the first season. (Dr. House is punished with every painful step he takes.)

But I don't think the "only good guys can win" accusation is fair. What we're seeing is a different cultural approach to fiction, nothing more complicated than that. This is simply the style of American TV drama that has evolved over the decades, and it has some roots in Greek tragedy—a genre preoccupied with showing the causality and consequences of our actions. I spend more time talking to Americans than I do Brits most days, and it's clear to me that it's more a matter of taste than belief: there's no naïveté, no subconscious belief that the world really is the way American TV depicts it. It's just what Americans watch to relax. Just because someone reads Harry Potter doesn't mean they believe the universe runs on magic, after all.

Turn this national stereotyping on its head, and it's equally easy to accuse British TV of being unnecessarily gloomy, of ignoring the statistical incidence of nice, normal folk in soap operas, and offering no uplifting message to viewers. We're a nation of whining misery-guts, always bemoaning the decline of everything and how it's bound to get even worse. We nod knowingly when bad things happen to other countries, because "that'll learn 'em." We're joyless.

It's even too crushing for me sometimes. One of the many reasons I don't watch the wrist-slashingly downbeat BBC soap *EastEnders*, for example, is that if I want to see low-life scumbags robbing, cheating, and fornicating their way through the day, I can just drive back to the dog-rough city where I grew up and stare at my former neighbors. Except, of course, that 99 percent of them never indulge in the doom-laden excesses of the soap world anyway. The soap is a fantasy about how much worse life could be, to make you feel lucky by comparison: it's dark and apparently tricked out with the props of reality, but fantasy nonetheless. Dark and depressing doesn't equal authentic any more than unalloyed happy endings do.

Actually, there's one area where British TV *does* slide into over-optimism—and that's in its medical dramas. Despite daily evidence to the contrary in our own state-run National Health Service, we tend to like our medical dramas populated by clever doctors and caring nurses who always have time to get involved in patients' problems. *Casualty* and its spin-off *Holby City* are classics that have their roots firmly in the respectful and uncritical *Emergency Ward Ten* of the 1960s. These long-running series are all set in big, busy hospitals and focus on emergency medicine, with a little topical controversy to spice it up. Staff make mistakes, nurses shag their way through the doctors' rotation, and management gets in the way—but, basically, they're all depicted as good competent folk trying hard to get through the day without killing too many patients, with varying degrees of success. It's sympathetic, and it's obviously set in an alternate universe where time operates differently, because the doctors and nurses can all spend a lot of quality time finding out the very smallest details of their patients' private lives. Such are the demands of drama, though: nobody can make a decent medical series without fabricating that excessive degree of involvement.

But let's return to Greg House and the divine in hospital drama.

Using the Greek tragic model, House has been burdened with a gift from the gods. He's a brilliant diagnostician. He's not just good at his job: he's much, much smarter than anyone else around him, and, in a way, he's treading on divine turf because he's so very good at unraveling the mysteries of life.

But he's not a god, and we never see him deluding himself by thinking that. Being a rude, cocky, patronizing pain in the arse isn't a God complex, not in House. His relationship is with the puzzle rather than the patient. He doesn't appear to get off on having that power over people's lives, which is the hallmark of the god complex: "Your life is in my hands!" That kind of power—a staple of medical fiction—is all about influence over people. The act of finding stuff out and of being right isn't the central pivot of that mindset.

No, House is more Prometheus: the smart-arse who got a bit too cocky with his flaming power from the divine, his red-hot gift of diagnosis, and whom the gods decided to slap down with a perpetual dose of pain, except in his case it's a necrotic muscle rather than eagle-eating-your-liver syndrome. House has paid, and keeps paying, for being such a clever dick and making everyone else look dumb. That's his main crime.

If House's sin were being handsome, he wouldn't have to pay the price. If he were rich, he'd get away with being happy with it. If he were a brilliant athlete or elite spy, we'd grant him his ticket to enjoy life. But House's sin is being *clever*. He's intellectually brilliant. And, in our cultures—American and British—society abhors extreme intelligence, especially intelligence that dispenses with false modesty. Nobody loves a smart-arse. The clever must be put in their place and cut down to size.

House's chronic pain problem is integral to this. You want to be that smart all the time? Well, take *that* all the time. No wonder House has made nasty into an art form; he started out charm-challenged, and when the pain started, he had a head start in the curmudgeon stakes compared to most folks. He's in constant agony. Chronic pain erodes you, exhausts you, and makes you irritable. Of *course* he's going to be short with self-pitying, noncompliant patients or dim-to-average colleagues. He has to suffer fools *and* pain. And what has he done to deserve it? He's on the far end of the bell curve when it comes to brains. It's the revenge of the average, not the wrath of the gods. And they deny him respite.

Much has been made of House's Vicodin habit, which can baffle British viewers. Until I spoke about this to friends with pain problems, I wasn't aware of a moralizing attitude toward painkillers in the U.S. that we just don't have over here; at times, it looks almost religious to me, that pain is good for your soul, and . . . well, maybe you deserve it, so why should we offer you a palliative? There also seems to be a fear that pain relief will create a junkie—witness Dr. Wilson trying to get House off Vicodin—that bewilders us.

In Britain, we don't have to beg the doc for analgesics; it's likely to be all we get prescribed. So Vicodin isn't as meaningful to the plot for us. We can buy codeine over the counter here and get bombed out of our skulls any time we like, just so long as we don't expect real treatment (although for the stop-a-rhino doses we need to get a prescription). My elderly mother, who suffers from chronic pain, came back from her last visit to the doctor with large boxes—yes, I do mean large—of several hundred high-dose codeine tablets. She gets that every time she visits. She could run a drugs cartel if she weren't in so much pain. No treatment, of course, and no referral to a consultant for tests, but she gets plenty of painkillers, because they're cheap and budgets dictate treatment in the U.K. health service. Maybe House needs an exchange visit with a National Health Service hospital to stock up on his meds—but that'd kill the series. A smiling zombiefied House dispensing goodwill just wouldn't work.

So House can't be a bastard because he has a good reason to be as awful as he is, and most real bastards don't. He's in pain. And the stupid system—the medical system he's part of, ironically—doesn't enable those in pain to be soothed. This is the chicken and egg circle of House's cycle of gracelessness; his hubris and his contempt for those around him are exacerbated by chronic pain that fellow doctors are reluctant to relieve.

Apart from the fact that he's played by the utterly adorable Hugh Laurie—who, despite his acting talents, could never come across as wholly bad to a Brit audience even if he were playing Hitler—House is redeemed by being unafraid and always willing to do what's right rather than what's socially or professionally convenient: and the right thing for a doctor is putting the welfare of the patient first—before budgets, before colleagues' reputations and feelings, and before administrators' tidy procedures.

He serves as a reminder that people who do the right thing aren't always comfortable to be around. Laurie wearing the House character is, in fact, a signpost to the nature of House: the apparently unpleasant person with the genuinely decent chap visible beneath.

House is rude, patronizing, arrogant, and abusive to patients and colleagues alike. But he *cures* people while all the polite doctors are standing around in white coats just Not Getting It. This is the price: this is how his karma stays in balance. His loutishness—which is exacerbated by circumstance anyway—is offset by his devotion to curing illness. He's a bizarre example of a holistic approach that isn't remotely touchy-feely or connected to the suffering sick, just good at covering all the angles.

However misanthropic, House would never sneak off for a round of golf or give priority to a more lucrative patient if he could save a life. The human relationship with the patient is missing, but if you're the one with the catheter in your arm waiting to die, the motive and bedside manner of your savior is irrelevant. House wants to win. A patient doesn't have to love him to feel the benefit of that.

He's also honorable in a way that appeals to grumbling, not-very-deferential U.K. audiences: he won't toe the party line. Expected to make a cozy statement about the benefits of a drug program at the hospital, he stands his ground and delivers a withering speech about a colleague being in the pocket of the pharmaceutical company running the drug trials, which House said was to the detriment of patients. What a guy. Wouldn't you be willing to put up with dismissive rudeness in the examination room from a man with scruples like that? He's never going to leave a swab inside you when he closes, or put you on a dubious medication because the company sent him on an expenses-paid trip to Venice. And he won't keep quiet when he knows a colleague isn't competent.

Greg House is super-skilled and eye-wateringly outspoken. But even if he weren't such a whiz at diagnosis, he'd still never make a proper Bastard, because he's *honest*. The doctor who tells you he hasn't a clue what's going on is inherently nobler than the one who tells you not to worry your little head about it because he's clueless and scared to admit it. Tell us the truth, Doc. We can take it.

House is, of course, more of a science fiction series than a medical one for some Brits, in that it's fiction about what science might be able to do. The luxurious standard of hospital care is way beyond what most NHS patients can expect here, and the concept of a health service where you get treatment soon after you've asked for it is also a novel one for a country whose well-being is in the hands of a crumbling National Health Service with waiting lists that can run into years.

But rather like the BBC's home-grown white-coat drama, *Casualty*, where we see staff getting personally involved with patients' pain and misery and spending time on them, we know it's just make-believe and adjust our believometer accordingly.

There's a lesser-known BBC series set in a hospital which is *much* nearer the reality mark in terms of how hospitals behave. In *Bodies*, there aren't many heart-of-gold House characters. Plenty of the nurses are lazy, self-centered, obnoxious harpies who care more about their tea breaks than the needs of patients, the doctors won't speak out when they know colleagues are botching operations, the bureaucracy is a dead weight, and the surgeons aren't remotely amusing and spend their time jockeying for position. In the end, the patient doesn't come first.

Those are *true* Bastards. Those are characters you can look upon and say, "Yes, they're nasty people. They should be saving lives, not feathering their own nests." It's a different kind of drama, and I'll freely admit that given the choice, I prefer to get my entertainment from the constantly redeemed Greg House than the all-too-real *Bodies*. I stopped watching *Bodies* when its unflinching reality became too harrowing; the scene of a woman who couldn't eat unaided being left to go hungry because no nurse was prepared to feed her was too much like real cases I've actually witnessed, and I just changed channels forever. I'm a writer who specializes in gritty realism, but I really don't want it as a consumer of fiction. I know bad things happen in the health service, so I like TV that lets me relax, not that makes me want to rush to the barricades and overthrow the government. I can get plenty of that from factual programming.

Greg House, for all his acid tongue and general lack of social graces, has a conscience. I'm not sure he even has a truly repellent character. He's abrasive, yes, but he's *funny*. He gets all the best scathing one-liners. His abuse is creative, and his reservoir of vitriol is kept to chivvy staff into striving for higher standards of care, and the patient into helping themselves more. There's nothing gratuitous about his abuse; the end justifies the means.

If anything, he's more like the heavy drama version of Dr. Cox in *Scrubs* than a real anti-hero. Cox is a bully, but he's a good doctor, a lonely and wounded man, and has the best insults of any character on TV. As with House, you tolerate the stream of invective because you know that underneath it is a man who puts all he's got into making people well again.

In the end, House fails the Bastard test because he keeps faith with the sick. Nothing is more important to him than finding a cure, or—sometimes inevitably—the least unpleasant death. It doesn't matter that he isn't a people person and has no interest in the patients themselves, or that he's driven by professional pride. He gets results. That's the most patient-centered approach I can imagine.

KAREN TRAVISS is a *New York Times* bestselling author of military science fiction whose critically acclaimed Wess'har novels have been nominated for the Philip K. Dick and Campbell awards. She also writes Star Wars novels for Lucasfilm, where she explores the same themes of identity, species, and political and personal corruption. A former defense correspondent, and TV and newspaper journalist, she has also served in the Royal Naval Auxiliary Service and the Territorial Army. She lives in Wiltshire, England. You can visit her Web site at www.karentraviss.com.

It's impossible to imagine House *(or House) without Hugh Laurie. Though, having seen his previous work, it's hard to imagine the show with him. The path from the foppish Prince George to the dour, sarcastic Gregory House is a perplexing one — but one that, as Geoff Klock shows, is in some ways remarkably direct.*

HUGH LAURIE'S HOUSE

GEOFF KLOCK

regular dictionary has maybe 50,000 entries; a good one has 100,000 entries. The *Oxford English Dictionary* has half a million entries — every word used in the English language since Chaucer. It does more than define words; it gives definitions across time, tracking changes in the usage of a single word across centuries, illustrated with quotations from the literature of each historical period. The *OED* is important in the study of poetry, because poets are sensitive to the history of words and invoke that history to get the most charge out of the language. Robert Frost's "Directive," for example, describes leading the reader to a secret goblet of which he may "[d]rink and be whole again beyond confusion" (379). In his book *Genius*, literary critic Harold Bloom remarks, "Frost . . . seem[s] to have known that the Indo-European root of 'confusion' initially signified the pouring of a libation to the gods" (361). The history of the word comes into play to determine the meaning of the poem.

Just as poets think across time to chose the word that will bring, in its history, the proper meanings to a poem, a good casting director will select an actor that carries, in his career, the best meanings for a show.

Steve Martin, for example, is a fascinating choice to play the villain in David Mamet's *The Spanish Prisoner*—as a con man we feel there is something going on beneath the surface of this character; a comedian in a straight role is an interesting way of communicating this to the viewer, who cannot help but expect another side to emerge. Every actor's career is like every word's history—an important factor in our appreciation of television or poetry. This is why certain actors become totally unusable: Erik Estrada will never be more than that guy from *CHiPs*, which is why when you see him now, he only spoofs that character.

Everything about Hugh Laurie's career as a goofy, friendly British comedian before *House* suggests that he is totally inappropriate to play a brilliant, cynical American doctor. And yet his earlier roles inform his portrayal of Doctor Gregory House in surprising and canny ways. House is even more important on *House* than main characters usually are, even in shows named after them: like Hamlet making his way through a generic revenge tragedy that is beneath his obvious charisma and intelligence, Hugh Laurie's House is an amazing, compelling, and surprisingly complex character trapped in a repetitive and formulaic hospital version of *CSI*. Like *CSI*—and like *Law & Order*—*House* can be counted on by viewers to be pretty good most of the time, but never amazing; Hugh Laurie as House, on the other hand, is always stunning.

Hugh Laurie's Biography and Career

Laurie was born and raised in Oxford, England. His education was top notch—he attended a prestigious English preparatory school, Eton, and Selwyn College, Cambridge, where he studied Anthropology and Archaeology. His father was an Olympic gold medalist as well as a doctor. Hugh Laurie himself admitted the primary reason he attended Cambridge was for rowing, but he had to give it up because of a glandular fever. In the late 1990s, Hugh Laurie realized he was clinically depressed when he was in a race car and felt neither scared nor excited. His depression was treated successfully.

After giving up rowing, Laurie joined the Cambridge Footlights, a comedy group, where he started lifelong friendships with Emma Thompson and Stephen Fry (Laurie's real-life daughter appears for a single scene in

Thompson's *Wit*, as the main character's younger self). The jokes in the Cambridge Footlights are already extraordinarily high-brow, including brainy word play ("He walked with a pronounced limp. L-I-M-P, pronounced 'limp'") and a parody of a Shakespeare master class. Their production of their annual revue *The Cellar Tapes* won a Perrier Award for comedy, and it was transferred to London's West End and eventually to television. From there the three of them starred in a sketch comedy show called *Alfresco*, which ran for two seasons. As Thompson pursued other work, Laurie and Fry collaborated on three major projects together in the 1980s and 1990s—the *Blackadder* series, *A Bit of Fry and Laurie*, and *Jeeves and Wooster*.

Fry and Laurie was a sketch comedy show that ran from 1989–1995. At a time when being posh Oxbridge-educated young men could not have been less popular in comedy, Fry and Laurie were more Oxbridge than Oxbridge. They used their position to poke fun at the upper class, and many sketches, including one around a very high-class dinner, involved advanced word play, posh accents, and jokes about vacationing in Venice. In one recurring sketch, Fry and Laurie spoof high-powered American execs in the Gordon Gekko mode; managing something as small as a health club, they drink all day and shout, at every opportunity, such elaborate curses as "Damn! Double damn! And an extra pint of Damn for the weekend!!!"

Blackadder is actually the generic name for four BBC television series: *The Black Adder*, *Blackadder II*, *Blackadder the Third*, and *Blackadder Goes Fourth*. Each series was set in England in a distinct historical period—the Middle Ages, the Renaissance, the Regency (the late eighteenth and early nineteenth centuries), and World War I. Rowan Atkinson played Blackadder, a cowardly, cynical opportunist reincarnated anew for each age. He became smarter with each incarnation, but it did him no good, as he never had more power than the insane and stupid people who controlled the destiny of the age. Hugh Laurie played major characters in the third and fourth series—in the Regency period he was the idiot fop Prince George, and in World War I he was the dim-witted Lieutenant George. Both roles were essentially the same—stupid people such as Laurie reigned over smart people such as Blackadder, who were cynical from seeing how stupid the world is.

Jeeves and Wooster began as a series of stories by P. G. Wodehouse; Laurie has said that reading P. G. Wodehouse saved his life when he was depressed. The stories were adapted for television from 1990–1993. The episodes varied in quality—the show's reputation rested almost entirely on its perfect casting, as Laurie's Wooster and Fry's Jeeves were definitive and flawless. The show revolved around Laurie's dopey upper-class gentleman Bertie Wooster getting himself into various kinds of difficult social situations (such as accidentally being engaged to two women at the same time); Fry's Jeeves was his impossibly intelligent and wise valet who regularly got him out of trouble.

As Mr. Palmer in *Sense and Sensibility* (1995) we see Laurie as an unpleasant character, a new turn in his repertoire. Laurie plays a completely silly criminal bungler—a puppy-napper—in the live action Disney film *101 Dalmatians* (1996). That same year he wrote a loving, half-serious half-spoof crime novel, *The Gun Seller*, Laurie's only novel to date. In *Spice World* (1997)—the Spice Girls movie—Laurie appears briefly as a character listed as Poirot (the Agatha Christie detective) in a throwaway scene where he accuses a character of a crime in a drawing room. His 1998 *Friends* cameo ("The One With Ross's Wedding, part 2") reprised his *Sense and Sensibility* meanness in an overtly funny vein, making fun of American comedy characters: his disdainful use of the name "Pheebes" made the scene famous.

The Path to Dr. House

The seeds of Dr. House were already in Hugh Laurie's biography outside of the roles he has played. Though it was not necessarily something a casting director would take into account, having a powerful and important doctor for a father, completing a top-notch Oxbridge education, losing his physical prowess to illness, and dealing with serious clinical depression already inform Laurie's portrayal of Dr. House.

Dr. House is brilliant, and at least one aspect of Laurie's career feeds into this perfectly: *Fry and Laurie* established Laurie's obvious intelligence for the viewing audience. Fry and Laurie were upper-class young men out to lambaste the upper class, just as the educated, powerful House uses his brilliance to show his "superiors" up. Because his collaborations with Fry were comedy programs, he played off of this established intelligence in two ways: his characters have been either brilliant and pompous or very, very stupid, but rarely in between. House is no exception.

Fry and Laurie, *Blackadder*, and *Jeeves and Wooster* all paired Laurie with a foil, someone for him to play against, and so Laurie became associated, in various ways, with the qualities of his antagonist or friend as much as the qualities of the character he played. In these shows we saw two sets of opposing terms that would organize Laurie's career and culminate in House: intelligence and stupidity, heart and cynicism. The relationship between House and Blackadder is clear—in *House*, Laurie has shifted from playing one of the idiots in power to a character much more like his foil Blackadder: cynical, brilliant, and exhausted with his inadequate help. The path from *Jeeves and Wooster* to *House* is exactly the same: Laurie has moved from being the hapless idiot to becoming a version of his brilliant foil (here Jeeves). Like Blackadder, House is cynical; like Jeeves, House has (arguably) an essentially good heart.

In retrospect the darker Mr. Palmer in *Sense and Sensibility* was the turning point for Laurie—after *Sense and Sensibility* his idiot fop personae began to be filtered through the crime genre, where it led directly to House. There is precedent in his earlier career for Laurie being connected to the crime genre. A recurring bit on *Fry and Laurie* was a spoof of 1970s thriller television, in which Laurie played Alan, hired as a secret agent by something only known as "The Department." Another recurring sketch on the show had Fry and Laurie as secret agents who were far too nice to each other and totally ignored matters of national security; in one episode they telephoned a Russian spy and just asked him politely if he would stop spying on them (he did).

These early, silly crime genre roles get picked up in the 1990s three times, all for comic effect. Laurie is once a criminal and twice a detective: a puppy-napper in *101 Dalmatians*, Agatha Christie's Poirot in the Spice Girls movie, and author of *The Gun Seller*, Laurie's one and only novel. While *The Gun Seller* is not, of course, a "role" for Laurie the actor, it is impossible not to hear his voice, and the voices of the characters he has played, as you read this first-person novel. You can't miss Laurie's British comedy voice in a line like, "She . . . pointed a pair of grey eyes at me. I say a pair. I mean her pair. She didn't get a pair of someone else's out of a drawer and point them at me" (13). *The Gun Seller*, it must be said, is a genuinely good novel; it is a spy thriller that could stand tall in the genre even if the jokes were removed, and the jokes are good enough that it would still be a very fun read if the plot and characters were no more than excuses for jokes. *The Gun Seller* spoofs the detective genre in much the way the Hitchhiker's Guide to the Galaxy series spoofs science fiction: Laurie writes "there's an undeniable pleasure in stepping into an open-top sports car driven by a beautiful woman. It feels like you're climbing into a metaphor" (133).

One of the main objects of satire in the novel is the hard-boiled detective in the Philip Marlow vein, typified by the Sam Spade character in *The Maltese Falcon*. Unlike the "golden age" detectives such as Sherlock Holmes and Hercule Poirot, the hard-boiled detectives were marked more by toughness than brains. In his novel, Laurie gets it both ways, as his detective thinks (and narrates) in quite a smart way, making fun of his own stupid, often thug-like, actions. Here is the main character narrating about a fight he is in the middle of:

> So I inhaled deeply, through my nose, straightened up to get as close as I could to his face, held the breath for a moment, and then let out what the Japanese martial artists refer to as a kiai—you'd probably call it a very loud noise, and that wouldn't be so far off—a scream of such blinding, shocking, what-the-fuck-was-that-intensity, that I frightened myself quite badly (6).

In *The Maltese Falcon*, Sam Spade is deeply cynical on the outside—as a private detective he has seen all the corruption the world has to offer, and, at least at first, does everything he can to keep from getting personally involved. But at heart Spade is a romantic, who ultimately falls for the female client he wants to protect from the dark conspiracy he has uncovered.

In terms of Laurie's career, it is with *The Gun Seller* that we see the four aspects of Laurie's earlier roles (intelligence and stupidity, cynicism and heart) in a single character: as a highbrow spoof (a mode he perfected in

Fry and Laurie), Laurie's detective is both smart and stupid; as a participant in the hard-boiled tradition he is both cynical and romantic. We are at this point only one step away from Dr. House, who combines intelligence, cynicism, and heart; House spends his free time making fun of stupid people and deflating their pretensions, which is exactly Laurie's attitude toward the genre of the hard-boiled detective novel and his main character. Dr. House matches the hard-boiled detective on many points: like Sam Spade, he has a cavalier, cynical, cruel, and occasionally thug-like exterior, but this exterior conceals a troubled man, lonely and in pain, who cares deeply and passionately about his patients and friends. The hard-boiled detective, notably, was a violent break in the crime genre from his dapper and brainy golden age counterpart. In creating House, the show's creators use Laurie to take these two very different kinds of detectives and fuse them, while looking back to the origin of both.

Hugh Laurie as House

House creator David Shore has admitted House was inspired by the most famous character in crime literature—Sherlock Holmes. Laurie spoofed the second most famous golden age detective—Agatha Christie's Poirot—as well, in the Spice Girls movie. Experience spoofing Poirot is an odd way for Laurie to invoke the detective genre in House, but that is exactly what he does.

In the most clear and obvious nod to Holmes, House's address is 221, a reference to Holmes's famous 221B Baker Street address. Another stark allusion to Holmes is only visible in the script—the man who shoots House is not given a name in the first episode of season three, but in the script he is listed as "Moriarty," the name of Holmes's nemesis. The less obvious connections between the most famous golden age detective and House, however, are the most important and illuminating. Like Holmes, House is brilliant, egomaniacal, and misanthropic; House solves bizarre cases with intelligence rather than muscle; House's only real friend is a down-to-earth doctor sidekick (Holmes's Doctor Watson becomes House's Dr. Wilson). Like the violin-playing Holmes, House is a musician (Hugh Laurie is an accomplished musician who can play piano, guitar, and harmonica). Sir Arthur Conan Doyle based Holmes on a famous surgeon, Joseph Bell, and so David Shore's creation of a Holmesian doctor brings the genre full circle.

The pilot of *House* is a phenomenally good start, one that contained a good first case and also established a host of characters without hitting the audience over the head with the exposition stick. By the end of the pilot we had seen Wilson, Cameron, Chase, Foreman, and Cuddy in action, and we understood the basics as to what made them tick. In House's case, we had seen all of the qualities of Sherlock Holmes. We saw House take painkillers four times, and we see him order and then steal a bottle of painkillers—this was handled with enough subtlety that we don't immediately register that House, like Holmes, is an unrepentant drug addict, but it is clearly there. His first response to the idea of a twenty-nine-year-old woman dying of a brain tumour was the caustic, "Boring." "Humanity is overrated" and "Everyone lies" came in short order, and he was cruel to a woman whose son had asthma because he thought she was stupid. He deduced that a patient with orange skin had a wife who was cheating on him in an instant, a lightning-fast and advanced Holmesian deduction. Rather than look for proof, House looks for the idea that explains all the symptoms—in the pilot he had to prove what he believed to his patient, though he would have rather not dealt with her ("Shouldn't we be speaking to the patient before we start diagnosing?" Foreman asked. House replied, "Is she a doctor?"); this is one of the main methods Holmes employs to solve crimes—by searching for that one unifying idea, no matter how bizarre.

Once we realize that House is derived from Holmes, we can see how all of Laurie's roles culminate in House: the Oxbridge intelligence, the smart-dumb pairing (Jeeves and Wooster, Blackadder and Prince George, House and the legion of inferiors he must deal with), the criminals and the detectives (and House is certainly both). Two very different kinds of detectives collide in House—the golden age British fop genius Sherlock Holmes and the hard-boiled cynical-on-the-outside, romantic-on-the-inside Sam Spade. This is why Laurie is perfect as House—because his experience spoofing British fops and the hard-boiled American detective are equally needed to make House work. House is not a spoof of the detective novel. But the relationship between *House* and the detective genre is not unlike the relationship between a spoof and its source: the latter version tweaks elements we are already familiar with to make us see old things in new ways, to make an old genre seem fresh. Laurie reinvents the detective genre in *House*, combining two very different detectives in a single character and giving both a much-needed sense of humor.

———————————

GEOFF KLOCK is the author of *How to Read Superhero Comics and Why* (Continuum 2002) and *Imaginary Biographies: Misreading the Lives of the Poets* (Continuum 2007), based off of his doctoral thesis at Balliol College, Oxford. The first applies Harold Bloom's poetics of influence to comic books; the second argues that the bizarre portrayal of historical writers in nineteenth- and twentieth-century poetry constitutes a genre (and will be followed by a companion book on film). His blog—Remarkable: Short Appreciations of Poetry, Comics, Film, Television, and Music—can be found at geoffklock.blogspot.com. He lives in New York City, where he is a freelance academic.

REFERENCES

Bloom, Harold. *Genius*. New York: Warner Books, 2002.

"The Cambridge Footlights Review," special feature on *A Bit of Fry and Laurie: The Complete Second Series*. BBC2, 2006.

"Episode One, Season Two." *A Bit of Fry and Laurie*. BBC2, 1990.

Frost, Robert. *The Poetry of Robert Frost*. Ed. Edward Connery Latham. New York: Henry Holt, 1975.

"House." *Wikipedia.org*. 1 Dec. 2006. <http://en.wikipedia.org/wiki/House_(TV_series)>

"Hugh Laurie." *Wikipedia.org*. 1 Dec. 2006. <http://en.wikipedia.org/wiki/Hugh_Laurie>

Laurie, Hugh. *The Gun Seller*. London: Arrow Books, 1996.

O'Hare, Kate. "Building House Is Hard Work." *tv.zap2it.com*. 5 Jan. 2005. <http://tv.zap2it.com/tveditorial/tve_main/1,1002,271%7C92770%7C1%7C,00.html>

M*A*S*H's Hawkeye Pierce was an icon, a prank-playing, antiestablishment hero for a generation. House has those first two—the prank playing and the establishment anti-ing—down; it's that "hero" part some would argue with, no matter how many lives he saves. Lois Winston draws a line between the two doctors, and comes up with a surprising explanation for their similarities and their differences.

IS GREGORY HOUSE THE HAWKEYE PIERCE OF THE TWENTY-FIRST CENTURY?

LOIS WINSTON

They sure don't make TV doctors like they used to.

Gone are the days of the benevolent doctors James Kildare, Ben Casey, and Marcus Welby. Those patriarchs of bygone medical dramas, those god-like miracle workers with their compassionate bedside manners, must be turning over in their prime-time graves at the likes of Gregory House. But just as the baby boomers, the first generation to grow up on television, have matured over the decades, so has the drama we've watched. When Bob Dylan said, "The times they are a-changin'," he had no idea just how much they would change over the next four decades. And once we lost those rose-colored glasses we purchased in Haight-Ashbury or at Woodstock, we were confronted with medical dramas that were more realistic. Edgier. More cynical. And nowhere is this more evident than in the character of Gregory House.

But we didn't leap out of Alex Stone's home office from *The Donna Reed Show* to land in Princeton-Plainsboro Teaching Hospital. The transition, at first, was gradual. Then came 1972 and a groundbreaking comedy with serious overtones. In the television version of Robert Altman's *M*A*S*H*, we were introduced to Captain Benjamin Franklin

"Hawkeye" Pierce, a very different doctor from what we were used to seeing on television. *M*A*S*H* dealt with the highly incendiary issues of the day and managed to stay beneath the censor's radar by masking its cynicism and political indictment of the Vietnam War in a police action from thirty years earlier. In creating the brutally honest character of Hawkeye, the writers of *M*A*S*H* set the stage for House.

Much has been written about the comparisons between House and Sherlock Holmes, but when I watch House, I'm bombarded with reminders of Hawkeye. I'm drawn to House in much the same way I was drawn to Hawkeye. Both characters are richly complex and skillfully developed, but for me the similarities go so far that I believe the writers are paying homage to Hawkeye in much the same way they pay homage to Holmes. And yes, there are differences between the two characters, but those differences are far outweighed, I believe, by the similarities. So let's discuss House in relationship to Hawkeye.

What You See Is Not Always What You Get

Neither House nor Hawkeye are proponents of the "Dress for Success" doctrine. Both are more like poster boys for The Morning After the Night Before, always looking like they've just rolled out of bed in the same clothes they wore the previous day—or throughout the previous week. A perennial five o'clock shadow along with uncombed hair in desperate need of a date with a pair of scissors accentuate the constant state of dishevelment of both men. Hawkeye looked more like a combat soldier after a two-week bunker encampment, while House can easily be mistaken for one of the indigents treated at the Princeton-Plainsboro clinic. Wear big boy clothes like Wilson, Chase, or Foreman? Never. It's House's way of sticking it to the establishment in general and dean of medicine Dr. Lisa Cuddy in particular.

With few exceptions, the only time Hawkeye "cleaned up" was for a date, and then he usually went overboard, donning a tux he kept pressed under his mattress for a rendezvous in the supply tent. House? We finally saw him wear a suit for his dinner date with Cameron in "Love Hurts" (1-20) toward the end of the first season.

Hawkeye usually walked around the 4077th in a bathrobe over an army issue T-shirt and trousers. Often, he didn't even bother with the trousers, wearing only boxers under his robe. For less casual attire, he slipped into one of many Hawaiian shirts. House walks around Princeton-Plainsboro Teaching Hospital wearing jeans and graphic T-shirts of rock bands such as Mötley Crüe or shirts sporting skulls and skeletons or advertisements for obscure businesses, like the one that touted car loans for people with questionable credit. "Dress for Success" is definitely neither man's mantra.

There are further outward similarities between the two men. House twirls his cane almost as often as he uses it to help him walk. Hawkeye often strolled around the compound twirling a golf club, although we rarely saw him actually playing golf . . . but then again, golf and mine fields aren't exactly compatible.

When House isn't puzzling through the symptoms of some strange illness, he spends his downtime watching either *General Hospital* or porn. Occasionally we see him engage in a higher form of entertainment—playing piano. When Hawkeye wasn't standing knee deep in blood and wounded bodies in the OR, we often found him reading the latest issue of one of his prized nudist magazines. Articles—or more precisely the pictures from those articles—on women's nude volleyball were of particular interest to him.

Okay, so I suppose it's not that far-fetched to find a doctor hooked on watching a medical soap opera. Hawkeye, however, had no such luxury. There wasn't any TV in South Korean *M*A*S*H* units back in the early 1950s, and he left the piano playing to Father Mulcahy. Had porn been available to him, I'm sure he would have traded in all his nudie volleyball photos for some Grade-A blue flicks. His choices of mindless brain candy were decidedly limited. But both men, as brilliant as they are, seem to need escapist entertainment of some form, and that form often leans toward ogling naked women.

I Don't Have To, and You Can't Make Me

In "DNR" (1-9), House said, ". . . there's no 'I' in 'team.' There is a 'me,' though, if you jumble it up." The next season in "House vs. God" (2-19), Wilson stated, "They could build monuments to your self-centeredness." In those two quotes we see exactly what House thinks of himself and what others think about him. House's world revolves around House. He knows it and everyone else knows it.

Both Hawkeye and House mock authority and refuse to play by the rules. Their wardrobes are but one reflection of their disdain for authority and act as a protest against that authority. Hawkeye railed against the war and the politics that sent him to Korea, but he did so in a way that often made us laugh. He used humor and sarcasm to alleviate not only his own misery at being in a situation beyond his control but also the misery of those around him. In the pilot episode he told Frank Burns, "I happen to be an officer only because I foolishly opened an invitation from President Truman to come to this party."

Here is where Hawkeye and House truly begin to differ. House rails against authority of any kind, believing he is answerable to no one. His sarcasm lashes out at those around him and rarely does anyone laugh — because he's not funny. He's cruel. He's angry at the world for his own personal circumstances and no one is safe from being the target of that anger.

Refusing to play by the rules is a recurrent theme in both characters. Although a captain in the army, Hawkeye adamantly refused to carry a gun. He also refused to turn over injured North Korean soldiers to the MPs until he'd treated their wounds. His unwillingness to play by the rules was based on his compassion, his deep convictions, and his medical ethics: a doctor is supposed to save lives, not take them, and a doctor's first duty is to the patient, no matter who that patient is. Hawkeye's third finger salute to authority and army regulations was ultimately for unselfish reasons.

House, on the other hand, is completely egocentric. He refuses to play by the rules because he believes he's above them. Although clinic duty is required of all doctors at the hospital, House will do anything to get out of it. The patients who come to the clinic don't interest him. Their complaints are run-of-the-mill and beneath him. As such, he'll resort to anything from lies to bribery to blackmail to avoid clinic duty. And when the lies and bribery and blackmail fail and he's forced to attend to the clinic patients, his contempt for their sniffles and rashes is apparent.

It was only a matter of time before he pissed off the wrong patient.

And boy, was Michael Tritter the wrong man to piss off. At the end of "Fools for Love" (3-5), we learned that Tritter was a cop. He was so furious with the way House treated him in the clinic that he arrested House for possession of a controlled substance (the Vicodin pills he observed House taking while on duty in the clinic).

But even after House spent a night in jail, he was so convinced of his own superiority and self-righteousness that he didn't consider Tritter a serious threat. Tritter, we soon learned, was a bully who would stop at nothing to get back at House for his perceived indignities, including blackmail and coercion of the other doctors in an attempt to get one of them to rat House out.

Tritter claimed he just wanted House to find another way to cope with his leg pain before House, practicing medicine under the influence of drugs, made a mistake and a patient died. However, it's hard to accept such an altruistic motive when we saw the hell Tritter put the other doctors through in order to get his way. Still, House believed that Tritter was no more than a bully who, if ignored, would eventually tire of the game and go away. Tritter was not going away, and House was too wrapped up in his own self-righteousness, his feelings of superiority, and his contempt of Tritter to see that.

The Misanthrope Factor

In "Fidelity" (1-7) Cameron told House, "You're a misanthrope, not a misogynist." House has a decidedly antisocial personality and a negative opinion of everyone. His acerbic, brutal honesty doesn't border on cruelty; most of the time it is downright cruel. The more someone reaches out to him, the more House abuses them. This is one of the ways in which he differs from Hawkeye the most. Hawkeye was a prankster who didn't suffer fools or hypocrites lightly. Although both men resort to sarcasm and adolescent pranks, Hawkeye's were escape mechanisms to maintain his sanity within the confines of an insane situation. Even when he was at his cruelest, we still laughed because his targets—usually the hypocritical Frank Burns and his pompous ass replacement, Charles Emerson Winchester III—were so deserving of what Hawkeye dished out.

When Hawkeye turned his attention to the army, he always had a higher purpose, like when he invented a fictitious Captain Tuttle so that the man's salary could be donated to a local orphanage. His chicanery about to be discovered, Hawkeye killed off Tuttle in a fictitious act of heroism and had the entire camp mourning the loss of a hero that no one would admit never having met.

Hawkeye blackmailed a lieutenant into allowing a corporal to marry a local Korean girl. He taught a bigoted sergeant a lesson in prejudice. He badgered a general into allowing the enlisted into the Officers' Club. He instigated a riot in the mess tent after several weeks of "a river of liver and an ocean of fish," then schemed with Radar and Trapper to get ribs delivered from Chicago for the entire camp. Even when Hawkeye was at his juvenile worst (or best, depending on how you look at it), his antics, for the most part, had a higher purpose.

House, on the other hand, is a control freak who is so afraid of any emotional connection to another human that he goes out of his way to alienate people, deliberately lashing out at anyone who crosses his path. In "DNR" (1-9) Cuddy told him, ". . . when I hired you, I also set aside $50,000 a year for legal expenses. So far you've come in under budget." In real life she'd need a lot more than $50,000 a year. In real life House's sexist and racist comments to his staff, his patients, and their families would not only get him fired, but slapped with lawsuit after lawsuit. And that doesn't even begin to address his questionable medical ethics. We're only talking personality here. Lucky for him, television allows for a bit of artistic license.

The biggest difference between Hawkeye and House is that Hawkeye cared deeply about the patients he treated, while House shows no regard for his. To him it's all about solving the mystery of the illness *du jour*. In "DNR" Wilson told him, "You know how some doctors have the Messiah complex; they need to save the world? You've got the Rubik's complex; you need to solve the puzzle" (1-9).

House would much prefer to sit in his office, puzzling out the cause of symptoms, than enter a patient's room. If it were up to him, he wouldn't even speak to his patients. When he does reluctantly interact with them, he browbeats, intimidates, and insults them. He lies to them. He's downright nasty, even to children. In episode after episode he repeats his belief that "everybody lies," especially patients, so what's the point of speaking with them in the first place? He went so far in the pilot episode as to say, ". . . treating illnesses is why we became doctors, treating patients is what makes most doctors miserable."

Hawkeye cared so deeply about his patients that he often volunteered to go to the front during a battle, putting his own life in jeopardy, to save a soldier. Each time he lost a patient, he took it personally, losing a little bit of himself in the process. In the final episode, when he believed himself responsible for a Korean mother suffocating her infant, he suffered a nervous breakdown.

Not only would House never get close enough to a patient to be affected by his death, he believes the end justifies the means. He'll risk a patient's life to prove he's right. And he knows this about himself. In "Meaning" (3-1) he said, "I had no objective reason to think I was right. Just needed the puzzle." He practices a form of medicine where the patient may become a battlefield casualty, but that's fine with him as long as he's proven right in the end.

When I was doing research for this essay, I spoke with author C. J. Lyons, a physician, to get her take on House from a medical perspective. She concurred as to House's lack of regard for his patients: "Often the methods he employs are sloppy science, cause harm and/or pain to his patients, are done without [his] patient's knowledge or consent, and violate medical ethics. He's meant to be brilliant because of his deductive abilities and observational skills, but he's really practicing the same kind of medicine they practiced in the 1700s—trial and error."

House apparently wouldn't debate C. J.'s take on him. As he said in "Occam's Razor" (1-3), "Tests take time. Treatment's quicker." It's all about solving the puzzle to House. The patient be damned.

She Loves Me; She Loves Me Not

Both men have had one true love in their lives. For Hawkeye we learned that love was Carlye Breslin, a nurse he lived with while in medical school. When he was briefly reunited with Carlye for one episode in "The More I See You" (4-22), we learned that Carlye left Hawkeye because he was so committed to his work that he was unable to commit fully to their relationship. Hawkeye, for all his one-night stands and womanizing while in Korea, admitted to Carlye that there had never been anyone since her. When asked why she left, Carlye said, "I had to survive."

We saw the same theme in House's relationship with Stacy Warner. Like Hawkeye and Carlye, House and Stacy lived together. In "Three Stories" (1-21) Stacy reappeared after a five-year absence, and we learned the circumstances surrounding House's leg injury and Stacy's involvement: she was responsible for House's limp and leg pain. After House suffered an infarction in his leg, Stacy waited until he was in a coma, and then gave the go-ahead for a middle ground procedure that saved House's life but left him permanently injured. It's an option House would have refused. It was also the act that wound up destroying their relationship, and Stacy, too, left in order to survive.

Both women married other men. Both, when reunited with their former lovers, were confronted with feelings they'd buried but never lost. Both couples faced their *Casablanca* moment, with the women tempted to leave their husbands. In the end, neither did—though Stacy stayed with hers only because House told her she should.

Hawkeye was a glib master of small talk. House admittedly is incapable of small talk. In "Love Hurts" (1-20) he told Wilson, "I don't know how to have casual conversation. You think you're talking about one thing, and either you are and it's incredibly boring, or you're not because it's subtext and you need a decoder ring."

Hawkeye used meaningless small talk to distance himself from others. He was afraid to get too close, afraid to care about anyone other than his patients, afraid to lose his heart to another woman. House does much the same, but instead of casual hook-ups and clever banter, he resorts to curmudgeonly behavior to build barriers between himself and others.

For all his compassion, Hawkeye feared feeling too deeply and too much about anyone of the opposite sex. House fears feeling anything toward anyone.

Physician, Heal Thyself

Finally, we come to the issue of addiction. For Hawkeye, it was his alcohol. Hawkeye needed to drink to relieve the horrors of what he saw on a daily basis in Korea. When he wasn't in the OR, we rarely saw him without a drink in his hand. He had his own gin still set up in the Swamp, and he spent much of his time in the Swamp getting drunk. He raided Henry's liquor cabinet. He was a regular at the Officer's Club. Bottom line? Hawkeye was an alcoholic. And like many alcoholics, he refused to admit his dependency.

There were episodes that dealt with this issue throughout the series's eleven years, and from time to time Hawkeye would reluctantly admit that he was drinking too much and cut back. Or he'd be forced into abstinence when some general ordered the camp to go dry and his still was confiscated. He always insisted, though, that he never let his drinking affect his performance in the OR. Until the day a hangover forced him to walk out of the OR. Then he finally admitted to a *possible* problem. However, the boozing picked up in the next episode.

House is hooked on Vicodin. He's so hooked that he had a secret stash of 600 pills in his home. He's so hooked that he forged Wilson's signature on prescriptions. He's so hooked that when Officer Tritter confiscated his stash and cut off all his sources of supply, House began to go into withdrawal. He's built up such a need for the pills, which he had taken to popping like M&Ms, that when Cuddy began doling out a normal regimen of meds to him, they had no effect on House's pain. He's a junkie, and like all junkies, if you thought he was a mean SOB when his pain was manageable, he's a hundred times worse when it's not.

We begin to wonder if maybe Tritter was right, even if his motives were skewed more toward revenge than a concern for the patients House treats. Is the Vicodin controlling House's decision-making abilities?

In "Finding Judas" (3-9), House nearly subjected a five-year-old to a double amputation because he was convinced it was the only way to save her life. Luckily, Chase intervened just as the surgeon was about to remove the girl's arm. House was wrong in his diagnosis, but at first he refused to admit it, going so far as to punch Chase out when he dared to challenge House's diagnosis and attempt to present the correct one.

Was House's brain clouded by pain and withdrawal or, worse yet, as Foreman suggested earlier, had the withdrawal caused House to develop paranoia? Would he have made the same misdiagnosis had he been popping Vicodin throughout the episode? Are his abilities, as he insists, unaffected by the drug use? These are questions left unanswered. But at the end of the episode we saw Wilson caving and striking a deal with Tritter. So even Wilson, who had stood by House to the point of committing perjury to save his friend from going to prison, finally realized that House had become his own worst enemy.

Hawkeye + Thirty Years = House

So let's go back and examine the initial premise of this essay. Is Gregory House the Hawkeye Pierce of the twenty-first century? Forget that M*A*S*H was about the Korean War and that by now Hawkeye would either be long dead from Pickled Liver Syndrome or spending his retirement playing golf in some assisted-living community in Palm Beach. Suspend disbelief for a moment and assume that, through the magic of television, Hawkeye hasn't aged at the same rate as the rest of us. It's 2007 and Hawkeye Pierce is now head diagnostician at Princeton-Plainsboro Teaching Hospital. Except he's changed his name to Gregory House.

Hawkeye Pierce would have left Korea a changed man. In order to survive, he would have had to build a titanium bunker around his heart and emotions. He'd have come home to more senselessness. The Korean War ended, but it took with it more than the lives of those embroiled in it. America didn't lose its innocence in the turbulent sixties; the seeds were planted in the men and women who returned from Korea.

Hawkeye came home to what baby boomer Gregory House grew up in: the Cold War and McCarthyism. The assassinations of John F. Kennedy, Bobby Kennedy, and Martin Luther King, Jr. Watergate. Vietnam. Irangate. Bosnia. Somalia. 9-11. Afghanistan. Iraq.

As my friend C. J. so aptly put it, "Hawkeye was a very (psychologically speaking) healthy person adapting to a very unhealthy environment. House has a very unhealthy psyche and finds himself unable to adapt to a nurturing and friendly atmosphere because he's broken."

Was House ever as healthy as Hawkeye?

We are told that his bitterness existed long before the infarction in his leg. In "Detox" (1-11), Wilson said, "You alienate people." House responded, "I've been alienating people since I was three." (Wilson also claimed House had changed since the infarction, that he'd become miserable and afraid to face himself, but maybe the infarction only acted to magnify what was always within House's personality.) And Stacy on more than one occasion reinforced the notion that House's disposition was far from sunny prior to his infarction.

His childhood could be the culprit. We know that House's father was stationed in Japan when House was fourteen, and we know that an incident that happened in a Japanese hospital set House on the road to becoming a doctor. We also know, though he rarely talks about his parents, that he has issues with his father and has probably had them for most of his life. Wilson suggested that House thinks he's a disappointment to his father, but again, we don't know why.

In the end, though, because of this, House is a more realistic character, a Hawkeye without the magical make-believe of Hollywood. We all know a House, a man jaded and embittered by life. We've probably never met a Hawkeye. House is Hawkeye without the sugar coating we were fed for the first three or four decades of television. Gregory House is Hawkeye Pierce when viewed through the lens of realism and not the rose-colored lens of Hollywood—a Hawkeye Pierce for the twenty-first century.

Award-winning author LOIS WINSTON is not a doctor, nor does she play one on TV. Instead, she writes humorous, cross-genre contemporary novels, often drawing upon her extensive experience as a consumer crafts designer for much of her source material. Her first book, *Talk Gertie to Me*, a combination chick-lit/hen-lit/romantic comedy with a touch of the paranormal, was released in 2006. She follows that up in 2007 with *Love, Lies, and a Double Shot of Deception*, a mom-lit romantic suspense. When not writing or designing, Lois can be found trudging through stacks of manuscripts as she hunts for diamonds in the slush piles for the Ashley Grayson Literary Agency. Visit Lois at www.loiswinston.com.

It's not exactly a secret that the inspiration for House was nineteenth-century master of deduction Sherlock Holmes. Watching the show, you practically trip over the parallels: the brilliance, the drug addiction, the apartment number. So why, Nick Mamatas asks, do we love one, and love to hate the other?

WHY WE LOVE HOLMES AND LOVE TO HATE HOUSE

NICK MAMATAS

It should be no surprise to any careful observer that Dr. Gregory House is based on the famed fictional detective Sherlock Holmes. The names themselves are reminiscent of one another, with House being named, it seems, in the same way that Rex Stout's fictional detection Nero Wolfe was. ShErlOck HOlmEs and NErO WOlfE, as John D. Clark pointed out, have names in which the O-E vowels appear in the same place[1]—further, Clark suggested that Stout was hinting at the possibility that Wolfe was the son of Holmes. Well, GrEgOry HOusE fits the pattern too. And, of course, what is a House but a "home"—a homophonic punnish reference to Holmes.

The episodes are littered with such hints. House, the character, is even a fan of Holmes, as we saw in "Whac-A-Mole" (3-8) in which House wrote on an envelope "The Game's A Itchy Foot." Like Holmes, House was nearly killed by a man named Moriarty (in the second-season finale, "No Reason" [2-24]). Like Holmes, House is a drug addict—

---

[1] Ellery Queen, in *In the Queen's Parlor*, refers to Clark's note as the "Great O-E Theory" and further suggests that the vowels were a tribute to the founder of the detective genre, Edgar Allan POE (4-5).

Holmes is addicted to cocaine, and House to Vicodin. House even lives in a home with a street address 221B (as seen in "Hunting" [2-7]), the same apartment number as Holmes's famed Baker Street address. Both have broken the law in pursuit of their goals and have what a modern psychologist might call "issues with authority."

There are subtler connections as well. In Arthur Conan Doyle's stories, the narrator is a doctor named Watson, of course. What's his first name? If you said "John," you're correct. However, you're also correct if you said "James," as he is called in "Man With the Twisted Lip." House has a boon companion too: Dr. James Wilson. Wilson, like Watson, was oft-married and a bit of a lady's man.[2] Wilson moves in with House, then moves out, reflecting Watson's own time at 221B Baker Street.

Watson and Wilson also have concern for their friend in common. Watson takes credit for ending Holmes's drug addiction in "The Missing Three-Quarter," saying:

> I knew by experience that my companion's brain was so abnormally active that it was dangerous to leave it without material upon which to work. For years I had gradually weaned him from that drug mania which had threatened once to check his remarkable career. Now I knew that under ordinary conditions he no longer craved for this artificial stimulus; but I was well aware that the fiend was not dead, but sleeping; and I have known that the sleep was a light one and the waking near when in periods of idleness I have seen the drawn look upon Holmes's ascetic face, and the brooding of his deep-set and inscrutable eyes (387).

In *House*, Wilson formerly enabled House's addiction, but finally stepped in and went to the police in an attempt to convince House to enter rehab and finally kick Vicodin. Both the detective and the doctor need either

---

[2] Of course, the main issue with Watson is that Doyle didn't keep many facts about the good doctor all that consistent. Trying to reconcile all of the inconsistencies in Watson's story, even to the point of suggesting that at one point "John" was replaced by a man named "James," is one of the major preoccupations of Sherlockians.

their drugs or a challenging case in order to be fulfilled; otherwise the characters fall into a brooding funk. House even temporarily abandoned his morphine stash when Cuddy came in with a case at the beginning of the episode "Who's Your Daddy?" (2-23).

Holmes is a genius, but not omnicompetent. In *A Study in Scarlet*, Watson notes, "His ignorance was as remarkable as his knowledge. Of contemporary literature, philosophy, and politics he appeared to know next to nothing" (15). In "Sports Medicine" (1-12), House sarcastically declares, "It's a shame I don't vote." Both Holmes and House have had only one major woman in their lives, though both have otherwise dallied. Both have whacked opponents with canes.

There are, however, some significant differences. Holmes has no problem committing burglary, lying, and even promising to marry a woman simply to solve a case. Legality is a secondary issue, as Holmes explains in "The Adventure of Charles Augustus Milverton": "I am never precipitate in my actions, nor would I adopt so energetic and, indeed, so dangerous a course, if any other were possible. . . . Since it is morally justifiable, I have only to consider the question of personal risk. Surely a gentleman should not lay much stress upon this, when a lady is in most desperate need of his help?" (195–196).

House, of course, also breaks the law and violates medical ethics all the time. However, his motivations are rather more important to the post-Victorian mind than the obligations of middle-class gentlemen to defend the honor of ladies. Holmes enjoyed the challenge of solving puzzles and fighting crime, but his motivation was always reinforced by the traditional values of his era—which also excused many of his methods. He could abuse a maid by creating a false identity and wooing her, but that's all right, we're told, because the honor of a *lady*, a far more important woman, is at stake. And anyway, the maid will likely marry someone else once Holmes vanishes from her life.

House saves lives. Indeed, he saves the lives of people he knows to be liars, adulterers, and murderers, because he believes that everyone has a right to life. In "Acceptance" (2-1), he even took the case of death row convict Clarence, while the "good" characters on the show, Cuddy among them, were eager to ignore the murderer's symptoms so that he might be sent back to prison. Dr. Cameron, who was struggling with a terminal patient of her own, even criticized House for trying to extend the murderer's life and not the life of a cancer patient whose imminent death was beyond forestalling. She said, displaying the sort of sentiment House despises, "When a good person dies, there should be an impact on the world. Somebody should notice. Somebody should be upset." House would rather save, or at least extend, a life than prove himself to be a kind, caring, compassionate person by letting a man die while weeping for a good woman.

This brings us to a question central to the comparison of the two characters: Why is Holmes a hero, while House is an anti-hero? We love Holmes, but we love to hate House.

Presentation is key. Holmes is, to begin with, a proper gentlemen. The iconic image of the detective traipsing around London in a deerstalker aside, the detective is generally described as dressing in the manner of a middle-class Victorian gentlemen. House, on the other hand, is scruffy and dresses casually. He's rude to women as a matter of course, and only slightly less dismissive of other men. Whereas Holmes generally saves his arrogant remarks for either bumbling authorities or after-the-fact asides to Watson, House is endlessly sarcastic to all and sundry.

Holmes, while eccentric, falls short of deviance—his opinions were designed to please Doyle's audience. He even believes in God, explaining in the story "The Naval Treaty," "There is nothing in which deduction is so necessary as in religion. . . . It can be built up as an exact science by the reasoner. Our highest assurance of the goodness of Providence seems to me to rest in the flowers. All other things, our powers, our desires, our food, are all really necessary for our existence in the first instance. But this rose is an extra" (2). Published in 1893, Holmes's opinion was surely soothing to the members of the reading public. Their society had already been shaken by the blasphemous philosophies of Darwin and Marx. That the cleverest man in fiction had declared himself for God was surely a comfort, and also offered them a ready-made argument to make if confronted by one of those horrid atheists.

American society today is surely interested in faith, and atheists are one of the "acceptable" targets of public scorn and castigation. And yet Gregory House, in "Three Stories" (1-21), said of life itself, "I find it more comforting to believe that this [life] simply isn't a test." House also dealt with God and disbelief in "House vs. God" (2-19), and not for a moment even gave believers the dubious pleasure of a foxhole conversion. There are few atheists in television, and while House is depicted as both spiteful and damaged—the atheist cliché—he is never put in his place by a writer's *deus ex machina*. "House vs. God" ended in a draw. No miracles occurred. House wasn't even told off by a self-righteous believer. House is given an opinion that much of the viewing public would find distasteful, and isn't even punished for it.

The Holmes stories also are generally narrated after the fact by the sympathetic Watson, who takes great pains to present Holmes in the best light possible. Even when the characters conflict, as they do over Holmes's criminal activities—and emotional abuse of that maid—in "The Adventure of Charles Augustus Milverton," Watson quickly comes around. Holmes fills the narrative; he is larger than life and larger than any individual story or turn of plot. We cannot help but see morality, law, and criminality through his eyes. Because Watson is a sympathetic audience and partner, so too are the readers.

House has no such luck. Television naturally eschews the first-person point of view. The camera's gaze tends to be external and closer to objective than a story being related by a single subjective narrator. So we get to see all the negative reactions to House, from Cuddy, Cameron, Wilson, and, of course, the patients. Despite the moral failings of the various patients—in that they are similar to the many criminals and even some of the clients Holmes dealt with—we are naturally sympathetic as viewers toward people in pain. We can more easily see ourselves in a bed, confused, suffering, and trying to keep our business to ourselves than we can see ourselves attempting to kill our stepdaughters with a deadly snake.

This is not to say that there aren't some aspects of perspective that *do* work in House's favor. The third season and the introduction of Tritter, the vengeful cop that brought *House* up on drug charges, did serve to make House rather more sympathetic. Were this season of House boiled down into an episode of *Law & Order* or some similar cop show, of course, we'd surely loathe House and all the arrogant doctors who are willing to bend rules and even break laws to protect their brilliant friend. We'd spend forty minutes of our viewing time with Tritter as he begged for the power to freeze accounts and end Dr. Wilson's power to prescribe medicine. If we saw House at all, it would have been for a few minutes of sneers and prevarications, followed by a moral collapse after one pointed question too many. Seen from the point of view of House and the hospital, however, the police tactics seemed aggressive, intrusive, even unbelievable.

Tritter's claim, throughout the story arc, was that House had to be stopped because he's an addict, and one day he'd kill a patient thanks to drugs and hubris. (Of course, what doctor hasn't lost a patient, and what trial lawyer hasn't suggested that the doctor was at fault somehow?) But House doesn't kill people, though he has helped people die to save others. He saves lives, and that is all he is interested in. Wilson and his underlings often accuse House of being only interested in the "puzzle"; Wilson in "DNR" (1-9) even coins a psychological term for the House's fascination: "Rubik's complex." But this is not the case. House takes on only those cases that interest him, this is true, but there are many puzzles and mysteries he ignores. House does no pure research, is disinterested in pathology, and doesn't spend any time tangling with the seemingly intractable problems of etiology or public health.[3] Were he simply interested in solving puzzles, he could do so easily without the constant struggles to get his way, and feed his neuroses simply by retiring to the lab. As he doesn't, he must want something more than just the rush of achievement and validation for his own intelligence.

Ultimately, House loves life . . . he just hates people. Life to him isn't just a test for the afterlife, and the only score that matters is the number of lives saved, the number of hours lived, and the quality of those hours. As he said in "Finding Judas" (3-9) when asked about the quality of life a young girl about to lose her arm could have, "One thing about life—it's got qualities."

He is willing to put himself on the line for life, and cares nothing for the niceties, casual deceptions, and foolish rules that allow people to die when they could be saved. He's not shocked when he finds out that people are liars, or cheaters, and never lets his moral judgments of his

---

[3] In this way, too, he is again much like Holmes, who is no social reformer or student of social psychology; the detective just wants to help victims.

patients, or anything else, interfere with keeping them alive. Where there's life, there's meaning. The morality of the other doctors, and even of the viewers, is at its base dependent on the idea that our lives are in fact just a test, and that in the afterlife we shall be rewarded or punished. As an atheist and a medical man, House just wants to give everyone he encounters a second chance. Most doctors can handle the typical cases, but House knows that generally only he can correctly diagnose the cases he's attracted to. Most other doctors would not only get it wrong, but would often simply *give up* rather than confront a patient, the law, or the fellow-feeling of their medical colleagues. When life is more important than anything, then the constructs of law and decorum become trivial.

Unfortunately for House, but fortunately for television drama, House has no advocate except for himself. And he's not interested in defending himself, even to the point of ignoring the swirling economic and social chaos around him, in order to do his job: save lives. The rest of the cast fails to advocate for House as well. Cuddy admires House and his results, but ultimately doesn't see the method to the madness because of her obligation to the hospital. Wilson is no student of human nature; not only can he not keep a relationship together, he is wrong about every single claim he makes regarding House—from Asperger's Syndrome to willful loneliness. Cameron's feelings for House lead her to see him only as a victim in need of help. Foreman has no personal interest in House, and Chase is simply looking for (another) distant father figure. Then there is Stacy Warner, who herself has that same impulse to save lives, notably House's, but whose interest in advocacy stops there.

Ultimately, *House M.D.* is a study of the Holmes character as he would be treated in the twenty-first century, in a broadly egalitarian culture. In Victorian England, gentlemen were given wide latitude, litigation was fairly rare, and those treated poorly by their social superiors never had a platform to complain. Now, in postmodern America, we're all equal, and simply being right and doing good doesn't give anyone any free rides. The peculiar American form of politeness, wherein everyone treats one another as if they were casual friends and absolute equals, is merciless. And, of course, lawsuits are common and terrible. The reason House is loathed while Holmes is loved comes down simply to context: if Holmes were solving crimes in the modern era, he'd be hounded by the police, hated by the Baker Street irregulars, and declared a borderline autistic too.

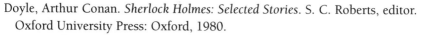

NICK MAMATAS is the author of the Lovecraftian Beat road novel *Move Under Ground* (Night Shade Books, 2004) and the Marxist Civil War ghost story *Northern Gothic* (Soft Skull Press, 2001), both of which were nominated for the Bram Stoker Award for dark fiction. He's published more than 200 articles and essays in *The Village Voice,* the men's magazine *Razor, In These Times, Clamor, Poets & Writers, Silicon Alley Reporter, Artbytes,* the *UK Guardian,* five Disinformation Books anthologies, and many other venues, and more than forty short stories and comic strips in magazines including *Razor, Strange Horizons, ChiZine, Polyphony,* and others. *Under My Roof: A Novel of Neighborhood Nuclear Superiority* (Soft Skull Press) was released in early 2007.

REFERENCES

Doyle, Arthur Conan. *Sherlock Holmes: Selected Stories.* S. C. Roberts, editor. Oxford University Press: Oxford, 1980.

___. *A Study in Scarlet.* Oxford World Classics: Oxford, 1994.

___. "The Adventure of Charles Augustus Milverton." *The Return of Sherlock Holmes.* A. Wessels Company: New York, 1907.

___. "The Naval Treaty." *The Baker Street Connection.* Retrieved 19 Dec. 2006. <http://www.citsoft.com/holmes/memoirs/naval.treaty.txt>

Queen, Ellery. *In the Queen's Parlor.* Simon and Schuster: New York, 1957.

HOUSE'S BRAIN
The Psychology of Gregory House

Robert T. Jeschonek thinks we should all be more like House. It's a bold statement—
one that I suspect not even House would be willing to let go unchallenged. . . .

BE LIKE HOUSE!

ROBERT T. JESCHONEK

Which television character makes the best role model?

From *Bonanza*'s Ben Cartwright and *Star Trek*'s Captain Kirk to *24*'s Jack Bauer and *CSI*'s Gil Grissom, we have plenty of heroic characters from which to choose—paragons of strength and decency . . . courage and honor . . . altruism and self-sacrifice.

But I'll take Dr. Gregory House over every one of them.

I think there's a lot we can learn from House. In fact, I think we should all try to be like House.

Great intro, Snorebringer. Was that the best you could do?

Excuse me?

Who's there?

Your old buddy, O. J. Simpson.

What? Really?

Nah. I'm your inner House. I thought this would be a good time for us to do our nails and talk about boys.

You mean you're part of me?

Hence the term, "inner." I'm the part of you that's already gone over to the dark side of the House force.

But don't let me throw you off your game. Not that you have any game.
Keep writing, and I'll throw roses when you get it right.

Um . . . okay then. I guess.

Where was I?

Those Family Circus kids were blaming the murders on "Not Me,"
"Nobody," and "Ida Know"?

Forget it. Let me see if I can get this rolling again. . . .

In my opinion, House makes a hell of a role model. When you get down to it, he's an admirable figure with a lot more to teach us than the difference between amyloidosis and angioedema.

Let's take a look at some of the lessons we can learn from House.

Pig-Headedness Can Help Us Overcome Limitations.

Whether pushing through a controversial treatment for a patient or dealing with his own disability, House makes an art form out of pig-headed stubbornness. He refuses to back down, even to a point that some might consider childish or self-defeating . . . and it works.

Instead of giving up his leg after suffering an infarction, House fights to keep it and remains whole. Instead of living like an invalid, he leads a productive life, continuing to succeed in his career and riding a motorcycle instead of a wheelchair.

When he thinks he's right about a diagnosis (which is most of the time), he'll stop at nothing to follow through with the treatment . . . no matter how unpopular. Time and again, House opposes the judgment of his team and the hospital administrator, Dr. Lisa Cuddy, and his patients benefit. Those in his orbit are lucky that he never backs down.

Tell that to the little girl in "Finding Judas." The little half-girl, if House had had his way.

That was an exception, not the rule.

Little Halfy would have lost an arm and a leg if Chase hadn't caught House's mistake!

That's true, but those were special circumstances. House's Vicodin supply had been reduced, and he wasn't thinking clearly. Normally, House's stubbornness is a good thing.

So his coworkers gave him a big wet kiss when Tritter went all bad-cop on them? Because House could've de-Trittered them if he'd just manned up and apologized.

Let's say that *most* of the time, it's a good thing House never backs down.

Never? So what was that called when he tried to take Wilson's deal with Tritter? "Backing up"?

Wait a minute! Aren't you my inner *House?* Shouldn't you be on House's side?

Never said I wasn't, Skippy. Now move on.

Not Caring What Other People Think Can Free Us to Focus on What's Important.

Worrying about other people's opinions can distract us from the facts and evidence that lead to effective problem-solving. It takes energy to make others feel comfortable. Putting on a good front can make you more popular, but it can also impair your performance . . . especially in a profession like House's, where objectivity is vital.

By acting without pretense, House is able to focus all his energies on medicine. By distancing himself from the people he treats, House is able to observe them scientifically, classifying them as collections of symptoms and factors instead of human beings whose opinions and truthfulness matter.

Quick! We have to tell all those doctors who think they can save lives and treat patients like human beings!

It's not House's job to make people "feel" better. In the first season episode "Occam's Razor" (1-3), he explained his philosophy like so:

> HOUSE: What would you prefer—a doctor who holds your hand while you die or one who ignores you while you get better?

I'm glad he isn't really an arrogant bastard at heart.
Well . . . I guess he is arrogant.
And it's a good thing he doesn't have a god complex. Doesn't think he can work miracles.

Maybe he does, a little.

Stop disagreeing with me!

You're the one disagreeing with *me.* You're arguing with everything I say!

No, it's just that I don't really care what you think. It frees me to focus on what's important.

Cynicism Helps You Make Better Decisions and Save the Day.

"Everybody lies." House lives by that mantra, and it pays big dividends.

Again and again, he sees human dishonesty in action. People of all ages and walks of life lie to cover up wrongdoing and to cast themselves in a better light. As a result, the true causes of symptoms can be occluded.

Secrets and misleading lies are often knowingly perpetrated by patients, like the seemingly sympathetic wife in "Clueless" (2-15), who was secretly killing her husband. Mistruths are also innocently perpetuated by patients who don't know any better, like the married couple in "Fools for Love" (3-5) who didn't know they shared the same father.

House, by cynically rejecting every statement made by patients as a lie, is able to concentrate on hard, physical evidence instead of hearsay when conceiving diagnoses. Cameron might think the wife in "Clueless" is innocent, and Foreman might be distracted by the biracial heroism of the "Fools for Love" couple, but House digs until he finds the facts . . . and saves lives.

Hey! I just thought of another example! How about when House asked the woman with Munchausen syndrome in "Deception" if she'd taken any drugs he didn't know about?

Oh, wait. Actually, that's an example of House believing something that a patient tells him, isn't it? And this patient lied to doctors all the time.

But she told House the truth.

Lucky for House! Otherwise, the Munchausen chick would've bitten the big one when he shot her up with those drugs.

But most of the time, House stays cynical, and that enables him to reach a higher level of accuracy than blind trust.

What about deaf *trust? Or hearing-impaired trust?*

What's your *problem?*

A burning sensation, an itchy rash, and a steadfast refusal to believe that Tupac is dead. I mean, come on! How many posthumous CDs can one man release?

Brutal Honesty Will Earn You Respect and Results.

Even as House demonstrates the benefits of not trusting others, he wields blunt, brutal honesty like a weapon. Again and again, he uses the truth to shock people into doing what he wants.

If a patient hesitates to undergo a procedure that House is convinced will help cure his or her illness, House isn't afraid to tell the patient in graphic detail exactly what he or she can expect if the illness runs its course. If Cuddy or another physician tries to block a procedure, House does the same for them, breaking down their resistance with the terrible truth about what could happen if he doesn't perform the procedure.

As a result, House gets his way. His recommendations might not lead to an immediate cure, but they always contribute to the successful resolution that inevitably occurs.

In other words, he almost kills *'em before he* cures *'em.*

Isn't there something in the Hippocratic Oath about that? Or am I thinking of the Constitution?

In addition to saving lives, House's brutal honesty earns him the respect of patients and coworkers. Once the short sharp shock of the initial revelation wears off, patients seem to appreciate House's bluntness.

Like the woman House forced to admit she was bumping nasties with her husband's best friend in "Fidelity," right?

Okay, not her.

I know! How about the married half-brother and sister in "Fools for Love"?

Maybe not everyone appreciates his bluntness.

I could really feel the love in "Skin Deep" when the father who'd been molesting his teenage supermodel daughter found out she was a *he!*

Enough already.

What's the matter? Can't handle the truth?

Being Manipulative Will Help You Succeed.

To get what he wants—which is often to solve a medical mystery and save a life—House manipulates those around him. He has gotten so good at it, in fact, that even those who are most alert to his manipulations aren't always aware that he's using them.

You are so right.

House uses all the tools at his disposal—sarcasm, mind games, political incorrectness, reverse psychology—to manipulate his patients and coworkers.

I couldn't have said it better myself.

When patients hesitate to take his advice, House insults and badgers them until they take it. When Cuddy won't give him what he wants, House hounds her until he wears her down and she gives in to his demands.

You go, girl.

When Cameron, Foreman, and Chase don't live up to House's expectations during the differential diagnosis process, he hits them with racist, sexist, and personal attacks that get their blood flowing and inspire fresh insights.

Exactly!

What are the results of House's manipulations? Solved puzzles, saved lives, medical breakthroughs, and. . . .

Yes?

I can't take it anymore! When are you going to say it?

Say what?

Spiro Agnew? OxyContin? Sexyback?

When are you going to bring up Trittergate? When are you going to remind me that House's manipulations finally failed when Tritter turned up the heat?

After all, when Tritter focused police attention on House and his inner circle, House reached a point where he couldn't even get Vicodin. As Tritter punished Wilson, Cameron, Foreman, and Chase, House became increasingly unable to get them to do what he wanted. House even found himself unable, in spite of his drug-seeking savvy and medical know-how, to score painkillers from an emergency room doctor.

So go ahead and say it! Point out that House's manipulations ultimately break down when outside pressure becomes too great.

Stop trying to put words in my mouth! You're nothing but a big, fat manipulator!

I feel so used.

Ignoring Rules and Regulations Can Mean the Difference between Life and Death.

I already know what you're going to say about this one, inner House.

Cool. Lay it on me.

Whatever I say, you'll shoot it down.

Aw, c'mon. Give me another chance.

Why bother?

Why else? We're both soldiers in the KISS Army.

But it's just a waste of. . . .

I ain't too proud to beg, bro.

Try me. Please?

Okay, okay.

In House's world, rules and regulations are meant to be ignored. Time and again, they stand in the way of his unorthodox diagnostic and treatment techniques . . . and time and again, he ignores them.

Disrespectful of any authority but his own, House hates all rules and will toss them aside without a second thought. He uses tests and treatments that are banned by hospital administrators and in some cases downright illegal.

The result? Lives are saved.

Hey, Skippy. You're right.

About the lesson?

About me shooting it down.

First off, lose the "He's a Rebel" shtick. Big, bad House only blows the rules down when they get in the way of his personal agenda.

Need Vicodin? Forge a prescription.

Stumped for a diagnosis? Run an illegal test behind Barney Fife Cuddy's back.

Otherwise, viva la status quo!

But at least when he breaks a rule, his colleagues benefit, right?

Hold on. My finger puppets have a thing or two to say about that.

What's that, Dr. Cuddy? You're sick of being on the hot seat all the time because of House's rule-breaking?

Yes, Dr. Wilson? You what? You lost your practice and went through hell because your so-called good buddy stuck it to a cop?

Cameron? Foreman? Chase? Oh, my. Who would like to have their careers on the line every day because of a whack-job boss?

So tell me again why the rule-breaking's a good thing?

Hello?

Skippy, are you there?

Yoo hoo! You have one more House lesson on the list.

Applying the Principles of Differential Diagnosis Will Help You to Analyze and Solve the Problems That Come Your Way.

Don't you want to talk about this one?

What's the use?

The satisfaction of rubbing my nose in it if you're right?

Wouldn't showing me up rock? Every kid in the neighborhood would pick you first for stickball!

I'm tired of being badgered. Now I know what Foreman, Cameron, and Chase feel like.

You don't see them giving up, though, do you?

All right, all right. I'll do it just to get you off my back.

Differential diagnosis. Every time House works a case, he applies this systematic approach to unraveling medical mysteries.

Working with his team, he lists the symptoms exhibited by a patient. Then, he lists the possible causes. Through the process of elimination, House and his teammates narrow down the possibilities to the most likely cause, then apply the treatment that best targets it.

The cool thing is, they're always wrong the first few tries, and they almost kill the patient before they cure him or her.

By employing the techniques of differential diagnosis, House saves lives. His methodical approach enables him to succeed in time-critical situations driven by complex and unpredictable biological phenomena.

In House-Latin, "methodical" means "trial-and-error," doesn't it?

It's not trial and error.

Whoops! I meant to say trial-and-error with educated guesses.

Based on his education in symptomatology, House makes guesses and tries treatments until he stops making errors.

What would you call it? Error and trial? Rodgers and Hammerstein? Ren and Stimpy?

Just forget it.

You win.

No! Don't let an idiot like me ruin things for an idiot like you!

Make your point. You were going to say differential diagnosis provides an excellent model for problem-solving in our everyday lives. Right?

I said you win. I give up.

What? Wait. . . .

You're right. House *isn't* a good role model. Instead of being like House, we should try to be *unlike* House in every possible way.

House is a browbeating, drug-addicted, misanthropic bully. He's crude, condescending, sexist, and racist. He's a selfish jerk with no filters or consideration for the feelings of those around him.

He cares only about himself and his own gratification. The only reason he helps patients is because he's addicted to the intellectual thrill of solving medical mysteries.

House returns the kindness of others with abuse. He repays friendship with contempt, respect with disdain. He mistakes his own genius and power for a license to act outside the limits of the law and decent human behavior.

As Foreman once said about House, in "Deception" (2-9):

FOREMAN: He's an anarchist. All he stands for is the right for
everyone to grab whatever they want whenever they want.

What about the lessons I said we could learn from House? Are they valid at all?

Not the way House teaches them.

Being pig-headed, cynical, brutally honest, manipulative, and not caring what other people think might help House solve puzzles and save lives . . . but it also makes him hated, hateful, lonely, bitter, and cold. Ignoring rules can save lives . . . but it also adds to the breakdown of a system designed to protect patients from abuses.

And applying the principles of differential diagnosis is fine on the dry-erase board, but it leads to a trial-and-error approach to treatment that causes human suffering and avoidable mortality.

That's enough!

Huh?

Cut it out!

You should be happy! I'm agreeing with you!

You've totally missed the point!

Paging Doctor Oblivious.

You're not making sense.

I give you the chance to nail House's diagnosis, and what do you do?

Know what? I think it's time for me to type a big, fat "The End" right here.

House challenges people.

What?

He challenges the people around him. Patients, friends, colleagues. He won't let them take the easy way out.

It's the noblest thing about him. It's the best lesson we can learn from the crusty old pill-popping cripple.

Wait a minute. You mean you *do* think we can learn from House?

Then why did you keep shooting down every idea I had?

Dear Diary: I had another dream about clubbing a baby seal today. When I woke up, I realized I was just hitting some moron over the head with a point that would be obvious to a baby seal.

I was illustrating a point. I was challenging you!

But I don't. . . .

Oh.

Theeeere we go.

I get it.

Brothers and sisters, let me tell you about the gospel of Saint Gregory House.

Once upon a time, there was a perfect little planet where complacency, laziness, shallowness, and impatience were not the most powerful forces.

The people weren't obsessed with instant fame and effortless success. They didn't crave easy answers and quick solutions to complex problems.

Unfortunately, we live on the Bizarro opposite of that planet.

Luckily, we have Saint House to show us the way.

Can I get an "amen"?

House won't let anyone off easy. He pushes himself and his team until they exceed his expectations and surpass their limitations.

Will he accept anything at face value? Or will he challenge every idea, preconception, and conclusion?

Say it with me now: Give me a "C"!

Give me an "H"!

Give me an "-allenge"!

That spells "Step up, you wuss!"

Defend yourself or come up with something better. Prove you deserve to participate. Better yet . . .

. . . challenge him right back.

This is why we gather each week to witness the word of House. Not because of his rugged good looks. Not because we're too lazy to change the channel after Idol.

It's because we recognize the greatness in the way House brings out the best in other people.

He pushes everyone around him to challenge the status quo, internal and external . . . to aspire to become more than they are . . . and not to let personal suffering prevent them from attaining their goals.

And that, I say that, deserves an "amen," a "kajagoogoo," and a "fo' shizzle" wrapped up in one.

So what do you say to that?

Wow.

I got through to you?

You sure did.

Sometimes I amaze myself. I ought to be on a postage stamp.

Better yet, paper money. They should put me on the front of the. . . .

There's just one thing.

Ruh-roh.

About what you said.

There's one thing you don't agree with?

There's one thing I *do* agree with.
The thing you said about challenging everyone. I like that part.
But the rest of it?
You can do better.

———————————

ROBERT T. JESCHONEK has written Star Trek fiction for Pocket Books, including a story that won the national grand prize in *Strange New Worlds VI*. His original fiction has appeared in magazines and Web sites including *Postscripts* and *Abyss & Apex*. His comic book work has appeared in *War*, *Commercial Suicide*, and *Dead by Dawn Quarterly*. He has worked in radio, television, and public relations and currently works as a technical writer for a defense contractor. Visit his Web site at www.robertjeschonek.com for news, original fiction, and *The Flog*, a fictionalized blog with an emphasis on fantasy.

House's mind, for most of us at least, is a mystery. But so, in a way, are the minds of all doctors, the ones on House and the ones to whom we trust our health in our own lives. Psychologists Linda Heath, Lindsay Nichols, and Jonya A. Leverett and explore medical decision-making, and reveal the connections between House's diagnostic process and your family doctor's.

HOW HOUSE THINKS

LINDA HEATH, LINDSAY NICHOLS, AND JONYA A. LEVERETT

medical dramas have long been a staple of television programming. From *Marcus Welby, M.D.* to *ER* to *Grey's Anatomy*, television doctors grapple weekly with obscure and heart-wrenching diseases. And it's easy to understand why medical shows are so popular. Medical dramas, similar to crime dramas, follow a basic mystery format: a puzzle needs to be solved under significant time pressure, clues keep emerging, and dead ends (no pun) need to be re-thought. Instead of the "who-done-it" of crime dramas, medical dramas focus on the "what-is-it?" And, like other good mysteries, the answer is never the obvious one—or, at least, not the obvious one in the obvious way.

A new member of the medical doctor pantheon is Gregory House, M.D., the main character in the series *House*. But House's personality sets him apart from the intensely sincere, kind, and sometimes cloyingly sweet doctors who populate most medical dramas. House is gruff, sarcastic, contentious, and disdainful of hospital policy. His personality is played off those of the other doctors in the series—the idealistic Dr. Cameron, the self-serving Dr. Chase, and the ambitious Dr. Foreman—and together, the group diagnoses and treats rare and complicated diseases each week.

Clearly this is not a snapshot of the typical doctor's typical week. Realistic medical shows would not make riveting television; television medical series that showed sore throats that turned out to be strep or nausea that was really morning sickness would be no more successful than a crime series in which the butler (or spouse) always did it. Similarly, few of us have experienced a doctor who is as gruff or as brilliant as House (or even as kind as Marcus Welby). So the cases and the personalities on medical series are, of necessity, atypical and overdrawn. But are the methods used to make diagnoses realistic? Do the doctors on *House* reach diagnoses in the same way as real doctors? How *does* House think?

The recent book *How Doctors Think*, by Jerome Groopman, M.D., outlines the actual decision-making processes followed by medical doctors, based on Groopman's own experience as well as interviews and case histories from other doctors. His conclusions map nicely onto the psychological literature on decision-making. Real-world doctors, he discovered, rely on stereotypes, schemas, cognitive short-cuts, and "gut instinct," as well as the formal decision-tree methods taught in medical schools. In the television version, House and his colleagues at Princeton-Plainsboro Teaching Hospital make extensive use of the standard whiteboard differential diagnosis method, but do they also use the messy, more human decision schemes used by real-world doctors? Within the overblown personalities and the obscure medical maladies, does House show us real-world medical decision-making?

The most obvious decision-making process used by Gregory House is what is known in the medical community as *zebra hunting*. This phrase comes from the common medical school saying, "When you hear hoofbeats, think horses, not zebras," meaning consider the typical explanation before the exotic one. Some physicians are accused of being in *zebra retreat*, meaning they shy away from unusual diagnoses or ways of framing a medical problem. House, on the other hand, is a *zebra hunter*, someone who is always looking for the obscure diagnosis, the brilliant insight that everyone else missed. (According to Groopman these doctors are also sometimes referred to disdainfully as "flamers.")

The show does a good job of revealing the frustration other doctors can feel toward *zebra hunters*—especially administrators concerned about the expensive tests that are needed to check for zebras. Dr. Cuddy accuses House of zebra hunting regularly: House is always looking for some rare, complicated cause for things that are actually mundane, or, as she claimed House saw them, boring. In the real world, a physician who routinely diagnosed a headache as a tapeworm in the brain would probably not be very popular or very successful, because rare events like brain tapeworms are, by definition, rare. On television, on the other hand, rare diseases are the norm. Further, House and his team of crack diagnosticians are only called in when a zebra is suspected. House, however, manages to find zebras even in the clinic: one woman came in with what she thought was a rash, and House's diagnosis was that, in reality, she was unknowingly having sex in her sleep.

House and his crew also reflect real-world medical decision-making in their use of *stereotypes* to make medical diagnoses. In "Histories" (1-10), Foreman did not want a homeless person to be admitted because, based on his stereotype of homeless people, he believed the patient was just trying to scam a place to stay for the night. Similarly, in "Detox" (1-11), the diagnosis of a teenager was initially—and erroneously—driven by the stereotype of teens as recreational-drug users. In "Daddy's Boy" (2-5), the stereotype of teens as binge drinkers initially set the diagnosis of a Princeton graduate suffering from seizures on the wrong path. On *House*, these stereotype-based misdiagnoses are frequently used as a way of complicating the medical mystery, and they are often quickly proven to be wrong by speedy laboratory tests or new and conflicting symptoms.

In the real world, incorrect stereotype-based diagnoses can stubbornly resist correction. Once a real-world diagnosis is started down the wrong path, the doctor who made the original, stereotype-based diagnosis, as well as doctors consulted for second—and third—opinions, often continues along the same incorrect path. Groopman describes the case of a young woman who suffered for years from vomiting after eating. The original doctor diagnosed bulimia and referred the woman for psychological treatment. In spite of the woman's unwavering protestations that she was not inducing herself to vomit, doctor after doctor looked at her symptoms and lab results as verification of the initial bulimia diagnosis. This diagnosis provided the *patient frame* for the original and subsequent doctors, and the frame naturally led repeatedly to the wrong diagnosis for her symptoms: the woman was bulimic, so of course she had bulimia.

Only after fifteen years and many consultations did a physician finally break away from the patient frame that was provided by the initial diagnosis and correctly diagnose the woman's problem as celiac disease, which was causing her to vomit whenever she ingested gluten.

One reason original diagnoses are so difficult to correct is that real-world doctors (and other real-world people) fall prey to something psychologists call the *confirmation bias*. A large body of psychological research has shown that when trying to solve a puzzle or make a decision, we are much more likely to seek information that confirms our hunches than information that disconfirms them. For example, if we are trying to determine if someone *is* a nurse, we are more likely to ask if he works in a hospital rather than if he works in a factory, even though if he works in a factory there is little chance that he is a nurse. If he works in a hospital, he might be a nurse, or a doctor, or a food server, or any one of dozens if not hundreds of other jobs. Consequently, determining that a person works in a factory is very diagnostic that he or she is not a nurse, while finding out that a person works in a hospital is less diagnostic that he or she is a nurse. To make matters worse, this confirmation bias—or "cognitive cherry-picking" (Groopman 65)—leads us not only to test for confirmations more than disconfirmations but to remember the confirmations more than the disconfirmations. In Groopman's example, the physicians fell prey to the confirmation bias by looking to see if the symptoms and lab results matched bulimia, which they did—except for the woman's adamant insistence that she was not making herself vomit. But even this last fact was interpreted as a sign of bulimia, since denying one is making oneself vomit is a frequent characteristic of the disease.

Do the doctors on *House* fall prey to the confirmation bias? House generally avoids this mistake because of his profound lack of confidence in other physicians' diagnostic abilities and his huge confidence in his own abilities. For example, in "DNR" (1-9), a legendary jazz musician who had been diagnosed with ALS was admitted to Princeton-Plainsboro but signed a Do Not Resuscitate (DNR) order because he did not want to suffer the slow death typical of ALS. House ignored the DNR order and eventually diagnosed the musician as having something treatable rather than ALS. Clearly, House is not influenced by the patient frames provided by other doctors . . . but he does fall prey to the confirmation bias when one of his own stereotypes sends him down the wrong diagnostic path. In "Hunting" (2-7), House is convinced a neighbor with AIDS has only an opportunistic infection, which House repeatedly refers to as "boring." But as with stereotype-based diagnoses, these mistakes are quickly made apparent by tests or symptoms, allowing House to move on in search of the correct diagnosis (which in the case of the AIDS patient was a rare disease contracted years before while fox hunting with his father).

"Deception" (2-9) showed a confirmation bias mistake that lasted through most of the episode, although it was one committed by the team rather than by House himself. A woman suffered a seizure near House when he was at an off-track betting facility, and the staff quickly realized that the woman had been doctored for many varied maladies over the years and had been hospitalized several times for seemingly unrelated illnesses. Some members of the team were convinced the woman had Munchausen syndrome, a psychological disorder in which people purposely make themselves sick so they can receive attention. Dr. Cameron even set up a test for Munchausen by leaving medication in the hospital room—and it worked. The woman really did have Munchausen syndrome. But she also had another serious medical problem that would have killed her had House not conspired to have her re-admitted to the hospital. The other doctors were so busy confirming the first disease that they failed to consider that the patient might also have another, unrelated problem.

The Munchausen episode also illustrates another decision-making process, called *satisficing*. Psychological research has demonstrated that for many types of decisions, people devote cognitive energy to the decision until they reach a decision that is "good enough," or that "satisfices" (a combination of "satisfy" and "suffice"). The option satisfies the need for a final decision sufficiently well, so the search for other options ends. This process is fine if one is selecting a kind of ketchup to purchase; one needn't do an exhaustive search of all the pros and cons of all the various ketchup options. Even with more expensive purchases such as automobiles, buyers don't need to consider every single option in-depth. They just need to find an automobile that meets their criteria well enough. When one is making a medical diagnosis, however, satisficing can be problematic, as Groopman points out; finding the very best diagnosis is crucial to proper treatment and cure. That doesn't mean satisficing should always be avoided, especially in areas such as emergency medicine or surgery where decisions need to be made quickly. Satisficing is often a necessary, though not optimal, strategy.

Satisficing is another area where the doctors on *House* differ from real-world doctors. In the real world, symptoms do not fit into neat packages. The first author's sixteen-year-old son totaled the family van (as sixteen-year-olds are wont to do), and received a small cut below his eye. The MRI done in the emergency room to check for bone damage revealed something in the eye socket and the doctors first thought it was cartilage fragments from the impact. Later inspection revealed the son had a minor sinus infection, which had begun before he slammed his head into the steering wheel. The emergency room doctors' assumption that spots on an MRI in the exact area where the kid had just smacked the steering wheel were related to the accident was reasonable. Fortunately, the doctor did not engage in satisficing, but rather had another person look at the images, and so the error was quickly corrected; antibiotics rather than surgery were prescribed.

A child who has a skinned knee and a sore throat almost certainly has two unrelated problems, and two diagnoses satisfice, or fit the symptoms well enough. On television, however, the odd result or stray symptom that doesn't fit with the diagnosis is routinely explored, as it is most often the clue to the correct diagnosis. And on *House*, the stray symptom that doesn't fit the obvious diagnosis is not some minor, irrelevant illness but often the sole clue that the mundane diagnosis is wrong and the disease is really some obscure malady such as flesh-eating bacteria.

The most obvious decision-making strategy that House and his colleagues use is the *whiteboard approach to differential diagnosis*. In every episode, they list all the possibilities and eliminate them one by one as test results or new symptoms make them implausible as explanations for the symptom-set. This strategy is a variant of the approach which, according to Groopman, is currently taught in most medical schools. Medical students are taught to use *probabilities* to guide their diagnoses, which House et al. clearly use in an informal way. In "All In" (2-17), a young boy evidenced similar symptoms to a woman, Esther, who had died in House's care twelve years previously. Rather than write the boy's pain off as gastroenteritis as Dr. Cuddy did, House called his team in to search for the diagnosis that he had missed twelve years earlier. Several initial suggestions for the boy's diagnosis were eliminated because they don't strike the elderly as well as the young with great frequency—in other words, the probability of those particular disorders occurring in those particular patients was considered. Dr. Cuddy referenced the boy's potential probability ("It's just a stomach ache!"), but these arguments are seldom considered relevant by Dr. House, who is focused on the particular patient rather than statistical probabilities. Current medical students are taught to use probabilities in a much more intentional way than is evidenced on *House*. Diagnoses based on probability comparisons are valued by new doctors and insurance companies, Groopman reports. But not only is House unimpressed by statistical probabilities (i.e., horses, not zebras), he is also uninterested in keeping insurance companies happy—as evidenced by his regular tardiness in completing paperwork.

Another current decision-making technique used in medical schools is *decision-tree analysis*. According to Groopman, the use of this technique is also heavily endorsed by insurers, as it provides a scientifically based rationale for the diagnoses and treatments. With this technique, a doctor starts with a symptom, such as sore throat, and then proceeds through a series of yes/no decisions, such as "Are the lymph nodes swollen?" and "Does anyone else in the patient's family or workplace have this symptom?" (Groopman and other older doctors are often not fans of such a mechanistic, rote method of diagnosis, and lament the loss of the holistic diagnosis methods which they had been taught.) Although the doctors on *House* exclude possible diagnoses by pointing out the types of counter-indications that are present in the decision-trees, they certainly do not follow a pat formula for reaching diagnoses—in part because the diseases they see every week are so rare it is unlikely a decision-tree even exists for them.

What about the more intuitive, *holistic approach* to diagnoses that many doctors in the real world use? This is clearly House's forte, as evidenced by the episode in which he emptied out the clinic at closing time by making several diagnoses in under five minutes based solely on observations of seemingly irrelevant factors. The intuitive sense that something doesn't look right (which some M.D.'s call the *eyeball test* [Groopman 22]) guides many of House's diagnoses. Given that House plays an expert diagnostician, this TV presentation actually matches reality. Research has shown that experts arrive at an initial diagnosis within twenty seconds of meeting a patient, but can't really describe how they do it. Experts in a wide range of fields exhibit this pattern of knowing something (or recognizing a pattern) but not knowing how they know it. Experts are therefore usually not very good at teaching by explanation, because they cannot analyze and articulate the thought processes that led to their decisions.

House's kind of intuitive, holistic, incredibly rapid diagnosis strategy is well-suited for the television world, where patients need to be diagnosed and treated within forty-two minutes, excluding commercial breaks. In the real world, however, speedy decisions are not necessarily good decisions. As with satisficing, using cognitive shortcuts, or *heuristics*, to make decisions in everyday life leads to reasonably good decisions about mundane issues, but can fall short when dealing with more serious ones.

Take, for example, the *representativeness heuristic*, a mental shortcut in which people classify things according to how well those things match the typical case or prototype (Aronson et al.). In making a judgment about the likelihood that Barack Obama is a presidential candidate as opposed to a farmer, one would subconsciously call up the prototype of a presidential candidate and a farmer. My prototype of a farmer is someone who is male and physically strong, wears blue jeans, and, if he attended college, attended a state university with an agriculture program. My prototype of a presidential candidate is someone male, with good verbal skills who wears a suit and graduated from an Ivy League college. Based on this, I would say it was more likely that Barack Obama was a presidential candidate than a farmer.

Obviously prototypes are not always correct. Women are farmers and presidential candidates. Some presidential candidates (and even some presidents) are not verbally skilled. But matching an instance against a prototype often leads us to a correct decision with little cost if we are wrong especially in areas of low importance. For example, if I am gauging the odds that a new kind of cookie is delicious, I can match the new cookie against my prototype of delicious cookies (e.g. chocolaty and crisp) and make a judgment that is usually correct. If I'm wrong, I'm only out the price of the cookies. The potential cost of a heuristic-based mistake is obviously much higher in a medical setting, but the use of heuristics is still sometimes necessary. Both Groopman and Croskerry see the use of heuristics as a regular part of real-world medical decision-making, and it's especially useful in time-pressured settings such as emergency rooms.

House and his TV colleagues also frequently use the representativeness heuristic. In "Sports Medicine" (1-12), House was treating a young, very fit, professional baseball player. Because in House's mind the prototype of "very fit professional baseball player" included "steroid user," House continued to pursue steroids as a possible cause of his malady in spite of the player and his wife's insistence that the player had not used them. In some ways the case was similar to the case of the real-world woman who was misdiagnosed with bulimia, except, since this is *House*, it turned out the player was lying and had used steroids five years earlier. (Of course, the athlete's illness was actually caused by a different drug he lied about: marijuana.)

Another heuristic that frequently guides our judgments is *availability*, a mental shortcut whereby people form a judgment based on the ease with which particular instances are brought to mind (Tversky and Kahneman). Think of words that start with the letter R as quickly as possible. Then think of words in which R is the third letter as quickly as possible. Which was easier to think of, words that began with R or words with R in the third position? From that, would you assume there are more words in the English language that begin with R or that have R in the third position? Most people estimate that more words start with the letter R than have R in the third position, because they can more easily bring words that start with R to mind. In fact, R is more frequently the third letter of words than the first; here, the availability heuristic has steered us wrong.

The use of the availability heuristic, though, does generally lead to right answers. For example, to guess whether a particular teenager plays the cello or PlayStation, you could think of all the teens you know who play the cello and compare that number with all the teens you know who play PlayStation. Probably, you would come to the correct decision. The danger when using this heuristic comes when the user's or the subject's situation is atypical. If you were making a decision about a student at a selective arts high school, the availability heuristic might lead you astray. Or, if you routinely associated with students from an arts high school, you might more easily bring to mind cello players than PlayStation players, which would lead you to an incorrect decision about a teen in the general population.

Real-world doctors clearly use the availability heuristic to make tentative diagnoses. Some college health centers, for instance, require that every female student who complains of nausea be given a pregnancy test, even if she says she hasn't been sexually active. Few doctors who treat a mostly middle-age clientele would follow this diagnostic practice, because they would run into more cases of flu than pregnancy. (This is another way in which probabilities enter the diagnostic decision-making process [although the use of the availability heuristic is generally subconscious].) When physicians base diagnostic leads on some vague, unexplainable gut instinct, they might actually be using heuristics. And since the pattern recognition involved in the availability heuristic is distorted by the background or situation, when that "gut instinct" goes awry, heuristics might be at least partly to blame.

In "Kids" (1-19), House showed himself to be capable of either using or ignoring the availability heuristic when students whose high school had an outbreak of meningitis were either being vaccinated or treated for the disease. Amidst hundreds of teens and no small amount of confusion, House detected that one student had symptoms that were similar but not identical to meningitis.

One common theme among the decision-making strategies outlined above is that they do a pretty good job of identifying the correct answer in typical situations. In atypical situations, however, the correct diagnosis depends on *breaking set* or *thinking-outside-the-box*. House clearly excels at thinking outside the box, which is fortunate because his patients' illnesses are never typical. In "Heavy" (1-16), an obese ten-year-old had a heart attack. Initial attempts at diagnosis were based on identifying what diseases obesity would cause, to no avail. Finally House broke set and began thinking about diseases that cause obesity, reversing the causal ordering. Only then were the doctors able to diagnose the patient with Cushing's syndrome—the cause of both the obesity *and* the heart attack.

Finally, in understanding doctors' decision-making process, it's important to understand that no one makes decisions in a vacuum. Groopman describes the "uncontrollable storm" that surrounds doctors, particularly in specialties such as emergency medicine, and claims that doctors find "safe harbor" in the overconfident mind set and "culture of conformity and orthodoxy that begins in medical school" (Tversky and Kahneman 153). Physicians generally need to make decisions quickly based on inadequate or conflicting information, and such a setting can lead to a profound sense of vulnerability and one's own lack of control. To deal with this, real-world doctors often adopt a sense of great confidence in their decisions, recognizing that while not all of their decisions will be correct, most will be. Similarly, some physicians take refuge behind the white coat and assiduously follow the rules they were taught in medical school; if they are wrong, at least they are wrong in an orthodox manner. House certainly projects the overconfident mindset possessed by many real-world physicians, but he decisively rejects conformity and orthodoxy, secure in his belief that his way is the right way. But at least his egomaniacal and unorthodox approach pays off. He is, after all, a zebra hunter in a television world full of zebras.

DR. LINDA HEATH is a professor of psychology at Loyola University Chicago, where her teaching and research interests focus on media effects, research methodology, and psychology and law. She received her MA and Ph.D. from Northwestern University in social psychology and her BA from the Ohio State University.

LINDSAY NICHOLS received her Bachelor of Arts degree at Florida Atlantic University, with majors in psychology and English and a minor in writing and rhetoric. She is currently working toward her MA degree in applied social psychology at Loyola University Chicago, where she also intends to earn a Ph.D. Future plans include working in academia, teaching, and conducting research.

JONYA A. LEVERETT graduated from the University of Georgia with a degree in art history. Before entering the applied social psychology doctoral program at Loyola University Chicago, she worked in trial consulting. She is entering her second year of doctoral study at Loyola University Chicago, and her research interests include the manipulations and effectiveness of media and propaganda.

REFERENCES

Aronson, Elliot et al. *Social Psychology*. 5th ed. New Jersey: Upper Saddle River, 2005.

Croskerry, Pat. "The Cognitive Imperative: Thinking About How We Think." *Academic Emergency Medicine* 7 (2000): 1223-1231.

___. "Achieving Quality in Clinical Decision Making: Cognitive Strategies and Detection of Bias." *Academic Emergency Medicine* 9 (2002): 1184-1204.

Groopman, Jerome. *How Doctors Think*. Boston: Houghton Mifflin Co., 2007.

Tversky, Amos and Daniel Kahneman. "Judgment Under Uncertainty: Heuristics and Biases." *Science* 185 (1974): 1124-1131.

Knowing how *House thinks isn't the same thing as knowing how House thinks* so
well. *Cognitive psychologist Nancy Franklin has a couple of ideas as to what
makes House's theories so much more likely to match reality than our own.*

HOUSE CALLS

Why Are They Better Than Everyone Else's?

NANCY FRANKLIN

here's the scary news: When you have your medical emergency, if
you're lucky enough to make it to the hospital, you're likely to
get a doctor who's not as brilliant as the ones on *House*. In fact,
if you go to a teaching hospital, you're likely to be seen by a resident
who's recently out of medical school and who hasn't yet reached the
peak of his or her diagnostic skills. Add to that the possibility of you getting sick in July or August, just as residents are first starting out as full-
fledged doctors, and you better hope you've got something obvious and
easy to treat.

Even if you wind up with an experienced physician, don't let your
guard down. Diagnostic errors are still in the range of 10–15 percent,
and many of these cases are pretty run-of-the-mill compared to what you
see on *House M.D.* (Elstein). These types of mistakes, which can lead to
delay or failure to treat your problem—or to a treatment that causes
additional problems—constitute the second highest category of adverse
events in medicine (Brennan et al.). No wonder that diagnostic error is
the second most common basis for malpractice suits against hospitals
and the leading cause for suits in radiology, pathology, and emergency

departments (Bartlett). And no wonder those lawsuits don't tend to go well for the hospitals.

As you may have noticed if you've ever tried to take a class in logic or probability, humans, even the smart ones, aren't natural-born critical thinkers. And the ways we solve problems and make decisions in our everyday lives generally don't have much to do with logic. Amazingly, though, we seem to muddle through just fine, so there must be some guiding principles behind our thinking. In fact, cognitive psychologists Danny Kahneman and Amos Tversky did the pioneering work demonstrating this that led to a 2002 Nobel Prize.

The reality is that for a lot of situations, you simply can't use logic to make decisions. You have to act immediately, too quickly to figure out the right answer. Or you don't have enough information to be able to apply the mathematical algorithm that would get you the right answer. Doctors, of course, find themselves in this position every time someone walks in with a set of symptoms. In making their diagnosis, they try to go with the most likely possibility. So how do they determine what the most likely thing is, in the absence of further information?

As Linda Heath, Lindsay Nichols, and Jonya A. Leverett point out in their essay, Tversky and Kahneman found that people use an *availability heuristic* to assess probabilities. If examples of a particular kind of outcome are brought easily to mind, then people (including doctors) assume that there are lots of cases of it out there, and that it's a likely outcome. The availability heuristic is an excellent, quick-and-dirty way to come up with a reasonable estimate because normally, the frequency of a phenomenon is indeed correlated with the number of examples you can come up with in a brief period of time. But as we saw in Heath's essay, the availability heuristic can and sometimes does lead to the wrong answer.

Doctors—sadly—think like humans. They may be well-educated and careful, but they fall prey to the same pitfalls of human cognition as the rest of us do. Doctors typically search for the most likely (in scientific parlance, "parsimonious") explanation for a set of symptoms. So far, so good; this is a rational approach. But the explanation that is most available in memory isn't always the one that is most likely. Doctors use the availability heuristic without realizing it (as we all do), and this can easily lead to diagnostic errors (Groopman).

You've seen elsewhere in this volume how *confirmation bias*, a well-known phenomenon in human cognition, can lead to reasoning errors in both real life and in medical settings—that it is at least as informative to rule out other alternatives as it is to amass evidence in favor of your current hypothesis. Doctors are taught this in medical school, but again, doctors are still people. It's not necessarily arrogance that leads them to look for evidence that proves they're right. The problem is deeper than this; they're stuck with human cognitive machinery. Well, most are. Lucky for us, the most arrogant of them all, Dr. Gregory House, is different.

When Cameron thought a patient had Munchausen, while House thought it was a tumor pressing on the optic nerve, both accused the other of seeking evidence that would only support their own theory. If true, it was a reasonable criticism. But time and again, we see House going so far to rule things out that he actually would put the patient in danger if one of the alternatives turned out to be true. (This, of course, has its own problems. Even the best of doctors work in a problem space that is inherently probabilistic, and there is always risk of misdiagnosis.) But House has a superhuman track record already, and this is TV after all. So we can be confident that he won't kill the patient in "Detox" (1-11), when he uses Mendrol to rule out hepatitis E.

An Open House

House also seems to somehow have intuited the cognitive value of recoding a difficult problem. The classic example of this, from the problem-solving literature, goes like this: A monk begins a journey at 5 A.M. up a mountain path. Along the way, he varies his speed, sometimes stopping and enjoying the view, sometimes walking briskly, and sometimes plodding along. He gets to the temple at the top of the mountain at 5 P.M. that day. He fasts and prays overnight, and in the morning at 5 A.M., he begins his descent down the same path. Again, he varies his speed along the way, but he gets to the bottom at 5 P.M. The question is: Is there a point along the path where he is located at precisely the same time on both days? One way you can try to solve this problem is by constructing infinitely many equations with infinitely many unknowns, but you'll immediately realize that this will get you nowhere. Alternatively, you can envision him meandering his way up a path between 5 A.M. and 5 P.M., superimposing on this same mental image a duplicate monk starting at the top and going in the reverse direction between 5 A.M. and 5 P.M. You can't possibly know what time of day it will happen or where along the path it will be, but because both of these treks take place during the same time frame, there must be a point where the two monks meet. And so, yes, there is a point the monk will reach at the same time each day. A problem that's infinitely complex when framed mathematically becomes trivially simple when framed graphically.

Where do we see House reframing his thinking? Imagine you had an aphasic patient who says, "I couldn't tackle the bear! They took my stain!" ("Failure to Communicate," 2-10). Would you have the wherewithal to realize he might be referring to his bipolar disorder and brain surgery? If Sister Augustine claims to have God inside her ("Damned If You Do," 1-5), would it dawn on you to look for a copper IUD that may be poisoning her? Do you think you could spontaneously make the connection between your own romp through a fountain after a jog and the troublesome diagnosis of a wheelchair-bound patient who'd driven himself into a swimming pool because his hypothalamic dysregulation prevented body temperature control ("Meaning," 3-1)? Or spontaneously realize the patient who can't feel pain has a twenty-five-foot-long parasitic worm in her gut, simply because Wilson accuses you of enjoying beating other hunters to the food ("Insensitive," 3-14)? If so, good for you (you liar). Let's face it: you and I don't possess the creative thinking abilities that House does.

It's that same creative thinking that helps him avoid settling too soon on a decision. It's a rare doctor who does a full differential diagnosis from the symptoms and test results, whiteboard or not (Graber, Franklin, and Gordon). More typically, doctors move quickly to a conclusion (e.g., based on availability) and decide they're done. If your thinking isn't as flexible as House's or your knowledge about medicine isn't as broad, you're less able to do such a differential diagnosis in the first place. But House, as cocky as he is, knows to keep an open mind and make optimal use of information as it continues to come in. Even as he was about to cut into a fellow passenger on a plane, having concluded that the man was a drug mule with a burst cocaine pellet inside him, House was receptive to new information. He noticed the relief the man felt when his joints were squeezed, and he realized that the man, a scuba diver, was actually suffering from decompression sickness ("Airborne," 3-18).

Bringing Down House (Or At Least Trying To)

In fact, House seems happiest with his underlings when they're shooting down his opinions and offering their own, forcing him to think more critically about all alternatives. Where a lot of managers might resent this, House demands it. It's as if he somehow knows about the pitfalls associated with *groupthink*, a term used by psychologist Irving Janis to describe the pressure that JFK's advisors felt to just give in to the group consensus when deliberating strategy in the Bay of Pigs. When people who see potential problems with the way a decision is going fail to express those opinions, tragic results can follow.

There's a personal analogue of groupthink that we're all vulnerable to as well. In psychological jargon, it's called *mental set*. In layman's terms, it's the tendency to use the same approach to a problem that you've used in the past because it worked before. As you can imagine, this predisposition is a good one for most circumstances. In those unusual cases, though, where the habitual approach isn't the most efficient—or worse, is actually ineffective—people tend to not be very good at thinking of alternative approaches. In life, we encounter problems time and again that remind us of previous problems that we've solved successfully. In general, it's a good idea not to reinvent the wheel and to use the same mental approach this time as well. But sometimes a new problem, while it looks like something you solved before, requires a novel approach, and we're very vulnerable to the limitations that mental set effects create. In medicine, doctors are frequently faced with such situations, and in fact, it's experts who tend to be most vulnerable to this problem.

House Divided Against Himself

So what's a good way to avoid it? How about getting high and going into an altered state of consciousness? Although there isn't clear agreement in the field that consciousness-altering drugs can effectively increase creativity, they may disrupt the conventional thinking processes that would otherwise lead to mental set. It may be that the already intellectually superior House benefits from his pain-reducing opiates by being able to dodge the set effects that the rest of us fall squarely into.

In any case, since he's an addict, denying him his drugs will present a challenge to even his conventional problem-solving abilities. He'd be in what we can only assume would be excessive and distracting pain, plus he'd be going through withdrawal symptoms. Both because of this high level of physical stress (Yerkes and Dodson) and because of the priority of this biological need for the addictive substance (Lacey et al.), we wouldn't expect much from him cognitively. And indeed, when he was off the Vicodin he started botching his work and ignoring his patients, putting his colleagues in the difficult positions of having to either consider selling him out or help him feed his addiction. He even went so far as to fake brain cancer to get in on a clinical trial that involved an implant in the brain's pleasure center ("Half-Wit," 3-15). (Maybe we shouldn't doubt his creative skills even when he's strung out!)

Playing House

Which other controversial actions by House might be defensible from a cognitive psychology point of view? Well, let's look at his unconventional tendency to watch TV and take naps on the job. We know from the literature (e.g., Yaniv and Meyer) that unconscious processing can actually lead to greater success in some problem-solving situations. This has sometimes been referred to as the *incubation effect*. Problems, even some famous scientific ones like the discovery by Kekulé of the benzene ring's structure, seem to have been solved while they weren't actively being worked on. The lore is, in fact, that Kekulé's insight came while he was falling asleep. Dijksterhuis and van Olden showed that better decisions can be made when one is distracted from deliberating between sets of complex options, compared to when one is allowed to deliberate. The TV watching and naps may be an integral part of House's success.

Putting House in Order

When he is focusing his mental resources on a problem, though, he often does what psychologists recommend in cognitively demanding situations. One principle he demonstrates is the freeing up of working memory. When you're holding information (for example, a set of symptoms) in working memory, you have fewer resources available to think about them, integrate them, compare them, infer their implications, etc. But if you write the symptoms down—say, on a whiteboard—you have considerably more working memory available for the hard job of thinking. House takes advantage of this principle. When there's a whiteboard available, he uses it. Even when there isn't, he often improvises—as when he scrawled a list of symptoms on a wall in "Failure to Communicate" (2-10) and on an in-flight movie screen in "Airborne" (3-18).

House of Cards?

Focusing on a problem allows House to be less aware of his pain, consistent with what many clinicians and researchers have reported over the years about chronic pain sufferers. In fact, the emerging technology of pain distraction software tries to create the sort of engaging situations that House naturally encounters during his workday. To help people to tune out their discomfort, even if only temporarily. Wilson, who knows House better than anyone else, called him on self-inducing a migraine so that he could distract himself from the loss of Stacy ("Distractions," 2-12). In "Skin Deep" (2-13), Cuddy injected House with what he thought was morphine but was actually saline. His pain was relieved, but only for as long as he stayed focused on a difficult task. It may have been the distraction, and not a placebo effect from the shot, that gave him relief.

So, given this, does House really need the pain meds? Well, sure. He's an addict, as even he has admitted. But aside from that, and aside from the possible indirect benefit of disrupting conventional thinking, there may be more direct benefits that the drugs provide. Among these is state-dependence. If House encounters any aspect of a case when he is on his meds, he is more likely to remember those details if he's in that same state of consciousness when trying to retrieve them (e.g., Hill, Schwin, Powell, and Goodwin). And, if he previously solved a similar case while under the influence, the likelihood of him remembering details of that case, which may help him crack this one, are higher if he's on the same drugs. For the sake of the patient, then, it may not be right to meddle with House's pill-taking.

The Doctor in the House

Now, let's turn to that surly personality of his, which he blames largely on his pain. The closest he seems to have gotten to happiness was when it was the primary symptom of a case ("Euphoria, Part 1" [2-20] and "Euphoria, Part 2" [2-21]). In what way could his own curmudgeonliness possibly work to his benefit in coming up with the right answer? It's not that the rudeness makes him smarter; it's that being a diagnostician means treating the patient and illness as a puzzle to be solved, and caring, in and of itself, provides no edge in that process. In fact, it can distract the diagnostician from his or her main goal. A lot of us certainly put a premium on doctors who genuinely want us to feel better, but caring doesn't make them more likely to figure out what's wrong with us. Sure, it's great to have a caring doctor once the mystery of our condition has been solved and it's obvious what should be done to make us better. But give me a surly, successful diagnostician over a warm, intellectually average one any day. And in fact, whatever his or her diagnostic capabilities are, give me someone who will concentrate on the puzzle and not be distracted by their empathy. Examples of empathy leading to the wrong decisions abound in *House*. In "Humpty Dumpty" (2-3), Cuddy's affection for her handyman, Alfredo, led her to object to the medically advised procedure. House himself is reminded of this sort of misplaced loyalty every day as he limps around the hospital; his own bad leg is the result of Stacy's faulty decision as his medical proxy years before ("Three Stories," 1-21). And we saw a glimmer of House's humanity (and fallibility) when he refused to do a biopsy on Foreman's brain ("Euphoria, Part 2," 2-21) because he couldn't stomach the idea of doing such a dangerous procedure on a friend. Why House is so nagged by the old woman, Esther, he lost several years ago when he couldn't make the proper diagnosis in time will probably always be ambiguous ("All In," 2-17). Does he feel guilty over her, or does he just hate batting less than a thousand? (If you think it's because he can't bear to get it wrong, think about his decision to save the minor-leaguer from being banned from baseball for unauthorized substance use by making a public diagnosis of Addison's disease. Or his decision to tell Leona that Crandall was her real father in "Who's Your Daddy?" [2-23]. He knew these medical calls were wrong, but being right wasn't his top priority.)

On the one hand, we shouldn't really care about the reason for his preoccupation with Esther. But we tend to hold irrational values regarding medical care and we want to know the answer, as if it has some bearing on how good a doctor House is. Remember when Jeffrey Reilich angrily accused House of experimenting on his son, Gabe, without even meeting him? His implication was that House was unmotivated. That's not true. House is so highly motivated to address the puzzle that he avoids the faulty information and over-emotionality that come with dealing with patients in person; he considers it a waste of time. (And let's not exaggerate the difference between House's bedside manner and that of the average physician. According to a classic study by Beckman and Frankel, the average physician interrupts their patient eighteen seconds after the patient begins talking. House may do it fifteen seconds earlier, but that's hardly a world of difference.)

If we're going to continue slamming his social skills, though, we can point to the fact that House's approach is unconventional even when he's not in the room with the patient. He has been known to take illegal and questionable actions in order to procure information or treat people who are in danger. Some, including his own team, mistake that for immorality. But he's not immoral when it comes to medicine; he's amoral. Think about the time he told little Andie that she was going to die ("Autopsy," 2-2). His purpose wasn't to torment—it was to determine whether her fear center, the amygdala, was functioning properly. What better way to move closer to a true diagnosis and potentially saving her life, even if it meant making her unhappy in the moment? He sometimes lies to his patients, or drugs them, but it's only to get the information he needs or to make them agree to something medically necessary, as with Mark in "Honeymoon" (1-22).

Let's not forget that House does some pretty morally heroic things, too. Once his own pain was relieved, he took action to improve Richard's quality of life in "Meaning" (3-1). Facing an entirely moral dilemma after the puzzle-solving was over with Ezra he chose to help him die when it was clear that his illness was terminal ("Informed Consent," 3-3). And he helped Gabe sacrifice himself for Kyle, who needed a new heart ("Son of Coma Guy," 3-7).

How to Play Doctor

House is creative and flexible in a way that most of us can never hope to have the brilliance to be. But much of his greatness is something that can be learned through basic scientific method by any reasonably smart person. How he considers working hypotheses mirrors what we know about what makes a good scientific theory: It can explain known data (or symptoms), it can predict future data (or how a medical test will come out), and it is parsimonious (or is the simplest of the explanations that would fit). He looks for the single condition that can explain all symptoms, rather than five different conditions to individually explain five symptoms. His reasoning is elegant, if nothing else about him is. And in the rare case where the evidence suggests that the parsimonious answer may be wrong, as happened when Brandon appeared not to have mistakenly taken gout medication in "Occam's Razor" (1-3), House gets justifiably annoyed at reality for not being as elegant as theory.

Part of the formula for developing good theories is creating situations in which to test them. Unsurprisingly House has the good experimental skills necessary to do so, as well—sometimes to his colleagues' great distress. A good experiment, for example, typically needs a control condition to rule out alternative explanations. If three babies with an unknown urgent condition are showing the same symptoms, there are good scientific arguments for putting them on three different treatments and comparing their progress ("Maternity," 1-4). There are also scientific arguments for collecting data even when it's illegal or immoral. Where other doctors might let their ethical values or fear of punishment stop them, House goes on. In "Hunting" (2-7), House provoked a patient's father into punching him—only, we soon realize, so that he can be justified in hitting back. It was all part of House's grand plan to see if his well-placed blow would rupture a cyst, causing the man to collapse, and therefore confirm House's diagnosis, that father and son had the same condition. Once House shattered a vial containing Legionnaire's disease in Foreman's isolation room because he believed it would slow the progression of the mystery disease Foreman had contracted. He often has his minions break into people's homes to search for the likely cause of a condition. (Unfortunately, this tendency to collect data is hard for House to control, as when he rummaged through Stacy's psychiatric file in "Spin" [2-6], or Cuddy's trash in "Forever" [2-22], or the new nurse's locker in "Lines in the Sand" [3-4].)

But he's not without his standards, either. He does his experimenting in order to help the individual patient who has an immediate need, not for the greater good of science (or for the profiteering of drug companies or doctors who perform clinical trials). Although he's a model scientist, he's against using the hospital's patients for clinical trials ("Control," 1-14). In this way, he takes a moral stand that medicine and science in general don't.

We should be glad that our next generation of TV doctors is being House-trained. He shows that not just thinking but ignoring, sleeping, insulting, vandalizing, infecting, rummaging, and pill-popping may have their benefits in cracking hard cases. Of course, it's also important to have the appropriate training in medicine and scientific thinking. But the tough cases are considered tough because a conventional approach to them has failed. When they arise, the ability to use knowledge creatively may make all the difference.

NANCY FRANKLIN is an associate professor of psychology at Stony Brook University, specializing in human cognition and memory. She received her Ph.D. in 1989 at Stanford University, where she trained with Barbara Tversky and Gordon Bower. Her current research concerns false memory and emotional influences on memory and judgment.

REFERENCES

Bartlett, Edward. "Physicians' Cognitive Errors and Their Liability Consequences." *Journal of Healthcare Risk Management* 18 (1998): 62–69.

Beckman, Howard B. and Richard M. Frankel. "The Effect of Physician Behavior on the Collection of Data." *Annals of Internal Medicine* 101 (1984): 692–696.

Brennan, Troyan A., Lucian L. Leape, Nan Laird, Liesi Hebert, A. Russell Localio, Ann G. Lawthers, Joseph P. Newhouse, Paul C. Weiler, and Howard H. Hiatt. "Incidence of Adverse Events and Negligence in Hospitalized Patients. Results of the Harvard Medical Practice Study I." *New England Journal of Medicine* 324 (1991): 370–376.

Dijksterhuis, Ap and Zeger van Olden. "On the Benefits of Thinking Unconsciously: Unconscious Thought Can Increase Post-Choice Satisfaction." *Journal of Experimental Social Psychology* 42 (2006): 627–631.

Elstein, Arthur S. "Heuristics and Biases: Selected Errors in Clinical Reasoning." *Academic Medicine* 74 (1999): 791–794.

Graber, Mark, Nancy Franklin, and Ruthanna R. Gordon. "Reducing Diagnostic Errors in Medicine—What's the Goal?" *Academic Medicine* 77 (2002): 981–992.

Groopman, Jerome. *How Doctors Think.* New York: Houghton Mifflin Company, 2007.

Hill, Shirley Y., Robert Schwin, Barbara Powell, and Donna W. Goodwin. "State-Dependent Effects of Marihuana [sic] on Human Memory." *Nature* 243 (1973): 241–242.

Janis, Irving L. *Victims of Groupthink.* Boston: Houghton Mifflin Company, 1972.

Lacey, Charles F., Lora L. Armstrong, Morton P. Goldman, and Leonard L. Lance. *Drug Information Handbook.* Hudson, Ohio: Lexi-Comp, Inc., 2001.

Tversky, Amos and Daniel Kahneman. "Availability: A Heuristic for Judging Frequency and Probability." *Cognitive Psychology* 5 (1973): 207–232.

Yaniv, Ilan and David E. Meyer. "Activation and Metacognition of Inaccessible Stored Information: Potential Bases of Incubation Effects in Problem Solving." *Journal of Experimental Psychology: Learning, Memory, and Cognition* 13 (1987): 187–205.

Yerkes, Robert M. and John D. Dodson. "The Relation of Strength of Stimulus to Rapidity of Habit-Formation." *Journal of Comparative Neurology and Psychology* 18 (1908): 459–482.

One of the most elegantly, entertainingly written House *episodes to date was sea-son one's "Three Stories," featuring Carmen Electra and the back story behind* House's *limp. The episode was framed by* House's *lecture in front of a classroom full of medical students. But this isn't the only time we've seen House teach; techni-cally, he's teaching in every episode, training Foreman, Cameron, and Chase in diagnostics. Clearly they've improved since the pilot, so he must be doing some-thing right. But how good a teacher is House, really? Psychologist Susan Engel and Sam Levin discuss.*

BUT CAN HE TEACH?

SUSAN ENGEL AND SAM LEVIN

While people love the hackneyed aphorism, "Those who can, do; those who can't, teach," it would be more accurate to say, "Anyone can teach. Few teach well." Luckily, in the medical profession those who are unusually good at their work are also the ones who teach.

Though knowing a great deal about your topic is necessary to good teaching, it is nowhere near sufficient. What else do you need to be a great, rather than adequate, teacher? And does Gregory House have what it takes?

House Knows a Lot about His Topic

Good teachers must have thorough knowledge of their discipline; though this concept is essential, it is often overlooked in school settings. Not only is expertise a prerequisite for great teaching in and of itself—how can you teach what you don't know?—it also does something equally important: it frees teachers from using a script.

House knows more than most about his discipline. Some might say

133

that he is just very smart. Judging by his encyclopedic memory, razor-sharp analytic skill, expansive and precise vocabulary, and enormous processing speed, it's a fair guess that House's IQ is 150 or above (Neisser). However, a person can be smart without acquiring substantive knowledge within a particular domain. His character is premised not only on his impressive intellect but on his vast knowledge of medicine. House often acts as if he doesn't take medical convention very seriously. But equally often he demonstrates comprehensive knowledge of past cases, obscure medical techniques, and unusual but important diagnostic procedures. His knowledge is deep as opposed to superficial; he knows so much about medicine that he can easily see connections others don't, between seemingly disparate cases or between types of treatment. He knows the literature so well that he can draw upon obscure information just when it is needed. When teachers draw solely on a rigidly circumscribed set of procedures, definitions, and examples, it suggests that they have only superficial knowledge of their discipline. House is the opposite.

One way House's knowledge manifests itself is in his ability to make refreshingly rapid and useful distinctions between the ordinary and the exotic. When a man came into the clinic with a numb hand, rather than considering a long tedious list of possible medical causes, or wasting time with a thorough examination of unrelated aspects of the patient's health, House, with barely a glance, told the man his watch was too tight and moved on to the next patient. House often relies on these everyday explanations. When House removed a tiny toy policeman, a fire truck, and then a fireman from a toddler's nose, it occurred to him that something else, too, might be buried up there—and using a magnet he retrieved a tiny toy cat. It dawned on him that the child was sending in help to rescue the cat. He knows when everyday thinking, or explanations from everyday experiences, are more apt than esoteric medical information.

House is also able to combine everyday kinds of knowledge with more technical or obscure medical information. When a man visited the clinic concerned about impotence, House almost immediately traced the problem to the diabetic man's refusal to take his insulin. Many of the clues he used were common sense (powdered sugar on the patient's pants and two napkins in his pocket told House the man was probably eating too much sugar), but his understanding of the relationship between insulin and impotence was based on medical expertise. These moments of comical virtuosity reveal two important things about House's expertise: he knows so much that he can be playful with his knowledge, and his grasp of the highly specialized information is so profound that he can easily slip back and forth between that kind of knowledge and common sense.

This kind of expertise is critical to good teaching in many ways; the more knowledge the teacher has, the more he can offer his students. But it also provides the student with a model of expertise. In "Heavy" (1-16), the team was working with a morbidly obese ten-year-old girl who had begun to suffer life-threatening high blood pressure and necrosis. Toward the end of the episode, House, looking for an explanation for her strange cluster of symptoms, noticed that she was short while both of her parents were tall. He reasoned aloud that her shortness might therefore be a symptom of her problem, because it was probably not inherited; in that case, the most likely dignosis was Cushing's. Cameron, Chase, and Foreman disagreed, reminding House that in none of the books was Cushing's linked with necrosis. But House pointed out that there were in fact rare cases, under certain conditions, where Cushing's had been associated with necrosis. Clearly, House keeps current with a huge body of medical literature, and that erudition is essential to his intuitive leaps.

House is a perfect embodiment of what Jerome Bruner, an American psychologist specializing in cognitive psychology, referred to as skilled intuition—his deep knowledge of medicine provides a background for what often seem to be out-of-the-blue leaps and intuitions. But as Bruner argued in 1959, and subsequent research has proven, good intuition arises not from chance or God-given gifts, but from thorough and flexible knowledge within a domain. In other words, the more expert you are, the more you are able to trust your instincts. What seems fanciful or capricious on House's part is usually based on some incisive blend of medical and non-medical insight. When House bounces his yo-yo up and down, his focus intent on the movement, and makes a startling leap in which he connects two unlikely pieces of information to hit upon the exact diagnosis for mysterious symptoms, it seems as if his sudden inspiration is coming from the yo-yo. In fact, it comes not only from many years of medical practice, but from reading a wide range of medical journals and staying up to date with the newest advances in organic chemistry, pharmacology, epidemiology, and physiology. And when his students see him make those leaps, and discover how often they are correct, they have an opportunity to model their own medical practice on his.

A great teacher offers something beyond the obvious and plodding integration of material, something his or her students cannot learn simply by memorizing huge quantities of information in a book. House's knowledge and expertise allow him to be creative, responsive, surprising, and authentic as he transmits what he knows to his students. But his skilled intuition is invaluable to his teaching in another way as well—it allows him to elicit greater ability from the students he teaches.

Whether students are five, nineteen, or twenty-eight years old, their knowledge often presents itself in surprising, disorganized, novel, and disguised ways. A good teacher is one who knows the domain so thoroughly that she recognizes the kernel of knowledge—the good idea, the promising first step—in a student, and can lead that student to develop that kernel, idea, or first step in the right direction. The teacher who has only superficial knowledge of her topic is stuck following a script (the textbook, the outline, the primer she has only just read herself), and that leads her to dodge her students' questions, discourage deviations that could actually lead somewhere useful, or tell a student he or she is wrong when actually the student's clumsy or odd-sounding answer just doesn't match the answer in the back of the teacher's copy of the book. House knows medicine so thoroughly that he can not only share that knowledge with his students, but see the value in his students' answers even when his students themselves cannot.

House Teaches Using the Apprenticeship Model

Perhaps it doesn't stand out because it is so common in medical internships, but House's ability to draw his students into his own work process exemplifies one of the best teaching methods: teaching through apprenticeship. Lev Vygotsky, a brilliant Soviet researcher during the first part of the twentieth century, was perhaps the first to identify the process by which a child comes to know more, or develop further in his thinking, by solving a problem with the help of an older or more competent person. Jerome Bruner later coined the term "scaffolding," which he used to describe how a mother's verbal responses to her child create a scaffold that allows/pushes the child to try increasingly complex vocabulary and syntax as he or she learns to talk. But it was only in the last part of the twentieth century that these ideas really took hold, as developmental psychologists began to look across a range of cultures and saw that in many cultures children learned the most complex and valued activities of the community by working alongside experts. In one well-known study, Patricia Greenfield showed how expert weavers in a rural Mexican community teach young girls to become expert weavers by using the apprenticeship model. The girls work alongside the expert weavers so that they can see what the best weaving process looks like. Over time, as they show readiness, the girls are given more and more autonomy and responsibility for increasingly complex parts of the process, until they are able to weave on their own. The apprenticeship model has many virtues, among them the experts' serious interest in the novice's progress; the experts in the Mexican village want the cloth to be well-made.

Similarly, House wants his patients to live. So when he gathers his three apprentices in the meeting room and begins writing up all the symptoms, he not only demonstrates his own pattern of problem-solving but also brings Cameron, Chase, and Foreman into the process. House has even given each of his students a chance to be the one up at the whiteboard listing the symptoms. Like the weavers, these neophytes learn by doing—by taking on increasingly difficult and important pieces of the shared endeavor. In "Act Your Age" (3-19), House actually dueled with Cameron over getting a father to endorse or refuse a questionable treatment for his young daughter. All of a sudden they were interacting as peers rather than as teacher and student, showing what a good job House had done in helping his novices become experts. It also reflected his ability to shift his relationship to his students as they do become more expert.

Because House is teaching his residents in the context of real cases, he cares more about diagnosing and treating the patient than he cares about what his residents are getting out of it. There's a good side and a bad side to this. The good side is that the focus on the work itself naturally raises the bar for his students and gives him, as their teacher, strong motivation to educate them. An example taken from the world of schools may clarify the point. When a high school student is asked to write an essay that will be read and graded by the teacher, the student knows that in the end, the only value of the work is the value the teacher assigns to it. The student's work is therefore directed toward pleasing the teacher rather than doing a great job. The teacher is committed to detailed and rigorous feedback only to the extent that she is committed to her student's educational progress, which may be distorted by a variety of factors such as lowered expectations based on implicit assumptions about students' ability or motivation (Rosenthal and Jacobson).

But imagine for a moment a student who is writing an essay that will be read by those outside the school—an essay that will bear the teacher's name as well as the student's. Now the teacher has a stronger motivation to see that the student writes well. In addition, the student has a strong motivation beyond a grade for making sure the essay is as good as it can be. As some have noted, this may be why students who have trouble focusing on academic work work so much harder at their athletic and performance art endeavors; the stakes are higher than just a grade. By the same token, coaches and school theater directors are often more demanding and more intense with students than teachers are, because they share a goal that goes beyond approval of one person by another. House and his students are under a shared pressure to heal patients, making the learning situation as potent as it can be. House's interest in finding the right answer overrides his need to be the authority or even to instruct. The best part about this is that if one of his students has a better idea than he does, he will be more interested in the idea than in worrying about looking bad in front of his students. In the real world, all too often teachers begin to dislike students who are smarter than they are because it makes them feel insecure and diminished. Two qualities prevent that: confidence in one's expertise, and a greater interest in the solution of problems (whether those problems crop up in writing, history, math, art, science, or medicine) than in maintaining one's position as the authority with power.

The bad side of House's unrelenting focus on treatment rather than the education of his medical apprentices is that he sometimes runs roughshod over them, shooting down ideas which may be wrong in a given instance even if they reflect a smart or effective line of thinking. Good teachers in more conventional classrooms have more time and freedom to encourage a good thought process even when the specific answer a student arrives at is wrong.

Another strength of the apprenticeship model is that it puts students (and teacher) into more real learning situations than the ordinary classroom. The lessons students learn matter to them, because what they're learning matters to society.

American philosopher, psychologist, and educational reformer John Dewey first wrote about the importance of connecting education to the real concerns and activities of students' lives over 100 years ago. Since then research has shown that children are more motivated to draw upon their highest cognitive skills during activities that are valued and meaningful in the real world. In one classic study, five-year-olds who could not recall lists of words when asked to by an experimenter showed remarkably more sophisticated memory skills when they enacted a grocery store scenario in which they had to remember items to buy (Istomina). The psycholinguist Frank Smith has shown that children are more likely to learn to read with ease when they feel they are part of a community of children and adults who read and read for a range of real world purposes. Yet here we are in 2007, and few schools in technologically advanced societies have yet to take the idea seriously. House and his students provide a vivid reminder that learning is most effective when students feel that what they are learning is part of real life.

House Loves Medicine

Every third episode or so, Wilson or Cuddy comes to House wanting him to take a case. He immediately and adamantly dismisses them, sure that the case is too mundane, too obvious, or too much work for him to bother. Then Cuddy or Wilson delivers the punch—the detail or quirk that makes the case irresistible (a seven-year-old with a symptom that never appears in anyone under thirty, a man who has never been to the tropics showing symptoms of a tropical disease). They know he cannot resist a fascinating case, because he just loves medicine too much. That magnetic draw is part of what makes him such a powerful teacher. Passion for a topic (which is different from knowledge of a topic) is contagious. That kind of contagion is very powerful in a teaching situation—particularly if and when the students care about their teacher. House's ability to transmit both his love and knowledge of medicine stems in part from his very real interactions with his students. Though Cameron, Chase, and Foreman are often furious at House, and often actually dislike him, he is never an invisible or insignificant component of the learning situation. He is a person to them and with them, and this makes a huge difference in his impact as their teacher (see "House Is Vulnerable," below).

House Has Charisma

Teachers with charisma have a leg up, and House is swimming in charisma. Not only his good looks (piercing blue eyes, rangy physique, chiseled features), but his wit, his ferociousness, his periodic and unexpected humility, and his legion of quirks all draw people to him, even as his less pleasant qualities repel them. Research on the development of leadership suggests that charisma cannot be learned, and that it is a powerful component in determining a person's influence over others. There is no question that those who draw people to them through their intensity, their humor, and their sense of authority are more successful at both changing the minds of others and convincing them to do otherwise unappealing tasks (Goethals et al.). In other words, charisma helps with exactly those challenges that face teachers all the time.

House Is Vulnerable

House's charisma is linked with another quality that is essential to effective teachers—the ability to be human with one's students. House demonstrates a rare combination of authority and vulnerability, a mixture that is common among great teachers. House is a bit intimidating and very sure of himself; his students never lose sight of who is in charge, and if they begin to forget, he reminds them in dramatic and humiliating ways. After Chase made the mistake of thinking the Tic Tacs he found in a patient's apartment were irrelevant to the case, House brought his three apprentices into the patient's room and told Chase to smell the patient's mouth, which turned out to be seriously infected. Chase hesitated, looked warily at his teacher, and said, "You're trying to humiliate me. I know it." House, intent upon putting Chase in his place, insisted, "Come on, just put your face in his mouth" ("Love Hurts," 1-20).

But House is also human. He limps, he suffers chronic pain, he is addicted to drugs, and he periodically reveals his insecurity, his envy, and his lust. All of this makes it possible for his students to create real relationships with him (albeit vexed ones). The relationship between teacher and student has been shown, time and again, to be the single most important element in determining a student's experience and success within a classroom (Pellegrini and Blatchford).

House's relationship with Cameron is particularly interesting because one could argue that he crossed a line with her personally and sexually; they had a date at one point, though the audience never found out what they actually did or did not do, and he often makes remarks about her body. Though that kind of sexuality would be unacceptable in any current school setting in the United States, it does dramatize an underlying reality of the teacher-student relationship: the role of attachment in learning. In the first learning relationship, the one between mother and child, the bond leads to a finely tuned exchange which enables the baby to begin to parse the world; this interaction forms the basis of all later cognitive, linguistic, and social advances (Stern). Study after study has shown that most early learning happens in the context of relationships, and the same seems to be true about the learning that happens in the more formal settings of school. When children form an attachment to their teacher they learn more. One fairly straightforward reason for this is that children model themselves on people with whom they have a bond (Pellegrini and Blatchford). To the extent that a teacher is a model rather than a just conduit for information, the stronger the connection to the model the more likely the child will emulate him or her.

Furthermore, research has shown that students learn more when they are intrinsically rather than extrinsically motivated. In other words, students learn more when they are driven by their own thoughts and feelings rather than some unrelated reward (a grade, a gold star, a piece of candy). Earlier we showed that when a student's work has a value beyond the classroom, it promotes high motivation. But another way to achieve this is to get the student to identify with the teacher. Identification is one of the most powerful bases for the transmission of values, goals, and interests. When a student (particularly a child or adolescent) identifies with his or her teacher, the student is much more eager to please the teacher, earn the teacher's praise, and win the teacher's good opinion.

Because of his combination of charisma and vulnerability, House elicits strong feelings from his students, thus creating bonds that allow him to be even more effective at shaping what they learn and how they practice medicine. During "House Training" (3-20), when Foreman had to confront the fact that his misdiagnosis led to a patient's death, he didn't know how to handle his feelings of guilt and failure. At the end of the episode, House walked into his office to find Foreman waiting there, clearly seeking some wisdom or guidance despite his skepticism about House. Having developed such a complex and dynamic relationship with his student, House used the moment to be firm, clear, and directive. He told Foreman to go home, drink, pray, or do whatever he had to do to feel better, then sleep, and come back ready to try—and possibly fail—again. But he also reminded Foreman that doctors who take more chances cure more people suffering from rare afflictions. The cost of such risk-taking, however, is that such doctors are also going to kill more people than the average cautious, by-the-book doctor. House was reminding Foreman that to be as good as House is, Foreman has to accept that. In other words, while advising Foreman, he also identified himself as Foreman's role model, using their bond even as he strengthed it. The impact of House's advice to Foreman was predicated on how attached Foreman had become to him. In "Poison" (1-8), Foreman realized that he had unwittingly bought the exact same shoes that House wore. What more perfect expression of the student's wish to be like his mentor than that?

House Has Great Students

It is all too easy to underestimate the role that students play in determining the efficacy of the teacher. Great students help teachers be great, and the better the students, the easier it is to teach them. House's students are highly able and highly motivated. Because they have already accomplished so much (they were chosen, for instance, for House's highly selective fellowship program), they are confident. Clearly, they are also ambitious and resilient. In "Histories" (1-10), Chase came up with a novel way to restore a teenage boy's vision without sacrificing the team's focus on the bigger problem, the underlying disease. House was impressed and said so, but then asked, "Why didn't you suggest this earlier?" Chase, surprised and pleased at the unexpected praise from House, responded honestly that he hadn't thought of it earlier. House retorted, "Well, you should have." House is a hard taskmaster. But he is right to assume that his particular students can take it and may even benefit from such unrelentingly high standards.

This is a valuable reminder that teaching is never simply a set of practices or techniques that can be applied in a regimented or automatic way. Teachers, at their best, are complicated, interesting, interested, skilled, and devoted. They are individuals, whose personalities can never and should never be extracted from the process. So are students. Teaching, then, is an endeavor in which the feelings, experiences, and quirks of both teachers and students determine the outcome of the teaching process.

House might not be a good teacher for other kinds of students. He is self-absorbed and undisciplined in his reactions. He can be mean. He can also be ruthless, and in his quest to diagnose and treat disease, he often runs roughshod over his residents—mocking them, denigrating them, not listening to them, and shaking their confidence. If he were working with less confident or less able students he might do as much damage as good using this approach.

More relevant, House has neither the interest nor the skill to monitor the learning process of his students. He is unlikely to spend time coming up with creative ways to reach the disengaged student or the student who has trouble learning. He is unlikely to have a repertoire of techniques for solving the kinds of teaching problems which face most teachers all day long, day in and day out. He is not interested enough in his students' success to spend time observing them and calibrating his approach in response to what those observations tell him. He is not given to the kind of critical self-reflection and un-defensive self-scrutiny that is as essential to good teaching as the other factors we've discussed. He probably has no interest or ability in motivating unmotivated students.

House possesses almost all of the natural gifts required for great teaching—the ones money can't buy. But he possesses almost none of the interest and commitment that lead talented teachers to become skilled teachers.

The tired (and tiresome) debate about whether someone can learn to be a good teacher or must simply "have it" is actually a non-issue: good teachers need to have talent, but they must be educated and trained—just like good surgeons need sharp eyesight, dexterous hands, and steady nerves, but still need to go to medical school and do a surgery internship (as is often mentioned in *House*, the better the medical school and internship, the better the doctor). No one can be a great doctor without natural gifts and great training. The same is true of teachers. House is both a talented and well-educated doctor. But as a teacher he's only got the talent, not the education. This is why he shines with great students, and would be lost with the students facing most teachers in our society. Without Chase, Foreman, and Cameron, House would still be brilliant, captivating, and intense. He just might not be as good a teacher.

SUSAN ENGEL earned a BA from Sarah Lawrence College in 1980, and a Ph.D. in developmental psychology from CUNY Graduate Center in 1985. She is currently a senior lecturer in psychology and director of the Program in Teaching at Williams College. Engel has taught students from age three to adults. In addition to journal articles and book chapters, Engel has written three books, *The Stories Children Tell: Making Sense of the Narratives of Childhood* (W. H. Freeman, 1985), *Context Is Everything: The Nature of Memory* (W. H. Freeman, 1997), and, most recently, *Real Kids: Creating Meaning in Everyday Life* (Harvard University Press, 2005). She is also the co-founder and educational advisor

144

to an experimental school in eastern Long Island, The Hayground School, and writes a regular column on teaching, "Lessons," for the *New York Times*. Engel's research interests include the development of autobiographical memory, narrative processes in childhood, imagination and play in childhood, and the development of curiosity. She lives with her husband and three sons in New Marlborough, Massachusetts.

SAM LEVIN is currently a student who attends school in Massachusetts. He recently completed a natural history, *The Pond*.

REFERENCES

Bruner, Jerome. *The Culture of Education*. Cambridge: Harvard University Press, 1996.

Bruner, Jerome. *The Process of Education*. Cambridge: Harvard University Press, 1959, 2006.

Dewey, John. *The Child and the Curriculum*. Chicago: University of Chicago Press, 1902.

Goethals, George, Georgia Sorenson, and J. M. Burns, eds. *Encyclopedia of Leadership*. New York: Sage Publications, 2004.

Greenfield, Patricia. "A Theory of the Teacher in the Learning Activities of Everyday Life." In *Everyday Cognition*, edited by B. Rogoff and J. Lave. Cambridge: Harvard University Press, 1984.

Istomina, Z. M. "The Development of Voluntary Memory in Preschool-Age Children." In *Soviet Developmental Psychology*, edited by Michael Cole, 100–159. New York: M. E. Sharpe, 1977.

Neisser, Ulrich, et al. "Intelligence: Knowns and Unknowns." *American Psychologist* 51.2 (1966): 77–101.

Pellegrini, Anthony and Peter Blatchford. *The Child at School: Interactions with Peers and Teachers*. London: Hodder Arnold Pubs, 2000.

Rosenthal, Robert and Lenore Jacobson. "Teacher Expectations for the Disadvantaged." *Scientific American* 218.4 (1968): 19–23.

Smith, Frank. *Understanding Reading*. New Jersey: Lawrence Erlbaum, 1994.

Stern, Daniel. *The First Relationship*. Cambridge: Harvard University Press, 1977.

Vygotsky, Lev, M. Cole, V. John-Steiner, S. Scribner, E. Souberman, eds. *Mind in Society*. Cambridge: Harvard University Press, 1968.

It's House's job to take on the medical puzzles no one else can solve. But some-times, even House needs a consult. Here, psychologists Mikhail Lyubansky and Elaine Shpungin take on the biggest unsolvable puzzle of all—House himself.

PLAYING HOUSE

MIKHAIL LYUBANSKY AND ELAINE SHPUNGIN

Inside an outpatient psychological clinic . . .

Mikhail: [Entering Elaine's office, with a college student in tow] Hey . . . got your message about needing a consult. This is Jordan, a McNair[1] student I'm supervising this summer that I invited to sit in, if you don't mind. We went over confidentiality[2] on the way over, so we can get started immediately. What have you got?

Elaine: [to Jordan] I don't mind. Hope you find it interesting. [to Mikhail] Thanks for coming by on such short notice. You don't have to worry about confidentiality. This is an unusual situation. I got a call today from the editor of BenBella—you know,

---

[1] The national McNair Program is designed to identify and mentor exceptional college students from low-income backgrounds. The program is named after Ronald E. McNair, the son of an auto mechanic who went on to become an engineer, physicist, and *Challenger* astronaut.

[2] Psychologists are mandated to keep all client data and identifying information confidential, though exceptions are allowed for training and consulting purposes.

147

they put out those Smart Pop books you like. Apparently, they're doing an anthology and one of their expected contributors backed out at the last minute. They need a report with a psychological diagnosis and treatment recommendations for House by tomorrow afternoon. They sent over a chart.

Mikhail: A psychological diagnosis for a house?

Elaine: Not for a house, for Greg House. He's the main character of a television show called *House M.D.*, a kind of medical Sherlock Holmes specializing in infectious disease and . . . [looks at notes] nephrology who solves medical cases that no one else can figure out.

Mikhail: Yeah, sounds vaguely familiar, but isn't this whole thing a bit problematic? How are we supposed to diagnose a TV character we can't even interview, much less formally assess, not to mention that I haven't actually seen a single episode?

Elaine: I told you; they sent us his chart. [picks up a three-inch-thick binder stuffed to the limit] Everything they know about House is in here: summaries of all his cases, colleague comments, even transcript segments and photos.[3]

Mikhail: Good grief! You expect me to read all that?

Elaine: That's up to you. For what it's worth, it's great reading. Edelyn[4] and I spent all morning discussing it. She says he meets criteria for Narcissistic Personality Disorder and Substance Dependence.

---

[3] The premise is that everything from the TV show is in the chart, nothing more and nothing less.

[4] Edelyn Verona is a professor of psychology at the University of Illinois in Urbana-Champaign, where she supervises doctoral students in their clinical work with clients diagnosed with personality disorders. She has written extensively on externalizing psychopathology, especially antisocial behavior and aggression.

Mikhail: Great, you've already got a diagnosis. What do you need me for?

Elaine: Same reason I always need you: he's complicated. Nothing seems to fit just right. For example, DSM[5] criteria specify that a person must have a grandiose sense of self-importance, *without* commensurate achievements.

Mikhail: So?

Elaine: So, he assumes he's always right and thinks the hospital and everyone in it should bend over backward to accommodate his hunches . . . *and* he just might be the pre-eminent diagnostician in the country.

Mikhail: Interesting . . . a narcissist with an accurate self-concept. Is that possible?

Elaine: Edelyn says it is, that high achievement is not unusual in narcissists with high intelligence. His arrogance, sense of entitlement, lack of empathy, and willingness to trample on others to meet his own needs are still all indicative of narcissism.

Mikhail: To meet his own needs or those of his patients?

Elaine: She said it didn't matter, that his behavior was inflexible, maladaptive, and longstanding, and that even when he supposedly wanted something for the patient, his attitude and demeanor conveyed that he thought that he was the only one who really knew what was in the patient's best interest.

---

[5] DSM-IV is the *Diagnostic and Statistical Manual of Mental Disorders, Fourth Edition, Text Revision*. It is the primary classification system of mental disorders used in the United States.

Mikhail: Ok, let's assume he has NPD. What was that about substance dependence?

Elaine: The substance is Vicodin,[6] which he takes for chronic leg pain caused by an infarction in the thigh, but the substance dependence isn't the presenting complaint. If you believe the reports, he's a miserable SOB—a real ray of sunshine, if you know what I mean. Doesn't quite fit Vicodin dependence, even if you factor in NPD.

Mikhail: Let me see that chart. [reads for a few minutes] Sorry, I don't see the mystery. Miserable, carmudgeonly, irritable, middle-aged guy with no life outside of work: classic depression or dysthymia, typical of people with NPD. Tell BenBella he needs anti-depressants.

Elaine: I don't think so. He doesn't fit the DSM criteria for MDD.[7]

Mikhail: Are you sure? He seems to have at least some of the symptoms, and his colleagues are so convinced that. . . .

Elaine: Of course, I'm sure. Half the clients we serve here have depression. This guy doesn't. He might be sad and irritable, but he's not anhedonic,[8] and there's no evidence of significant weight or appetite change, sleep problems, fatigue, indecisiveness, feelings of worthlessness, or suicidal ideation. He's not depressed.

Jordan: You can tell from the chart that he has a healthy appetite?

---

[6] Vicodin is a combination of hydrocodone bitartrate (an opioid) and acetaminophen (Tylenol).
[7] Major Depressive Disorder.
[8] Anhedonia is a marked decrease in interest or pleasure in almost all activities.

Elaine: Actually, I can. According to the chart, he likes his food—and his patients' food—and seems particularly fond of his friend Wilson's cooking. Also, there are dozens of pictures in the file, and there's no noticeable weight change over a several-year period. Incidentally, he's a real cutie.

Mikhail: [sarcastically] There's a clinically relevant point. . . . What about suicidal ideation and preoccupation with death? Didn't his chart say he rides a motorcycle to work every day, despite his leg condition? Seems like a death wish to me. And the way he taunts patients and their family members . . . it's just a matter of time before one of them shoots him.

Elaine: One of them did shoot him. It's in the chart. But you're way off and you know it. House is *not* suicidal. He's just a risk taker. Not the same thing. In fact, if anything, his attitude toward death is pretty healthy. He isn't in denial about the fact that everyone will die but believes that life is worth living.

Mikhail: Okay, fine, he's not clinically depressed. This also rules out dysthymia, since it's basically just depression that's less severe but more chronic. Here, give me that piece of chalk. What are the differentials?

Elaine: Well, House is not your typical guy. We should consider *atypical* depression.

Mikhail: Interesting idea . . . MDD With Atypical Features.

Elaine: [picking up her DSM] Well—he's got the "long-term extreme sensitivity to perceived interpersonal rejection."

Mikhail: What are you talking about? According to the chart, the man couldn't care less about what others think of him. He seems to be the rudest, meanest, most inappropriate . . .

151

Elaine: . . . most politically incorrect. . . . All true, but look at his relationship with Stacy. He was totally devastated when she left him and was obsessed with getting her back for five years.

Mikhail: So?

Elaine: So, he actually cares *more* about what people think of him than most people.

Mikhail: How's that?

Elaine: Look—if he is sufficiently mean and rude to others, then he can attribute his lack of intimate interpersonal relationships to the fact that he deliberately pushes people away. Otherwise, he might have to deal with the possibility that they may reject him—the way his dad did—and that possibility is too painful for him to handle.

Mikhail: Ookay. . . .

Elaine: Don't you see? That actually makes him *more* sensitive to rejection than most of us, since most of us are willing to take the chance of being rejected for the possibility of being accepted and loved.

Mikhail: I see what you're saying, but you can't have it both ways. If he took the breakup so hard, then he must have been willing to risk rejection in order to be with her.

Elaine: But that was more than five years ago, possibly before all these symptoms emerged. You really have to read the full report. More than five years after she left him, House actually managed to win her back—despite the fact that she was married. After spending some time with House, she decided to leave her husband in order to be with House—with no expectations that House change in any way. You'd think he'd be all over that after pining after her for five years, but no. He told her that their relationship was bound to fail again and that she should stay with her husband. He rejected her, because he was too scared that things wouldn't work out and she would find him inadequate—again. He'd rather take the chance of never being with her than the chance that she would reject him!

Mikhail: Very interesting theory, but it's only relevant if he actually meets the other criteria.

Elaine: True, true. Let's see . . . in addition to the interpersonal oversensitivity, he'd also have to have "mood reactivity"—the capacity to be cheered up when presented with positive events—and the presence of at least one of the following: increased appetite or weight gain; hypersomnia; or leaden paralysis. He doesn't have atypical depression either.

Mikhail: [skimming the chart] Says here he's suffering from chronic pain due to nondiabetic thigh muscle infarction. How about Mood Disorder Due to a General Medical Condition?

Elaine: Nope. It only fits when the mood disturbance is considered to be the direct *physiological* consequence of a general medical condition. Far as I know, a thigh infarction has no effect on serotonin levels. Doesn't work.

Mikhail: Addiction to Vicodin could cause Substance-Induced Mood Disorder. That could explain all his symptoms, including the sadness, irritability, low social functioning, mood changes. . . . On the other hand, those are pretty rare side effects of Vicodin use. Besides, we'd have to get him off the stuff long enough to be able to tell if there is any change.

Elaine: The chart indicates a week off the Vicodin, on a bet, with subsequent worsening of the dysphoria and irritability—which is pretty impressive given his usual state of churlishness.

Mikhail: All right, let me think a minute. He is irritable on Vicodin and even more irritable off of it. That means the increased irritability has to be due to either Vicodin withdrawal or to the chronic pain.

Elaine: Or to neither one—if his symptoms emerged prior to the infarction. Unfortunately, the chart's not clear on that. Apparently House told Wilson that he's been "alienating people since [he] was three."[9]

Mikhail: Yeah, I'm sure those early memories are highly reliable. What do his colleagues say?

Elaine: Cuddy seems to agree with House.

Mikhail: They were in the same preschool playgroup?

Elaine: They don't go that far back, but she reported that House was the same miserable SOB before he and Stacy first got together. On the other hand, Wilson claims House did change. He actually insists he did. So, we can't rule out either substance-induced Mood Disorder or pain-induced Mood Disorder.

Mikhail: Sure wish we could wave a wand and make his pain

---

[9] "Detox" (1-11).

go away so that we could see if either the pain or the pain meds are the cause.

Elaine: [waves a pencil like a wand] Voila!

Mikhail: What does that mean?

Elaine: You're holding the chart; feel free to read some of it. When House was shot, he was placed into a ketamine-induced coma, which apparently can "reboot" the brain, thereby successfully eliminating severe chronic pain in many patients. When House recovered from the surgery to remove the bullets in his neck and abdomen, the pain in his leg was gone, and in the two months following surgery, he took up jogging and skateboarding. More to the point, he returned to work with a new attitude and demeanor: still sarcastic, but without the mean edge.

Mikhail: Okay, so why are we still having this conversation?

Elaine: Bad luck. The treatment is only effective about 50 percent of the time. House wasn't in the lucky half. As the pain came back, he started using Vicodin again, and the surliness and irritability returned.

Mikhail: . . . bringing us back to the same place as before. There's something we're missing. Let's call it a day and talk again tomorrow afternoon. In the meantime, I'll see if I can get through the chart.

That next day, back at the Psychological Services Center . . .

Mikhail: [walking through Elaine's door with Jordan] You were right . . . fascinating reading. We've been chasing the wrong symptoms.

Elaine: And "hello" right back at you.

Mikhail: Yes, yes, hello. . . . The misery and irritability are masking the real problem.

Elaine: Which is?

Mikhail: The people around him. House is perfectly happy, but they're all miserable.

Elaine: You think House is happy? This I've got to hear.

Mikhail: Well, the easiest thing would be to give him Ed Diener's Satisfaction with Life Scale[10] or some other measure of happiness. We can't do that, unfortunately, but we *can* compare House to people identified by researchers as "happy." According to the research, happy people are characterized by several specific traits: extraversion, strong social networks, high self-esteem, high senses of optimism and personal control, and flow.

Elaine: Strike one on the extraversion. House certainly isn't a "people person."

Mikhail: True, he's not an extrovert. But he's not really an introvert either. Besides, I remember reading somewhere that extraversion only accounts for about 8 percent of happiness. He doesn't seem to have a strong social network either, so that's strike two. But he's clearly got all the rest.

---

[10] Ed Diener, a social psychologist at the University of Illinois, has been studying happiness and subjective well-being for more than twenty-five years. His Satisfaction with Life Scale has been translated into over a dozen languages and cited by more than 1,000 journal articles. It is available at http://www.psych.uiuc.edu/~ediener/SWLS.htm. According to Diener, who was kind enough to consult on this essay, people who love their work but don't care much about their interpersonal relationships (like House?) are generally low on positive emotions (which doesn't say anything about their negative emotions), but sometimes report high life satisfaction.

Elaine: So, you're conveniently going to ignore the two traits that don't fit your theory?

Mikhail: It's like depression and NPD. He doesn't need to have all the traits to qualify. Every trait just increases the probability. Self-esteem and personal control go together, so let's start there: Happy people like themselves.

Elaine: He's narcissistic, of course he likes himself. But you make a good point about personal control.

Jordan: I'm sorry to interrupt, but I don't see how doctors can possibly feel like they're in control. It seems to me that House can't really control anything—not whether the patient responds to meds, not even whether the patient lives or dies.

Mikhail: No, no . . . it's not whether he *can* control the events in his life—it's whether he *feels* like he can. Seligman[11] and his colleagues demonstrated that people who believe that what they do makes no difference are more likely to experience learned helplessness and eventually depression. In contrast, happy people tend to feel in control. They feel empowered to make decisions and act on them, because they believe that they have the ability to affect the world around them. Furthermore, when they have failures—as we all do—they attribute them to some external event, not to some internal flaw. House *believes* he has the ability to affect his world, to figure out what is making patients sick, and, in so doing, save many lives. The fact that illnesses are somewhat unpredictable and that he is sometimes wrong, or even makes a patient worse, does not detract from his

---

[11] Marty Seligman is a professor of psychology at the University of Pennsylvania. He is most well known for his theory on learned helplessness and his contribution to and promoting of the fledging field of Positive Psychology.

sense of personal control, because he attributes these failures to circumstances external to himself.

Elaine: Like, "everyone lies," so he didn't have the right information. . . .

Mikhail: Or the administration got in his way. . . .

Elaine: Or it was his team's fault. . . . But isn't there such a thing as too much confidence, or too high a sense of personal control? I mean, the guy seems to think he can solve any medical case that presents itself in the hospital, and is so confident in his abilities that he usually starts treatment before even confirming his diagnosis with tests!

Mikhail: Exactly, but his pride and confidence are both well-earned. I know his colleagues accuse him of thinking he's God, but his supreme confidence is not delusional. In fact, if you look carefully, you'll even find a little humility.

Elaine: You've got to be kidding. He's narcissistic, remember?

Mikhail: I'm completely serious. Cuddy said she once asked House how it is that he always assumes he is right, even when everyone else disagrees. Know what he told her? He said, "I don't. I just find it hard to operate on the opposite assumption."[12] This means the confidence is at least partly strategic—which, incidentally, points against narcissism—and it lets him do his job better than anyone else. And I'm sure you noticed that he tries to instill that same confidence in his diagnostic team—you know, stand up for what you believe is the right thing to do. . . . Anyway, let's keep going. People with high self-esteem have a strong moral

---

[12] "Pilot" (1-1).

code and low prejudice. . . .

Jordan: Okay, so that's strike three. I read part of the chart this morning. This Dr. House seems like he does whatever he pleases whenever he pleases with no regard for anyone or anything, certainly not any rules. Isn't that what an anarchist is, someone who has no ethical or moral code? I think Dr. Foreman called him that.

Mikhail: "Anarchist" is sometimes used to describe a person who disregards social norms and the influence of authority, but you can disregard these and still have a strong moral code. There's a clear and consistent pattern in House's behavior, an ethical hierarchy in which the patient's life comes first, followed by the patient's health, and then by the patient's quality of life. He pisses people off because his ethical code has no place for his colleagues' feelings and no value for rules, guidelines, and regulations designed to protect the hospital and its doctors. You may not agree with his ethical code, but he certainly has one, and he clearly thinks it's superior. For example, when Foreman became deathly ill and turned into a patient instead of a colleague, House's entire attitude toward him changed. He was willing to do whatever it took to figure out what was wrong, and he was furious that Cuddy wanted to follow CDC guidelines and not let him perform an autopsy on the dead police officer who had the same condition, for fear that the condition might be contagious.

Elaine: Okay, I'll accept that *he* thinks he is more ethical than others, even if I don't, but there's no way even he can believe he is less prejudiced.

Jordan: I was wondering about that too. I saw that he called

Dr. Foreman "Blackpoleon Blackaparte"[13] and wouldn't let him write on the board because it was a *white*board. And he makes sexual comments about Dr. Cuddy . . .

Elaine: . . . and called Wilson in for a consult—for possible breast cancer—in order to show him an attractive set of boobs.

Mikhail: And yet, he's still not prejudiced. First of all, he insults and pokes fun at almost everyone he comes in contact with. Secondly, his use of racial[14]—not racist—humor in the presence of people of color suggests a comfort and familiarity with race and racial dynamics. His barbs are always directed at individuals, not groups, and his overall behavior suggests that he tends to evaluate people based on their abilities, not group membership. His colleagues understand this. They may be annoyed, but they don't seem to be especially offended by his comments. At one point, Cameron even tells him to stop pretending to be a misogynist, when he is, in reality, a misanthrope.

Elaine: Glad you cleared that up . . . wouldn't want to misdiagnose him.

Mikhail: Actually, I think he just pretends to be misanthropic because it gives him license to do what he wants. I realize he frustrates and exasperates his colleagues, but he also knows how to get along with them on a professional level. Until he fired Chase and Foreman and Cameron quit, he seemed to have productive working relationships with just about everyone in the hospital with whom he had to interact on a regular basis. Sure, not everyone likes House, but that isn't the point. The point is that he likes himself.

---

[13] "Deception" (2-9).

[14] Racial statements merely acknowledge the existence of race and racial categories. In contrast, racist statements are intended to denigrate one group or elevate another.

Elaine: Okay, so he has high self-esteem and sense of personal control—but that's only two of the six characteristics of happy people, and he already has two strikes against him. So far, I'm sticking with either drug-induced misery or NPD.

Mikhail: No problem. Fifth characteristic of happy people: optimism. I think I've already convinced you that House is confident in his diagnostic abilities, but his optimism extends to many other domains. He obviously believes that the treatments he prescribes will work. In fact, he is generally optimistic about his ability to beat the odds—both in horse racing and in the race against death. He also demonstrates this trait in his dealings with his boss and his colleagues. He is optimistic that he can get away with shorter hours, fewer cases, and an unusual interpersonal style—without losing his job.

Elaine: Yeah, but what about Stacy? Where is his optimism there?

Mikhail: True, he does not seem optimistic about changing himself. But he pursues Stacy for a long time against the odds, which demonstrates confidence, good self-esteem, a sense of personal control—and optimism. At the end, when she offered herself to him and he turned her down . . . he might have been running away from interpersonal rejection as we talked about earlier, but turning her down was also a way for him to be in control. He wasn't willing to just let things take their course. He had to take control, even when doing so was painful for both him and Stacy. I'm not saying he's always optimistic; I'm just saying that it's hard to argue that he does not demonstrate high levels of optimism and personal control in most things most of the time.

Elaine: Hmmmmm.

Mikhail: Great. The last characteristic of happy people is that they go with the flow.

Elaine: Well, there's your third strike. You just said yourself that he's not willing to let things take their course, and I'm not sure I've met anyone who insists on going *against* the flow more. House is like a salmon, always trying to swim upstream.

Mikhail: Nice metaphor, but I'm talking about Csikszentmihalyi's flow.

Jordan: Chicks sent you what?

Mikhail: Mihaly Csikszentmihalyi. He's the psychologist who invented the concept of flow. Did you see his interview in *Wired* magazine?

Elaine: Do I look like I read *Wired*?

Mikhail: Hold on . . . I think I have it here somewhere. [rummages for a while in some piles of paper and journals on the floor] All right, here we go. Let me find the page. Okay. Here. He describes flow as "being completely involved in an activity for its own sake. The ego falls away. Time flies. Every action, movement, and thought follows inevitably from the previous one, like playing jazz. Your whole being is involved, and you're using your skills to the utmost."[15]

Jordan: Like when you're on a date with someone and everything just clicks together and is effortless . . . and you are so totally in the moment that you look up and you can't believe that it's already evening. . . .

---

[15] Geirland.

Mikhail: Seeing someone new, Jordan?

Jordan: Ummmm. No, I was just speaking hypothetically.

Mikhail: Right . . . so, hypothetically, you know what he means. And get this, Csikszentmihalyi says that the possibility of experiencing flow is maximized when we confront difficult challenges that engage our highest level of skills. Admit it; it sounds just like this House guy. Based on my recollection, I'd say he experiences flow practically every day.

Elaine: I suppose it's possible.

Mikhail: Of course it is, and to experience flow, at least for that period of time, *is* to be happy. For House, this means a lot of happiness indeed. So, we got self-esteem, control, optimism, and flow. As Meatloaf would say, "four out of six ain't bad." Convinced?

Elaine: Look, I hate to burst your bubble, but your argument only holds up for his professional life. As long as you completely ignore his personal relationships, or how he feels when he's not working, you might be right about him being Mr. Happy. But if you consider him when he's not at work, he is as miserable as everyone says he is!

Mikhail: Come on, no one is happy all the time. Happy people can't feel sad or frustrated or angry?

Elaine: Yes, they can, but these are usually linked to life circumstances and daily stressors. And, as you know, happy people usually cope with such stressors by confiding in friends or family members, not seeking escape by calling a prostitute, betting on horses, or resorting to juvenile pranks, such as sticking a sleeping friend's finger in a bowl of water. He doesn't even have friends, besides Wilson.

Mikhail: Nothing wrong with having one good friend. That's more than many men have.

Elaine: Fine, but he has no romantic partner and has either lost or pushed away the only woman he's ever been in love with.

Mikhail: That could count as a "life circumstance or daily stressor."

Elaine: Stop interrupting. He also has no meaningful outside activities or hobbies.

Mikhail: What—gambling and whoring aren't worthy activities?

Elaine: Very funny, but House himself describes them as temporary distractions from being with himself—just like the pranks he plays on Wilson, and the bets he makes with his colleagues on things like patient paternity status. His life outside his work is empty, and these are all just pathetic attempts to fill rather than fulfill himself.

Mikhail: Gorky[16] said: "When work is a pleasure, life is a joy."

Elaine: Yeah, well, Gorky never met this guy, or he would have said, "When work is a pleasure, use it as an escape from your miserable life!" Come on, look at the evidence. You know how almost none of the MDD symptoms applied to House? That was only because work was part of the equation. Remove work-related activities, and House has both depressed mood and anhedonia. Add in the lack of interpersonal relationships and his lack of optimism about anything outside of work, and he meets DSM criteria for either MDD or dysthymia.

---

[16] Maksim Gorky was a Russian author and playwright.

Mikhail: First of all, the DSM doesn't work that way. We can't just pretend his high-functioning areas don't exist and make a diagnosis based only on the low-functioning ones. Secondly, we don't know as much about his home and personal life as you seem to think. The chart, the interviews with his colleagues, the summary of his cases—all focus mostly on his work. Maybe he has interests we don't know about. Maybe he has more friends. Besides, House isn't completely bereft of activities that he enjoys. I think his bike brings him significant pleasure, and I think he enjoys playing the piano, even if it's a melancholy type of playing. He also likes playing video games and watching TV—and although you may not approve of television as a "fulfilling" pastime, there is a lot of good stuff out there.

Elaine: Like *House M.D.*?

Mikhail: Exactly! Anyway, my point is that we really don't know how he spends most of his time outside of his work or how much he enjoys his own company—maybe quite a bit.

Elaine: Maybe not at all. Did you see what he pulled in order to keep Wilson from moving out?

Mikhail: That just shows he liked having Wilson live with him, not that he doesn't also like being by himself. If anything, it supports my theory that House enjoys a lot of different things. Even the pursuit of Stacy, which Wilson interpreted as House being emotionally devastated, may have been for House a somewhat enjoyable activity—another challenge to overcome, another puzzle to solve. Not to say that he did not feel emotional and physical pain when he turned her away—but his rejection of Stacy could simply mean that it was the hunt rather than the catch that was so appealing.

Elaine: Okay. But you can't argue that he has healthy personal relationships outside of work.

Mikhail: Why do they have to be outside of work? House's work involves constant interactions with people. He and Wilson share meals together, talk about their love lives, joke, consult on real and imagined cases for each other, and even have interchanges about their friendship (like what it means for House to borrow money or for Wilson to lie on House's behalf). Although House spends a lot of time reading and thinking, he spends even more time in dialogue with his team. These people know each other well. They're comfortable with each other. They even seem to grudgingly enjoy each other's company. Maybe they are not intimate in the classic sense of the word, but their interactions include teasing, disagreements, rivalry, and personal disclosures about pretty personal stuff: parental and spousal deaths, difficult family relations, spousal infidelity, serious illness.

Jordan: But Dr. House shows no support or empathy for these people when they go through hard times!

Mikhail: Yes and no. He wouldn't score very high on an interpersonal warmth scale, and he doesn't exude caring, like Cameron. But he is very observant of the people who are close to him, picking up on signs of distress that most good friends would not: the absence of a favorite piece of jewelry, the presence of a colorful new tie or ironed shirt, a teary eye after a routine patient interview. One can argue that attention to detail and curiosity about people's inner life is an expression of caring. I mean, would you really argue that he does not care about Foreman or Cameron—does not care about them as people, about what happens to them? Do you think *they* would honestly say he does not care about them? I'm not saying he'd win any friendship

166

contests or that his interpersonal relationships are the paradigm of emotional health. I'm just not convinced he's as miserable and lonely in his personal life as you make him out to be.

Elaine: Look, this is all fine and good, but "happiness" is not a clinical diagnosis. And if everything is so great in his life, then why did he fire Chase and get abandoned by Cameron and Foreman? If you ask me, he's in crisis.

Mikhail: You make a fine point. House is hard to diagnose because he is a clinical enigma, but in some ways, the fault is with the DSM itself, because it insists on discreet diagnostic categories when most people might be better described using dynamic, multidimensional traits. That said, I still maintain that, beyond some possible narcissistic features, there is nothing wrong with House. It's everyone else around him who has the problem.

Elaine: Well, that's great. But we still need a diagnosis, and it would be nice to include some treatment recommendations too. I mean, what are we going to suggest, anti-happy pills?

Mikhail: Ok, so what would *you* recommend?

Elaine: Well, the basic treatment for practically all adult psychological problems—regardless of whether they actually meet diagnostic criteria—is talk therapy or psychotherapy. As you know, outcomes for people who engage in therapy are quite good overall. Eighty percent report improvement.

Mikhail: That may be true, but you know how that silly light bulb joke[17] goes.

---

[17] How many psychologists does it take to change a light bulb? One—but only if the light bulb wants to change.

Elaine: Yes, yes. Psychotherapy works, but only if the client is committed to change or growth. But it's not that cut and dry. There is precedent for successful therapy with clients who are mandated to undergo treatment, by a judge, for instance.

Mikhail: I like the way you're thinking. Tell BenBella that our recommendation is mandated therapy for everyone.

Elaine: What are you talking about? What everyone?

Mikhail: Psychotherapy. Group therapy for all the people who have a problem with House. Isn't that what you were recommending?

Elaine: What??

Mikhail: Well, I thought we agreed that, despite his irritability and grouchiness, he is basically a happy guy with high self-esteem, a sense of control over his life, optimism, flow, and . . .

Elaine: . . . and Narcissistic Personality Disorder. What's your point?

Mikhail: My point is that House isn't really unhappy. And even if he's narcissistic, which I'm not convinced that he is, NPD, like many personality disorders, isn't really treatable. This means that the current crisis can't be resolved by treating House, which, in turn, means we need to treat those who experience distress when interacting with him and help them better cope with their feelings and reactions. Given the number of people involved, given that they all have the same basic concern—although from slightly different angles—and given that there is already a psychologist at the hospital who works in the group therapy modality, the most cost-efficient and effective recommendation would be for all of them—and any members of his future team—to undergo group therapy together.

Elaine: You want me to tell BenBella *that* . . . that we think that House is relatively happy, that he may or may not have NPD, which isn't treatable in any case, and that the rest of the hospital staff should seek treatment in order to be able to coexist with him?

Mikhail: Yep, that about sums it up.

Elaine: And you think they'll buy it?

Mikhail: I have no idea. My diagnosis and treatment recommendations are right, but people aren't always ready to hear what's right. You can lead editors to a manuscript, but you can't make them publish it. [gathers things] As House might say, do whatever you think is right. I'll see you later. [walks out]

MIKHAIL LYUBANSKY, PH.D., is a lecturer in the Department of Psychology at the University of Illinois at Urbana-Champaign, where he teaches Psychology of Race and Ethnicity and Theories of Psychotherapy, does research on immigration and race relations, and writes an occasional essay for BenBella. Like House, he thinks he's right about everything. Unlike House, he often discovers that he isn't. Fortunately, his optimism and high sense of personal control remain entirely unaffected.

ELAINE SHPUNGIN, PH.D., is the director of the Psychological Services Center, an outpatient community and mental health clinic and the training site for doctoral students in the clinical/community program in the Department of Psychology at the University of Illinois at Urbana-Champaign. She shares House's knack for reading people quickly, but usually manages to speak her mind with slightly more tact and diplomacy.

REFERENCES

American Psychiatric Association. *Diagnostic and Statistical Manual of Mental Disorders Fourth Edition, Text Revision.* Washington, D.C.: American Psychiatric Association, 1994.

Geirland, John. "Go with the flow." *Wired.* September 1996. <http://www.wired.com/wired/archive/4.09/czik.html>

Myers, David G. "Who Is Happy—and Why?" In *Exploring Social Psychology.* New York: McGraw-Hill, Inc., 1994.

For all that it's evident in almost every scene (in his persistent limp if nothing else), House's pain is perhaps the most unexamined aspect of the show—at least outside of each hour-long episode. What does it mean to be in constant pain? How does pain really affect cognition, mood, social interaction? James Gilmer knows firsthand—and gives us a real-world context in which we might better understand House and the ways he chooses to cope.

DOES GOD LIMP?

JAMES GILMER

t he Western world, especially America, has an interesting relationship with pain. Perhaps it's that old Judeo-Christian idea of suffering being good for the soul, with a dash of Puritan work ethic thrown in for good measure: the suffering of Adam and Eve, thanks to their fall from grace and all that. It also has an interesting relationship with the medical community: doctors are portrayed as stern authoritarian figures who know all and dispense god-like wisdom and healing from behind a stone-faced visage as they watch brave patients clutch the bed sheets in repressed agony, suffering through whatever malady may affect them.

Which brings us to Dr. Gregory House—the pill-popping genius who solves medical mysteries while crunching down Vicodin, an honest breath of fresh air in the often stale genre of medical dramas. House manages his pain with the help of Vicodin, a name-brand combination of hydrocodone and acetaminophen. The hydrocodone part is the thing that gets people uptight; it's a semi-synthetic opioid derived from codeine and thebaine.

So in our society, where relief is just a medicine cabinet away (as the commercials tell us), why is this drug such a boogeyman? Why is it a big deal that House, who obviously functions well on the drug, takes it to function and do his job? Why does his best friend constantly try to talk him into trying different avenues of treatment? Why does that friend, an oncologist who deals with pain all the time in his practice treating cancer patients, constantly fight with House over his use of Vicodin? With House's intelligence and knowledge, is he another doctor with a god complex, a crippled god à la the polytheistic pantheons who suffered human maladies but still soared above the masses, or just a very smart doctor who suffers from a horrible affliction?

> HOUSE: I said I was an addict. I didn't say I had a problem ("Detox," 1-11).

It probably doesn't help that House's bedside manner is less than cheerful, but that's not a result of the Vicodin, as his ex-girlfriend Stacy has pointed out. So why is everyone so upset that House takes the pill? What's the big deal about this little narcotic?

There's that magic word, narcotic. It conjures up images instantly, doesn't it? It's not a positive word—images of crack houses and stoners spring to mind. And yet narcotics are used every day in hospitals in the United States by people who suffer chronic and acute pain.

The term "narcotic" originally referred to drugs derived from the opium plant, but in U.S. legal context it also includes anything classified under the Controlled Substances Act, even if the drug is not chemically an opioid derivative.

Vicodin, which is just one brand name for hydrocodone, and the other brand and generic names that it is sold under are probably the most well-known and widely prescribed narcotic analgesics available. A person without chronic pain problems, having taken the drug, would probably enjoy what is conventionally known as a nice "buzz," as it counts euphoria among its side effects as well as the reduction of tension, anxiety, and aggression.

Doesn't sound like House? You don't think he walks around in a constant state of euphoria? Well, there's the rub—the thing with chronic pain sufferers like Dr. House is that they don't get to enjoy that lovely buzz. If he were to overdo it—take well over the level needed for pain control—he might, but during conventional treatment we see that he still limps and grimaces his way through the day. Not the sign of someone enjoying a euphoric buzz.

Yes, House has been shown on occasion to over-treat his pain and get a bit loopy, but he's also shown to stay away from that sort of behavior when he's on cases (as shown when he was about to inject a secret stash of morphine, but received a phone call from the hospital in time to put it aside and hobble in to do his job).

> HOUSE: What would you prefer—a doctor who holds your hand while you die or one who ignores you while you get better? I suppose it would particularly suck to have a doctor who ignores you while you die ("Occam's Razor," 1-3).

As so often comes up on the show, opioids don't get rid of pain, they just mask it. Well, yes, but until they can give House a new leg, one would think that masking the pain is a rather good idea.

Chronic pain isn't a constant. It doesn't stay at one level, and what works for one person isn't going to work for everyone. Maybe not everyone should be on opioid painkillers, but maybe not every kid on Ritalin should be on that either.

There's a reason that it's known as practicing medicine—there is no instant fix or magic bullet that can take the pain away or instantly erase it.

> HOUSE: I take risks; sometimes patients die. But not taking risks causes more patients to die, so I guess my biggest problem is I've been cursed with the ability to do the math ("Detox," 1-11).

Give a dying man marijuana to ease his stomach discomfort? Ah, Wilson has no problem rolling up joints for his patients. There is a grudging and growing acceptance of using narcotics in treating end-of-life or cancer pain and other symptoms like glaucoma and such, but it's treated with marijuana, which still doesn't quite have the stigma of Vicodin, or morphine, or Oxycontin (a.k.a., "Hillbilly Heroin").

Teenagers are selling their Ritalin to classmates for the buzz it provides, and while there's some concern, doctors aren't diving between teens and their Ritalin supply. There's a lot less evidence for how Ritalin works than for Vicodin, and it is a known fact that Ritalin can cause withdrawal symptoms if the patient isn't tapered off.

Most drugs result in withdrawal symptoms if they aren't tapered off. It's just a result of your body being used to having the drug in your system, and then having to adjust to it not being there anymore. Granted, those symptoms sometimes aren't as serious as they are with opioid withdrawal, but its only a matter of degree, not type. The health care industry and the general public are only now finally beginning to accept that there isn't a drug or procedure around that doesn't involve risk.

Any single episode of *House M.D.* will show you the many and varied side effects that the wrong drug can cause a patient, depending on their condition. One thing the show does very well is to show that the wrong drug at the wrong time can be fatal, and the team is constantly fighting side effects from drugs that are the right drugs to treat certain conditions.

Look at the reactions to pain on the show, or even better, look at the reactions of those around House to their own pain. In the season two episodes "Euphoria, Part 1" and "Euphoria, Part 2" (2-20 and 2-21), Foreman accidentally came in contact with a deadly condition that threatened to kill him . . . very painfully. The only way to save him was to discover what infected him while he was forced into quarantine with the other patient dying from the mystery illness.

Foreman is probably most like the doctors we're used to seeing on television. When he presents himself to his patients he is calm, rational, perhaps allowing a slight smile, but it's the smile of the beneficial medical god come down the mountain to heal the afflicted.

Foreman, the most rational of all of House's acolytes, was so afraid of not just death, but a painful death, that he violated oath after oath in the two-part episode. He stuck a college with an infected needle, likely damning her to his own fate. He followed House's orders over Cuddy's and attempted a biopsy on the other quarantine patient's brain after he had died. And that was after he nearly killed the other patient himself with a morphine overdose in an attempt to spare him his agony.

HOUSE: There's no such thing! Our bodies break down, sometimes when we're ninety, sometimes before we're even born, but it always happens and there's never any dignity in it. I don't care if you can walk, see, wipe your own ass. It's always ugly—always! We can live with dignity—we can't die with it ("Pilot" 1-1).

How many people have repeated the old maxim that they'd want to go in their sleep? That when they die they hope it's quick and painless? The idea of easing a person's pain when they're dying comes easier to our society than relieving a person's pain while they're living.

Pain and death are two things that often go together. In the season three episode "One Day, One Room" (3-12), Cameron treated a homeless man who wanted to die in agony, believing that his suffering would mean that his life had meant something. Pain, for many people, is supposed to be meaningful. Wilson often tells House that his pain could be a good sign, it could be nerves regenerating—but to House, no matter what the reason, it's still pain.

There is no such thing as dying with dignity, as House so eloquently put it in the pilot episode.

This isn't to make light of death or end-of-life pain, or to say that one type of pain is more important than the other, but rather it's to say that they are both the same. A person in pain is a person in pain, and yet we see characters on *House M.D.* go on about the need for people to die with dignity while paying little attention to whether House has a right to live with it.

At some point every doctor on the show has stepped forward to issue god-like proclamations on the rights of patients to die, or to discuss whether a certain patient is ready to die or not. If you're on the way out you get a ticket to morphine-land, but if you should happen to have to live with pain, you're supposed to suck it up.

Physical therapy, acupuncture, chiropractic therapy, acupressure, massage, psychological therapy, hooking electrodes to the back and running a current through the muscles to block pain impulses, even up to going under live x-ray and having steroids injected directly into the spine . . . these are the lengths people will go to, and doctors will subject their patients to, rather than give them a little white pill.

No pain, no gain. Walk it off. It's in your head. Pain ain't nothing but fear leaving the body. Give blood, play hockey.

> HOUSE: You can have all the faith you want in spirits, and the afterlife, and heaven and hell, but when it comes to this world, don't be an idiot. 'Cause you can tell me you put your faith in God to put you through the day, but when it comes time to cross the road, I know you look both ways ("Damned If You Do," 1-5).

A Buddhist would tell us "Life is suffering." Jewish and Christian worship turns to Psalm 23, the well-known Shepherd's Psalm, which tells us only God can lift our suffering. Islam treats the mortal coil as a vale of tears that we have to walk through as well. Suffering as redemptive comes up again and again in *House M.D.* and is also pretty evident in the real world.

The very word itself, "pain," comes from the Latin word *poena*, meaning pain, punishment, or penalty. Poena was the goddess of punishment in Roman mythology, so the idea of pain as a punishment or penalty from the gods, God, or the universe itself has shown up in almost every culture and is deeply ingrained in our society. House, not surprisingly, rejects that notion of pain as redemptive; he sees it in cold, scientific terms, where pain is simply a biological process indicating pathology.

Humans look for reason in everything, and so we assume that pain must have a reason. It's not surprising that among the religious pain is often seen as a penalty for a fallen world or a test to get back into the big boss's good graces. If religion is the opiate of the masses, it's clear that House prefers his opiates in pill form.

The funny thing about that is that there is a strong argument that House is who he is because of the pain. It's the remit of the show: the one constant in House's life is that he is always in pain and will be for the rest of his life. When the ketamine treatment administered between seasons two and three worked and he was briefly pain-free everyone was astounded by the change. Notably, Cameron, who once tried to force herself on him as someone to love, was no longer interested in the new, pain-free House.

> CUDDY: You know, there are other ways to manage pain.
> HOUSE: Like what, laughter? Meditation? Got a guy who
>   can fix my third chakra? ("Detox" 1-11).

When Tritter, the police officer who spent much of the first part of season three trying to bust House on drug charges, questioned Cameron, Foreman, and Chase about House's drug use, they all said that no person can know another's pain. But people as a whole—Cameron, Foreman, and Chase included—tend to be cynical about pain and the amount of pain a person is in. How many times does House's team comment that he is overdoing the Vicodin or that he may not be in as much pain as he claims to be in?

How many times have characters on the show seen House's limp or cane and asked the question "Does that hurt?" only to receive one of House's cutting remarks in reply? Even Wilson, his best friend and the one person on the show he confides in, seems unable to fully grasp the extent of House's pain; he continues to doubt whether or not House really needs the narcotics.

Also, chronic pain isn't the same as acute pain, and when a person in chronic pain has acute pain—what is sometimes known as breakthrough pain (because it breaks through the treatment and becomes severe pain to the sufferer)—the person may or may not be better equipped to handle it than someone who doesn't suffer the chronic variety.

House could inject enough morphine to kill his pain completely. He could obtain a pain pump that would put morphine directly into his bloodstream or spine. At those levels it would be doubtful that he'd be able to function, though. The goal of any pain program is to find the balance point between too much and not enough analgesic effect. In other words, it wouldn't do to have House passed out on the floor, the way Wilson finds him in "Merry Little Christmas" (3-10) when House, having been denied Vicodin, binges once he obtains a stash.

> HOUSE: But not to worry, because for most of you, this job could be done by a monkey with a bottle of Motrin. Speaking of which, if you're particularly annoying, you may see me reach for this. This is Vicodin. It's mine. You can't have any. And no, I do not have a pain management problem, I have a pain problem. But who knows? Maybe I'm wrong. Maybe I'm too stoned to tell ("Occam's Razor," 1-3).

Usually, House just seems happier when he's taking his Vicodin. Gosh, you have to wonder if that's because the intractable pain in his leg is muted. Is it an accident that when he's denied his Vicodin he's unable to think clearly? And while some of that is the physical effect of detoxification, there's certainly an aspect of pain involved. Even Cuddy, his superior, handed him a script for Vicodin at one point in season three with the rejoinder that he simply worked better on it than off it.

Pain becomes the center of House's universe. It traps him. It becomes the only thing in his thoughts. Forget about Vicodin maybe causing a little mental blurriness, try thinking while pain is shooting through all your limbs. Try thinking as hammers go to work on your spinal cord and hot knives stab into your leg. Try not sleeping for days on end as searing pain wakes you every half hour.

Wilson's attitude toward his friend's pain is stunning. He is more than willing to break the law and roll joints to relieve pain for his patients, but constantly insists that House's pain is psychogenic and that he has no need for Vicodin. While it may be true that House could live without the drugs, there is still the undoubtable fact that his pain is real, and it seems strange that Wilson, who does everything in his power to ease the suffering of strangers, would want to deny House the ability to alleviate his pain. Instead, he wants House to accept his pain and let it make him a better person. Does that sound familiar? Pain as transformation? Pain as redemption?

We saw how well that worked during season three when House, having temporarily regained use of his leg, started to suffer from muscle cramps that might herald the pain coming back. Denied Vicodin, his pain increased—and as it did, he seemed less and less able to focus on the case until finally, during an endorphin rush brought on by jogging, he took a guess at a treatment that he had no tangible proof on but that his every instinct told him he was right. It doesn't seem like a coincidence that the right answer came to him while he was experiencing a "runner's high," after he'd pushed himself to such a point that his natural endorphins and bodily pain-control mechanisms had kicked in and given him a rush.

> **HOUSE: Deep inside, Wilson believes if he cares enough, he'll never have to die ("Son of Coma Guy," 3-7).**

Once again Wilson stepped in to teach House a lesson: after House's treatment, initially refused by his superior Cuddy before she gave in and administered it to the patient, worked and the patient was healed, Wilson swore Cuddy to secrecy about the case, arguing that House needed to learn that he was not God and could be wrong sometimes.

In this same episode it became clear that House's pain was returning, and when he asked for Vicodin to ease it, Wilson scoffed at the idea and refused. This led to House breaking into Wilson's office and forging a prescription at the end of the episode.

In the episode that followed, House and Wilson confronted each other and Wilson, ever the helpful friend, explained that he was just worried about House: "So what was the plan? I'd feel so humbled by missing a case that I'd re-evaluate my entire life, question the nature of truth and goodness, and become Cameron?" Wilson could only reply that he was trying to help and made an allusion to Icarus and House's wings melting—to which House pointed out that God doesn't limp.

> **HOUSE: I'm sure this goes against everything you've been taught, but right and wrong do exist. Just because you don't know what the right answer is, maybe there's even no way you could know what the right answer is, doesn't make your answer right or even okay. It's much simpler than that. It's just plain wrong ("Three Stories," 1-21).**

House has no illusions about his place in the universe. He doesn't think he's God. He knows that sometimes you get it right and sometimes you get it wrong and the best you can do is play the hand you're dealt.

He struggles with his pain and wins most of the time. Sometimes he lies and sometimes he does the wrong thing. Sometimes he takes too many pills. Sometimes he's just human, and he'd probably be the first to admit it, although he undoubtedly thinks he's a smarter human than most.

> WILSON: You know how some doctors have the Messiah complex; they need to save the world? You've got the Rubik's complex; you need to solve the puzzle ("DNR," 1-9).

House seeks distraction from the pain, and finds it in his medical mysteries. He's not ready to lie down and die, or lie in a bed on a pain pump for the rest of his life, but he's also not about to go through life in physical agony, even if his bedside manner pushes those around him away and causes him emotional injury.

Fans of the show, and even House's colleagues and friends, look at his distraction-seeking as an aspect of his personality, completely missing the idea that he may be trying to distract himself from focusing on his pain. The things he does are common enough coping mechanisms: focusing on little games of skill that he devises with his cane, engrossing himself in handheld videogames, anything to stop him from fully being conscious of the pain that he endures.

In the end there are no simple answers. Every person's pain is different. Everyone goes through life alone with their pain, no matter if they have a support system of friends and family or not. Pain becomes a constant in their lives.

Pain is the axis on which House's life, and the show, turns. Pain is always there as a hidden character, and often serves as the motivator for the show's plots. All of House's genius and his quick wit can not help him escape the constant agony of his leg.

A little white pill can give House a bit of dignity, and yet it's pitted against centuries of viewing pain as punishment from on high. The show is unique in that it treats pain as a humanizing factor. We don't connect with House through his warmth, through his humanity, through his innocence, but instead through his pain. Far from the cold god-like doctors of television dramas gone by or the hapless interns of *ER* or *Scrubs*, *House M.D.* gives us a view into the humanity of a doctor through his pain—the one thing that brings House down to the level of the rest of the mere mortals.

JAMES GILMER is a radiographer (which is a fancy way of saying he takes x-rays) at Sparrow Regional Medical Center, a Level 1 Trauma hospital in Michigan, and is also a part-time writer. He is a graduate of Michigan State University and also the Clarion 2000 Science Fiction and Fantasy Writers Workshop. His short fiction has appeared in Webzines such as *Ideomancer* and book anthologies such as *Mota 3: Courage*. He has also been a newspaper stringer and contributed to magazines such as *Variants* from Variance Press.

He currently lives with his wife, Elise, and is awaiting the day when he can retire thanks to her new nursing degree and spend his days writing in a hammock.

Until that day, he is still pursuing both his fiction and non-fiction writing when he's not distracted by watching *House M.D.*

WILSON, CUDDY, AND THE COTTAGES
Other Characters of Interest

I can't help but feel bad for Wilson sometimes. Okay, most of the time. Maybe it's his own fault for sticking around, but does he really deserve all the abuse House sends his way? What's keeping Wilson from just washing his hands of House altogether? Joyce Millman has a compelling theory.

THE SIDEKICK

JOYCE MILLMAN

(NEW YORK) Researchers at the Ethel Mertz Institute of Behavioral Science have undertaken the first study of the chronic and socially debilitating condition known as "Sidekick Syndrome." For years, the syndrome was thought to affect only high-risk individuals, such as supporting characters on TV sitcoms. But researchers now believe that the psychological condition has been under-diagnosed in the general population.

Those suffering from Sidekick Syndrome exhibit an extreme interest in the life of a more charismatic friend ("MCF"), unusual susceptibility to that friend's influence, and a higher than average tolerance for humiliation and abuse. According to researchers, many historical figures and celebrities who were long regarded as boring or useless are now believed to have been victims of Sidekick Syndrome. The list of famous sufferers includes Ed McMahon, many vice presidents, and William Shakespeare's oft-forgotten friend "What's-in-a-Name?" who, historians say, never complained about being stuck with the pub tab whenever the playwright claimed he left his purse in his other pantaloons.

Dr. Gilda Morgenstern, lead researcher of the Mertz Institute study, revealed that her own mother, Rhoda, suffered for years with Sidekick Syndrome.

"Rhoda lived in the shadow of a slimmer, perkier friend who was able to turn the world on with her smile and take a nothing day and suddenly make it all seem worthwhile," said Dr. Morgenstern. "The stress took its toll. Rhoda sought refuge in food addiction, yo-yo dieting, and a disastrous marriage to a guy who was better looking than herself. Her low self-esteem finally resulted in a total loss of identity, as symbolized by her refusal to wear anything but the anonymous 'Scarsdale Burqa' — a colorful but shapeless caftan and tightly wrapped headscarf. My mother's heartbreaking struggle made me determined to unravel the mystery of Sidekick Syndrome."

Okay, so there is no such medical condition as Sidekick Syndrome. But there should be. Sidekicks are people too, although you wouldn't know it from the way they're often portrayed on TV. I'm not talking about equal, dynamic-duo partnerships like Cagney and Lacey, Laverne and Shirley, and the Odd Couple. I'm talking about shows where a secondary character is entrusted with the job of reflecting the spotlight back onto the star—in the solar system of celebrity, the sidekick is the moon.

Sidekicks exist mainly to make the hero look good. Or, in the case of the TV series *House*, bad. If there were such a thing as Sidekick Syndrome, *House's* Dr. James Wilson could be its poster boy. In many ways, Sidekick Syndrome is as much about the egotistical and controlling behavior of the More Charismatic Friend as it is about the sidekick, and Wilson couldn't ask for a more textbook-perfect MCF than Dr. Gregory House. A brilliant diagnostician, House is regarded as a legend, not only for his unusually high cure rate, but for his unorthodox methods and abrasive, at times offensive, personality. House and Wilson have been friends since medical school, where the cautious, sensitive Wilson found himself caught up in the orbit of his dashing, risk-taking friend. In recent years, House suffered an infarction which left him without full use of his right leg; he is dependant on a cane, in constant pain, and addicted to Vicodin. The combination of his disability, drug use, and considerable ego has made House angry, arrogant, self-centered, rude, eccentric, and manipulative. And yet, Wilson considers House his best friend. He repeatedly puts his own career in jeopardy in order to clean up House's messes. For this, Wilson is rewarded with abuse and ingratitude. Why would someone as intelligent, kind, and successful (he's an oncologist of some renown) as Wilson fall under the spell of a person as damaged as House? My diagnosis: Sidekick Syndrome. Wilson has all the classic symptoms.

Desire to please. The typical sidekick suffers from low self-esteem. From Barney Fife on *The Andy Griffith Show* to Xander on *Buffy the Vampire Slayer* to Ando on *Heroes*, sidekicks have been depicted as bland nerds with an urge to walk on the wild side—an urge that's fulfilled by hanging out with an MCF. Wilson, with his Tupperware-sealed lunches, old-man neckties, and *Ugly Betty* eyebrows, is no exception. He gloms onto the motorcyle-ridin', impeccably stubbled House, and House looks all the more wolfishly sexy in comparison.

The sidekick has a strong desire to please his MCF, but since the sidekick's role is often under-written, we don't know why they try so hard. Why does Barney Rubble submit to Fred Flintstone's every whim? Why does Gareth/Dwight on the British/American versions of *The Office* keep licking David/Michael's boots? Faced with House's snide insults and glib brush-offs, how can Wilson still look at him and say, "I've only got two things that work for me: this job and this stupid screwed-up friendship" ("Babies and Bathwater," 1-18)? Is it the need to stay in the reflected glow of a brighter, cooler MCF that keeps Wilson hanging on? Is it the fear of rejection? Or is it something more primal? Before *House*, actor Robert Sean Leonard, who portrays Wilson, was best known for his role in the movie *Dead Poets Society*, in which he played Neil Perry, a sensitive prep school lad pushed around by his stern, domineering father. Yeah, I know we're talking about two fictional characters here, but the earnest, sweetly gap-toothed Neil could almost be a teenaged version of Wilson. As you watch Neil trying in vain to please his cold, bossy dad, it makes you wonder what Wilson's father is like. Is he as distant and impossible to please as House? A one-sided father-son relationship could explain why Wilson is so driven to prove his worthiness by fixing all things unfixable, House included.

"Half the doctors who specialize in oncology turn into burn-out cases, but you—you eat neediness," House snarled at Wilson ("House vs. God," 2-19), and it's true. Wilson so needs to be needed that his bed-side manner has in the past extended to sleeping with one of his cancer patients.

An obsessive interest in an MCF's love life. Just as man-hungry Rhoda Morgenstern devours accounts of her friend Mary Richards's (modest) dating adventures, Wilson seems fixated on House's relationships. He's interrogated House with probing questions about his relationship with his ex-girlfriend Stacy, as well as about his feelings for Dr. Allison Cameron, the attractive young resident who has a crush on House. In the episode "Love Hurts" (1-20), Wilson hovered around House's apartment on the night of House's date with Cameron, advising him on what to wear ("The wide tie's too short, you're gonna look like Lou Costello"). Wilson also gave House tips on dating etiquette, telling him to "open doors, help her with her chair, comment on her shoes . . . then move on to D.H.A.—her dreams, hopes, and aspirations. Trust me. Panty-peeler." (Ah, so that's how Wilson has managed to peel the panties off of three wives and numerous sexual conquests, extramarital and otherwise. He may be a dork, but he knows how to be a good listener.)

Wilson engages in pre-emptive behavior toward women whom he perceives as a threat to House's happiness. Before her date with House, Wilson warned Cameron that it had been "a long time" since House "opened up to someone" and she had "better be absolutely sure, because if he opens up again and gets hurt, I don't think there's going to be a next time" ("Love Hurts," 1-20). He also confronted Stacy when she resumed her relationship with House, telling her, "The last time you left, I was the one stuck picking up the pieces!"—although, frankly, Wilson appeared to be more than a little proud of his role as House's chief piece-picker-upper ("Need to Know," 2-11).

While Wilson is so busily focused on his MCF's romantic exploits, his own relationships with women suffer. And House enjoys making Wilson squirm about it; he relentlessly teases him about his boyish romanticism and the affairs it has led him into. "I love my wife!" protested Wilson in "Fidelity" (1-7), to which House replied, "You loved all your wives. Probably still do. In fact, you probably still love all the women you ever loved who *weren't* your wives." The reason why Wilson can't sustain a long-term, monogamous commitment to a woman is obvious, and it has nothing to do with a wandering eye or a restless search for some romantic ideal: it's because he has a man-crush on House. I'm not saying that Wilson is gay (but that might make a neat, and not entirely implausible plot twist in the future—Wilson seems to know an awful lot about the Village People for a straight guy). No, it's more like the episode of *Seinfeld* where Jerry fell under the spell of his new best friend, baseball player Keith Hernandez. The emotional thrill-ride of Wilson's tempestuous friendship with House—the verbal sparring, the tension of following House from one risky adventure to the next, the excitement of watching that singular brain solve impossible cases—offers a high far superior to any he has experienced with wives and girlfriends. As he told House, "My marriages were so crappy, I was spending all my time with you!" ("Fools for Love," 3-5).

Protectiveness and loyalty. Wilson has a lot in common with the greatest sidekick of all time, Sherlock Holmes's assistant, Dr. John Watson. Is it a coincidence that the names "Wilson" and "Watson" are separated by a mere two letters? Wilson and Watson both toil at the side of genius. The quite ordinary Watson provides the all-too-human counterpoint to Holmes's deductive infallibility. And Wilson, with his sound but unimaginative professional thinking, represents the collective medical wisdom that always comes up short against House's flashy, maverick solutions to medical mysteries. Watson and Wilson are the loyal protectors of the flawed geniuses they serve. Without Wilson at his side, doggedly pricking his conscience and holding up both ends of their friendship, House might be even more cold and misanthropic than he already is (a frightening thought). Watson also displays staunch fidelity toward his aloof, overly cerebral (and, lest we forget, substance-abusing) friend. And while Watson may be no Sherlock when it comes to crime-solving, he holds a power of his own—it is Watson, after all, who is telling the stories. He is the gatekeeper of our knowledge of Holmes, and our perceptions of the great detective depend mainly on Watson's admiring narrative.

Wilson is not the narrator of *House*, but he expends a large portion of his dialogue psychoanalyzing House—in effect, he defines House, subtly possessing him as he influences our understanding of him.

"Several researchers have proven that psychological pain can manifest as physical pain," Wilson told House when the latter's bad leg acted up more than usual when ex-girlfriend Stacy returned ("Skin Deep," 2-13). Wilson often functions as the conduit through which the show's writers tell us what we need to know about House's personality and motives. Here, Wilson was telling us that we should regard House's crippled physical state (while very real) as a metaphor for his crippled emotional state.

When Wilson told House, "You don't like yourself. But you do admire yourself. It's all you've got, so you cling to it. . . . Being miserable doesn't make you better than anybody else . . . it just makes you miserable" ("Need to Know," 2-11), he wasn't just showing his MCF some tough love, he was showing us that he is not fooled or intimidated by House's suffering-genius routine, and that we shouldn't be either. Wilson's words bring House down to our level, make him easier to relate to.

As for the observation, "Religious belief annoys you, because if the universe operates by abstract rules you can learn them, you can protect yourself. If a supreme being exists, he can squash you anytime he wants," it pretty much nailed the psychology behind House's bravado ("House vs. God," 2-19). Wilson knows that House's biggest fear is loss of control, of being a victim of randomness—as he was when his artery blew and left him lame.

And Wilson perfectly summed up House (and the premise of the series) when he said, "You know how some doctors have the Messiah complex; they need to save the world? You've got the Rubik's complex;

you need to solve the puzzle" ("DNR," 1-9). Four lines, practically a *TV Guide*-listing haiku, for viewers with short attention spans.

Wilson is a highly empathetic physician; House is an extremely troubled individual. Together, they form a perfect storm of Sidekick Syndrome. As House becomes more brazen and self-destructive, Wilson becomes more intense and outlandish in his efforts to diagnose, define, and heal him. In the episode "Lines in the Sand" (3-4), Wilson suddenly became convinced that House was autistic, citing as proof his unfriendliness, refusal to accept societal rules, and resistance to change. Fortunately, Chief of Staff Dr. Lisa Cuddy brought Wilson back down to earth with a more credible differential diagnosis of House's behavioral problems: "He's a jerk."

Masochistic tolerance for abuse and humiliation. To the sidekick, any attention from the MCF is positive attention. As illustrated by the persistent, self-defeating clinginess exhibited by Smithers toward Mr. Burns (*The Simpsons*), Hank Kingsley toward Larry (*The Larry Sanders Show*), and E. B. Farnum toward Al Swearengen (*Deadwood*), many sidekicks lack the ability to sense when they have become annoying, even when their MCFs give them unmistakably hostile verbal cues. "At what point does a person endlessly lecturing someone make him a jerk?" snapped House when Wilson made yet another attempt to psychoanalyze him ("Lines in the Sand," 3-4). The problem is, sidekicks often thrive on just this sort of hostility. Wilson continues to shower his curmudgeonly pal with overbearing concern, even when House ratchets up his retaliation from withering put-downs to the occasional sharp blow to the kneecap with a walking stick. And so the cycle perpetuates itself.

Wilson exhibits unusual patience when faced with House's anger and rejection. He doesn't throw a punch, or vow never to speak to him again. Instead, he attempts to take the high road with silent looks of exasperation and pity. Or he hazards a verbal barb ("In Swedish, the word 'friend' can also be translated as 'limping twerp'" ["Histories," 1-10]) that rarely measures up to House's nimble, acerbic wit. There are also many occasions where Wilson is simply unable to stand up to House's intimidation. For example, House habitually pilfers from Wilson's lunch tray; he even loads his own tray, cuts in front of Wilson in the cafeteria line, and tells the cashier to ring it up on Wilson's tab, to which Wilson responds with a helpless shrug. And Wilson has yet to ask for repayment of the large sums of money (what are we up to, now, $30,000?). House has borrowed from him over the course of the series.

During the second season, while Wilson was in the process of separating from his wife, House allowed him to temporarily move in with him. However, House seemed to regard this period of cohabitation as an opportunity to torture Wilson for his own sadistic pleasure. House raided the fridge and stole Wilson's food, even though the containers were clearly (and anal-retentively) labeled "Property of James Wilson," and even though House thought that Wilson's healthy homemade concoctions looked like they'd "been rolled onto your plate by a dung beetle" ("Clueless," 2-15). House also mocked Wilson's lengthy morning grooming regimen ("You blow dry your hair?") and made him do all the dishes ("Clueless," 2-15). And he subjected Wilson to juvenile pranks, such as plunging his unfortunate sidekick's hand into a pot of water to make him urinate in his sleep. At the same time, the lonely House sabotaged Wilson's attempts to find an apartment of his own, deleting answering machine messages from realtors and effectively holding Wilson hostage.

House's torment of Wilson took on an intriguing psycho-sexual dimension when House hung a stethoscope on the outside doorknob— their old college signal that one was occupied with a woman and required privacy—and kept Wilson waiting outside the building for hours, perhaps as a boastful sign of his superior sexual stamina. However, when Wilson was finally allowed to enter, he discovered that House had not been with a woman, he was merely masturbating. I know that this essay is mainly concerned with the psychology of the sidekick and not the MCF, but I believe the medical term for House's emotional problems is, "Dude, you are so messed-up!"

Allows himself to be drawn into the MCF's schemes against his better judgment. Wilson is blinded by admiration for his MCF, and fears provoking his displeasure. Rather than jeopardize their friendship, Wilson often agrees to House's demands that he participate in questionable, even unlawful, activities. Let's call this symptom "Ethelitis," in honor of the most famous sufferer of Sidekick Syndrome, Ethel Mertz. (You might remember that Ethel's tragic inability to resist the influence of Lucy Ricardo, her wacky, redheaded MCF, led to marital discord, a near-fatal chocolate overdose, and arrests for fraud, disorderly conduct, and impersonating a Martian.)

The usually mature and responsible Wilson often reverts to juvenile behavior under the influence of House. The two doctors ogle Cuddy's cleavage like twelve-year-olds. In "Love Hurts " (1-20), Wilson teased House about his date with Cameron, singing the schoolyard tune about "sitting in a tree, k-i-s-s-i-n-g." Perhaps this goofy immaturity represents Wilson's innate desire to abdicate the responsibilities of adulthood, and who can blame him? But Wilson, like many sidekicks, sometimes seems only too willing to let House take the lead and do his thinking for him.

Wilson enters dangerous waters when he enables House's unorthodox behavior at work. In the episode "All In" (2-17), he occupied Cuddy in a game of poker during a hospital benefit "casino night" so that House could slip away unnoticed and administer a forbidden treatment to a patient. Wilson also protected House from censure by the hospital board for insubordination. Wilson resigned his position rather than join the board in voting to terminate House's employment, telling them, "Okay, he's screwed up. He's miserable. And he should probably reread the ethics code. But it works for him. He's saved hundreds of lives" ("Babies and Bathwater," 1-18). Most disturbingly, Wilson has prescribed Vicodin for House, even though he knows House is an addict who pops pills while on the job.

House also forged Wilson's name on Vicodin prescriptions for himself; when questioned about this by police, Wilson again went into mother hen mode and lied to protect House, insisting that the signature was his own. Placed under criminal investigation, Wilson's bank account was frozen and he was threatened with the suspension of his medical license, but he still refused to turn House in for forging the prescriptions. And while Wilson was displaying this extraordinary loyalty, House was, as usual, taking no responsibility for Wilson's predicament, offering no remorse or sympathy. He even failed to offer Wilson a lift home after his car was impounded.

Yet, even with his career in chaos, Wilson was still sufficiently in thrall to House to help him take a dying patient to Atlantic City for an ill-advised "last fling." Not only did Wilson go to great pains to locate the ingredients to make the patient a perfect last hoagie sandwich, he provided House with an alibi to cover for his part in the patient's assisted suicide. Wilson is a mirror of our own conflicted feelings about House. He sees the good in him, and knows that it is almost outweighed by the bad. Yet, he can't look away, and neither can we. House's abuse of Wilson's loyalty keeps you watching in fascination, to see how low this creep can go. But *House* would have gotten old pretty fast if House were just a creep. And in that respect, Wilson's loyalty is crucial; it signals to viewers that, even though House is a jerk, he does have one friend who thinks he's worth the effort. It grants us permission to give House the benefit of the doubt, and not completely withdraw our sympathy (and tune out).

Yeah, Wilson has some issues. But that's part of the territory when you're a sidekick; your neuroses and shortcomings are symbols of your less-than-heroic status. However, your neuroses and shortcomings can't be more interesting than those of the main character. If they are, then you have failed in your first duty as a sidekick: to lend support. Despite the modern ensemble-cast structure of *House*, the relationship between House and Wilson hews strictly to the old-school TV model of hero and sidekick. And like such old-school masters of sidekickery as Vivian "Ethel Mertz" Vance and Don "Barney Fife" Knotts, Robert Sean Leonard knows just how far he can let Wilson assert his presence without stealing House's thunder. He works quietly in his capacity as the dependable good boy to House's flashy bad boy.

Wilson is as open-hearted as House is aloof; he is as generous as House is selfish. He allows himself to be affected by the patients who pass through his life, while House sees them only as puzzles, not people. Compared to House, Wilson is a tad boring and a little preachy, but that's by design. We need Wilson's sweetness in order to appreciate House's tang. And we need Wilson's selflessness in order to see how stunningly self-centered House really is—it all goes back to the sidekick's job of making the hero as vividly heroic (or, in House's case, anti-heroic) as possible. House's disdain for and fear of human connection has never been more repellently depicted than in the episode "Autopsy" (2-2), when the heartless bastard sarcastically asked if he could watch Wilson deliver bad news to a courageous little girl with terminal cancer, because, "I want to see how brave she is when you tell her she's going to die." You may nervously snicker for a moment at House's lack of empathy, but you very quickly realize that House's behavior is meant to be appalling, and if you didn't realize it, you'd read it on Wilson's stricken face.

To the credit of the series' writers, Wilson is not a one-dimensional saint—just as House is not a one-dimensional sinner. In the third season, Wilson began to display some intriguingly devious behavior: he initiated a secret plan to "help" House, which rode the line between helping and passive-aggressive revenge. In the episode "Cane and Able" (3-2), House fell into a deep depression when he thought that he had failed to cure a patient's mysterious paralysis. What he didn't know was that his untested, reckless treatment had worked, but Wilson had insisted that everyone withhold this information from House in order to try to keep his ego and future recklessness in check.

"He got lucky, that's all that happened," Wilson told Cuddy. "Next time he won't get lucky. He'll kill someone." When House figured out that Wilson was behind the conspiracy he asked him, "So what was your plan? That I'd feel so humbled by missing a case that I'd re-evaluate my entire life, question nature, truth, and goodness, and become Cameron?" Wilson answered, "If we told you the truth, that you'd solved the case based on absolutely no medical proof . . . you'd think you were God. And I was worried that your wings would melt." Wilson's caring and concern were tinged with self-righteousness throughout this two-episode arc. Is this speech really about saving House from himself, or is it simply a case of Wilson's guilt talking? Is Wilson trying to tell himself he's acting in the interest of patients, because he feels disloyal over lying to his friend? Or is the guilt coming from a darker place? Perhaps Wilson feels guilty because a part of him enjoys holding House's fate in his hands and showing him a dose of humility, enjoys acting on his repressed anger and exacting payback for everything he has endured from House.

In Wilson's boldest gambit, he finally informed on House to the police detective investigating the forged Vicodin prescriptions, sheepishly telling him, "I'm going to need thirty pieces of silver" ("Finding

Judas," 3-9). The true nature of Wilson's action is open to interpretation. It could have been a straightforward betrayal. It could have been a concerned sidekick's last-ditch attempt to force his self-destructive companion to face his problems. Or could it have been an attempt to untangle himself from a toxic friendship?

In any case, by finally standing up to House and turning him in, Wilson emerged as a more complex character. But he still performs all the functions of a loyal sidekick. Like Watson, Ethel, and all the classic sidekicks, Wilson is our stand-in; he's a more or less average person allowed intimate access to a larger-than-life character, to observe all that genius and madness up close and be both awestruck and disappointed by it. Wilson is also a yardstick against which we can measure House's excellence and folly; he is morally superior enough to House to make us see the latter's flaws, but he remains inferior to him in all the ways that make House so charismatic and brilliant.

Most of all, Wilson humanizes House. House doesn't seem like an intimidating genius when he's taunting and tormenting Wilson, he seems like an ordinary grade-school bully. And in the rare home scenes where House is not moping in solitude, he is hanging out with Wilson, eating Chinese takeout for Christmas together, watching TV, drinking beer, like a couple of regular guys. Wilson is House's link to the world in all its beautiful mundanity. He is his confidant and his sounding board. And in being all of these things to House, Wilson recalls Tom Hanks's volleyball companion in the movie *Cast Away*. Sure, it was just a ball. But without it, the movie would have been two hours of a lonely man talking to himself, isolated from society, cut off from his own humanness, descending into savagery. It's worth remembering that the volleyball's name was Wilson.

Joyce Millman is the co-author of the book *The Great Snape Debate* (BenBella/Borders). Her essays on pop culture have appeared in the *New York Times*, Salon.com, the *Boston Phoenix*, and several Smart Pop anthologies, including *Neptune Noir* and *Getting Lost*. Read more of her work at www.joycemillman.com.

Joyce Millman's point about Tom Hanks and his volleyball brings up an interesting question: What if Wilson is really House's imaginary friend? It would explain a lot, actually, as Bradley H. Sinor suggests. Not least of which is why Wilson is House's friend to begin with.

THE LITTLE DOCTOR WHO WASN'T REALLY THERE

Bradley H. Sinor

i didn't start watching *House M.D.* when it first came on the air, mainly because my initial reaction was, "Oh no, not another doctor show."

When I did start watching the series, I found out how mistaken I was. That first episode I saw, maybe the sixth or seventh of the season, turned out to have a sharp story, interesting characters, and, to say the least, some very cool special effects.

Almost from that first view I also noticed something odd about one of the characters, or at least I thought it was odd. That person was James Evan Wilson, M.D., graduate of Montreal's McGill University. Besides being the head of the Princeton-Plainsboro Teaching Hospital's Department of Oncology, he also happened to be Dr. Gregory House's best and, perhaps, only friend.

The thing that struck me as odd about Wilson, almost from the very first episode, was that, at times, I found myself wondering if he was real. Yes, he was on screen, but there was something almost supernatural about him.

In several instances House turned around or looked up and Wilson was just standing there. There was no sign that he had walked in—i.e., the sound of a door opening or someone saying "Hello"—or any indication to show that Wilson had been in the room all along. At first it only seemed to happen when no one else was around. Then I noticed that there were times when others were in the room and didn't seem to notice him.

In "Occam's Razor" (1-3), when Foreman came into House's office with the results of a test on a lacrosse player, Wilson was sitting right there in front of House's desk. The two of them had obviously been talking, yet Foreman never acknowledged Wilson's presence in any way, manner, or form. You would think that a younger doctor would at least acknowledge the presence of a senior doctor, especially one who happens to head up an important department at the hospital, if only as a matter of protocol and job courtesy. (Though of course, in all fairness, Wilson also didn't turn around and look at Foreman, the normal reaction when someone walks into a room.)

In the opening sequence of "Damned If You Do" (1-5), something similar happened with Dr. Cuddy: Wilson and House were talking about a patient when Dr. Cuddy came into the room. She talked only to House and seemed to look right through Wilson.

We can come up with reasonable explanations for instances like these. Usually, it takes something urgent to convince someone to interrupt House when he's in the middle of something, and there isn't a lot of time for common courtesy when someone's dying. But times like these aren't the only ones in which others have failed to acknowledge Wilson's presence.

And sure, hospital employees might not speak to Wilson when House is around, unless it is on hospital business, because they don't want to have a run-in with House. (After being on staff at the hospital for eight years, House is no doubt known and feared by a lot of the people who work in the building, be they doctors, nurses, or support personnel. While it is unlikely that a new employee's orientation would include a warning about dealing with House, you can bet that within a few days veteran members of the staff would have passed on warnings to not cross paths with him.) But it isn't just the hospital staff that seems to ignore Wilson's presence. In "Damned If You Do," the patient's sister approached House and Wilson but spoke only to House, never once even looking at Wilson. During "Paternity" (1-2), House and Wilson were sitting outside on the patio having lunch. The parents of House's teenage patient approached him and want to know what the prognosis was for their son. Like Foreman, they talked only to House and never reacted, even with a nod, to the fact that there was another person sitting at the table with him.

"Maybe he's the little doctor who wasn't really there," my wife suggested when I mentioned my observations to her.

Given the evidence, even Sherlock Holmes would have had to consider the possibility: Wilson was House's imaginary friend.

Having imaginary friends isn't exactly unique, though having one when you're over the age of eight is a little more rare. (Then again, this wouldn't be the only way in which House could be said to act like a child.) Children often create imaginary friendships as a "practice ground" for real friendships . . . and boy, does House need practice. The reason it's such a good way to practice at relationships is that the child has control over the interaction, something that would be impossible with a real person. House does enjoy being in control.

Imaginary friends also act, often, as a source of companionship for a child, something House certainly lacks (and may want more than he lets on), but they also often embody personality traits that their creator lacks—they are the ideal version of the child himself. It's hard to imagine House wanting to be Wilson—but isn't it possible that he would sometimes wish that he were more kind or compassionate (or at least have more dates)?

An imaginary friend can also act as a confidant, someone with whom a child can share their secrets and problems. Wilson certainly acts in this capacity for House. And while Wilson might not give House the confirmation that his ideas about a particular case are right, he will often point out something that gets House moving in the right direction. In "Damned If You Do" (1-5), Wilson made a joke that the ailing nun might be allergic to God, causing House to order a full body scan on the theory that there was something physical inside of her causing her allergic reactions. During "Hunting" (2-7), it was a discussion with Wilson over the patient's sweating that caused House to realize that the illness could have been caused by an unsuspected parasite.

House wouldn't be the first fictional character to have an imaginary friend. One of the classic cases is Elwood P. Dowd, in the stage play and movie *Harvey*, whose best friend was a six-foot-tall invisible rabbit (named, appropriately, Harvey). More recently, the long-running comic strip *Calvin and Hobbes* featured the adventures of six-year-old Calvin and his best friend, the stuffed tiger Hobbes, who could only be seen as alive and heard by Calvin.

On television, imaginary friends have been turning up in a variety of shows. *M*A*S*H* had an episode featuring Hawkeye Pierce's childhood imaginary friend, Captain Tuttle ("Hey, when I got drafted, so did he" ["Tuttle"]). More recently, Hurley on *Lost* was shown to have an imaginary friend named Dave ("Dave").

Wilson, though, is real; there is absolutely no doubt about that fact. There are any number of people in the *House*-verse who can testify to his reality: the hospital administrator, Dr. Lisa Cuddy; the other members of Team House; Debby in Accounting; Detective Michael Tritter; and Grace, the patient Wilson moved in with, as detailed in "House vs. God" (2-19), after discovering that she was dying and alone.

But suppose he isn't real *all* of the time.

In other words, what if what we had were two Wilsons, one real, the other a product of House's imagination?

It's a compelling theory.

But *House* is a medical show, and so we should consider a medical explanation for the phenomenon. So let's do a differential diagnosis on House. Why might he be seeing someone who isn't really there?

One possible culprit might be schizophrenia; its symptoms include delusions and auditory hallucinations. That would explain House's ability to both see and hear Wilson. But usually a schizophrenic hears voices that torment and berate not only him, but the people around him — and Wilson tends to save his berating for House alone. (House, on the other hand. . . .) Also, the lack of concentration and physical unsteadiness of the schizophrenic mother from "The Socratic Method" (1-6) are pretty classic for schizophrenia, and they don't sound like House at all.

Having hallucinations of his best friend could be the result of drugs. The only drug that we see House take is Vicodin, for his chronic pain, and he does use a lot of it—he gobbles pills like they were M&Ms in some episodes. According to a number of medical Web sites, the recommended dosage for Vicodin is no more than five tablets in a twenty-four-hour period, accompanied by six to eight full glasses of water. When the police searched his apartment in season three, House was found to be in possession of over 600 tablets—and we see how often he needs a refill.

The problem with our drug hypothesis is that the side effects of Vicodin include euphoria, seizures, and dizziness (among others)—but not hallucinations. So that eliminates drugs as a possible explanation.

But if House's "hallucinations" aren't the result of mental illness or an overdose of drugs, what can we possibly be dealing with?

How about reality, of a sort?

House is a bit more than a "simple country doctor," as Wilson facetiously described him in the pilot. If he did begin to actively hallucinate, seeing Wilson in places his friend wasn't, House would more than likely realize he had a problem.

So what options would he have? He might go to another doctor at a different hospital, since his ego would not allow him to admit to his coworkers that he had a problem. Then again, he might present it to his own team, changing the name of the patient. House has no problem with conjuring up a good fantasy; witness his substitution of Carmen Electra in the episode "Three Stories" (1-21) to "disguise the identity of the patient. I got tired of using the middle-aged man, so Carmen seemed like a pleasant alternative."

Since he hasn't done either of those things, House must be aware that he sometimes talks to someone who isn't really there, and not have a problem with it.

In "No Reason" (2-24) after he was shot, House's subconscious conjured up a whole scenario with not just Wilson but the entire hospital staff, not to mention his assailant Moriarty, in order to figure out what he needed to alleviate the constant pain in his leg.

So, obviously, House is aware that the fantasy Wilson is nothing more than a projection of his subconscious, not an illness of any kind. Since he has done nothing to try to cure himself, House must recognize that his imaginary friend is actually his own mind speaking to him, in order to give him the push he needs to solve the mysteries in front of him.

It also, no doubt, pleases House's ego to no end, knowing that even though it might wear Wilson's face, he is in the end talking to the smartest person he knows: himself.

––––––––––––

BRADLEY H. SINOR has had three collections of his short stories published, *Dark and Stormy Nights*, *In the Shadows*, and *Playing with Secrets* (co-written with his wife Sue). His latest fiction can be found in the anthologies *Space Cadets*, *The Grantville Gazette*, *Places to Go, People to Kill*, *Ring of Fire 2*, and *Houston, We Got Bubbas*. He has also seen his non-fiction appear in a variety of magazines and anthologies such as *Stepping through the Stargate* and *The Cherryh Odyssey*. Visit his Web site at www.zettesworld.com/Sinor/index.htm.

The great adversaries of our time: Coke and Pepsi, Microsoft and Apple . . . House and Cuddy. Like the others, House and Cuddy's battles are often high stakes, and have produced some great entertainment. And also like the others, their struggle is, at heart, about profit. Virginia Baker explains the conflict—and why House wouldn't be the show it is without it.

HOUSE VS. CUDDY

Money and the Bastion of Painful Truth

VIRGINIA BAKER

Why *is* Greg House such a bastard?

It's a fair question to begin with here. Differential diagnoses, anyone? How *do* we find the truth about a man who hides it as cleverly as this one does?

Symptoms don't lie. He cheats, he steals. He fibs. Breaks the rules and plays everyone from patients to friends and even his superiors like tools to be leveraged in the pursuit of solving whatever medical conundrum has captured his attention. There are no limits to where House will go or how many boundaries he'll push to find the answers. Once House zeroes in on the weird, the baffling, or (especially) any disease the average doctor is not equipped to address, he is then driven—possessed, really—to take any measure, no matter how extreme, to solve the puzzle.

For a man driven by mysteries, House is himself the ultimate enigma. Why, really, is he such a bastard? Does he have to behave so badly to be so effective? Couldn't a more polite approach be just as valuable?

Well, no, actually. More often than not, it is his willingness to apply whatever leverage or machination he has to that solves the puzzle and saves the patient. And though he seems like the prince of freefall—a gleeful explorer of hypocrisies, vulnerabilities, and humanity's every weakness—if you look closely, you see that he rarely applies his manipulative tools without reason. Therein lies the ultimate mechanism of his success: House is willing to do, say, or risk anything to get to the truth, no matter how much—or who—it hurts. It's what makes him a bastard. It is also, ironically, what makes him so good at what he does.

But if House had *carte blanche* for his bad behavior without repercussion or question, there would be no friction in the show. Friction equals heat. Heat spins excitement, interest, curiosity. It's the challenges House faces, and how he gets around them, that are so riveting to viewers. And while the medical mêlées House takes on are interesting by themselves, they are most often illuminated in the frame of other confrontations—especially during the skirmishes between the business end of medicine and the purity of obsessive diagnostics.

Administration as a fulcrum for conflict brilliantly underscores the places where medicine and profit collide. It also sheds light on the reason House is so extreme as he pursues life-saving solutions: he doesn't care about legalities or profits or money. His bottom line is *The Answer*.

Dr. Lisa Cuddy's bottom line, as the hospital's administrator, focuses on the financial health and welfare of the hospital as its own living organism. Were she a typical version of the breed, Greg House would be working anywhere else but Princeton-Plainsboro Teaching Hospital. Administrators are, after all, a hospital's financial and legal safety net, its protector, and the director of its survival.

Ironically, sometimes Princeton-Plainsboro Teaching Hospital's biggest threat is also the man who helps give it the reputation of excellence it needs to thrive: Dr. Gregory House. Loose cannon. Manipulative, abrasive, even cruel. On the surface, at least, it seems like the only thing he's really good at is being a doctor. And while colleagues, friends and the Establishment often don't "get" the man, one patient at least caught on to the secret of what drives House:

> I know that limp. I know the empty ring finger. And that obsessive nature of yours. . . . You don't risk jail and your career just to save somebody who doesn't want to be saved unless you got something, anything, one thing. I got music, you got this. The

thing you think about all the time, the thing that keeps you
south of normal. Yeah, makes us great, makes us the best. All we
miss out on is everything else ("DNR," 1-9).

In this rare case, knowing House is obsessed with finding the answer—
and would do anything to get to it—makes it possible for this patient to
trust House as a doctor. The interchange also serves as a symbolic model
for the delicate (and sometimes precarious) balance of trust and misgiv-
ing between House and Cuddy, with House's obsession forming the
nexus of his credibility as he drives home success after success.

It soon becomes clear that it's his obsession that makes House so good
at what he does. At anything else, doing anything else, he fails. But as a
physician—the perfect computational healer—he shines. If it weren't for
his outrageous rudeness, someone might have done him the same honor
they did Clapton, and scrawled on a subway wall, "House is God."

House would not argue with that. But he often argues with Cuddy. It's
only appropriate. As players in the hospital's cultural infrastructure, they
should be diametrically opposed. Other shows have played it that way.
In fact, in most hospital shows, the administrator is not even a doctor,
much less Dean of Medicine. He (and it's always been a "he") would
have been a financial manager, coldly above mercy, unable to grasp the
suffering of patients or the hope that just a few dollars more put toward
their treatment could offer. And the doctor would have been the right-
eous crusader—heated, passionate, and most likely a fine physical specimen at the height of his powers. Superman vs. Lex Luthor engaged in
an eternal battle between balancing financial profit and human loss.

As House would say, *Puh-lease.*

Yes, the eternal conflict between administrator and doctor would be a
rich vein to mine for drama, for the kind of tension that winds a plot
tight and keeps it ticking. It has the added advantage of being the
expected relational paradigm, one that audiences are so deeply pro-
grammed for that they can accept it without thinking twice.

But thankfully, the show's creators didn't go for the obvious. There's
more to House vs. Cuddy than stereotypical (and macho) head-butting.
The realities of this relationship are more subtle, and are set up from the
start to grow from fractious uncertainty to outright dependency on the

part of both characters.

House is not Clark Kent in a lab coat. He has those gorgeous blue eyes, yes, but not the formulaic physique or lush dark hair. (That's Wilson, who has the looks but not the attitude.) House, as he himself puts it, is *crippled*. The physical handicap is obvious. Grasping House's other levels of impairment requires exposure, over time, to his vicious wit and hellacious antisocial machinations.

As for Cuddy, the first thing you notice is that she is not a he. And she isn't just the authoritarian macho stereotype in drag, either, which immediately makes her more interesting. The second thing you notice is that Cuddy knows who House is. Not only did she hire him anyway, she hired him because she could count on him to be who he is. She knows that House is no simple jerk. He's not mean for the hell of it (though he can be mean for the fun of it). There is, most often, a method to his meanness—and she can count on that method to bring results.

For instance, when House tells one of the hospital's financial donors that his wife is having an affair (which he deduces by noticing that the man has turned orange—something the wife has failed to note), the donor complains to Cuddy. She responds with a defense that defines the Cuddy / House relationship:

> You've been good to me and good to this hospital, but I don't see how this conversation can end well for me. Either your wife is having an affair, or she's not having an affair and you have come here because you rightly think I should fire him. But I can't, even if it costs me your money. The son of a bitch is the best doctor we have ("Pilot," 1-1).

Here's the thing: Administrators are good for business. They exist for a reason. They're the stop-gaps between the narrow vision of specialists and the big-picture view of profits. If a business—any business—isn't profitable, it doesn't *stay* in business. Salaries get cut, people get laid off. The economy, spreading out from neighborhoods to the whole world, erodes like the cells of a cancer patient, eaten away by a lack of cash flow.

House would understand that. Would understand the necessity of profit, how it feeds the economic body and keeps it healthy. What he wouldn't understand is putting it first. And he'll go to any measure to make sure that doesn't happen.

This puts him and Cuddy in an interesting position. Because to do the job she hired him to do, House has to push patients, doctors, and the hospital into places your typical administrator would rather not go. If he doesn't do that job, he's useless. If he does, more often than not, he gets into trouble with the Establishment. As a smarter-than-average administrator, Cuddy factored this paradox into her plans:

> When I hired you, I knew you were insane. I will continue to try and stop you from doing insane things, but once they're done. . . . Trying to convince an insane person not to do an insane thing is, in itself, insane, so when I hired you, I also set aside $50,000 a year for legal expenses. So far, you've come in under budget ("DNR," 1-9).

Still, even Cuddy couldn't have known how far House would go when she hired him, and that unknown has come between them many times, bringing the two characters into an elliptical orbit—a constant wary circling where proof of success is more often confirmed than denied and that foundational "nexus" of trust is built.

But audacious daring in the name of medicine and plain old uncooperative stubbornness are two different things entirely. Taken as a whole, the series clearly shows that Cuddy most often will support House when he's working through a perilous diagnosis, but does not appreciate him taking other duties lightly:

> Your billings are practically nonexistent. You ignore requests for consults. You're six years behind on your obligation to this clinic. The only reason that I don't fire you is because your reputation is worth something to this hospital. [That] won't last if you don't do your job. The clinic is part of your job. I want you to do your job ("Pilot," 1-1).

House, quoting Mick Jagger as a philosopher, tells Cuddy that, "You can't always get what you want," setting up the standard administrator vs. doctor challenge. But Cuddy's reaction provides a significant twist. Instead of bullying House with a display of aggression, she simply revokes his access to diagnostic technologies—and doesn't tell House. He finds out only when he tries to get access to an MRI machine. Humiliated in front of a patient and his three diagnostic assistants, House storms into Cuddy's office, furious, yelling about disrespect and embarrassment. Instead of yelling back (which an old-fashioned stereo-typical administrator would almost certainly do), Cuddy defuses House by calmly turning the tables on him:

> Is your yelling designed to scare me? Because I'm not sure what I'm supposed to be scared of. More yelling? That's not scary. That you're gonna hurt me? That's scary, but I'm pretty sure I can outrun you. Oh, and I looked into that philosopher you quoted—Jagger. And you're right, you can't always get what you want, but as it turns out, "If you try sometimes, you get what you need" ("Pilot," 1-1).

Cuddy has a point. Profit is the heart of any business. It's the star that businesses steer by, and unlike in *Peter Pan*, it isn't the first star on the right and straight on 'til morning. It's a place where the wild boys had better grow up, play by the book, and bring in the money that keeps the business alive.

House as rebel speaks to our own questioning subconscious. Over the last few years, there's this suspicion niggling at all of us, lurking just beneath the noise of all of our delightful consumerism: that quantity is not quality, and that most of what we are told to be the truth is either overblown confusion or deliberate misinformation—all for the sake of profit. Now, profit is not a bad thing. We like profit, both personally and on a global economic level. We like making a profit through our skills. We don't mind paying for goods or services rendered, allowing others to make a profit off of us. What we don't like is to be screwed over—for people to lie or to take undue advantage of us to make more profit than they fairly should. Or, in the case of medicine, to risk lives instead of the bottom line.

The conundrum between House and Cuddy is one we, ourselves,

engage in every day, albeit in different ways. Even as we chafe at the lies we are told by those trying to make a profit in this world, we know we are unsuspecting co-conspirators by buying into those lies without question. The show plays on this paradox in subtle ways, making House a hero because he does what we, as gullible consumers, fail to do.

So go ahead. Ask the uncomfortable diagnostic question: Why would so many people lie for money? In House's view, people lie all the time—it's a given. Anyone who doesn't approach life with that assumption is bound to get hurt. If you assume people lie, you can't be disappointed, and are less likely to be fooled. House assumes that patients lie, so he looks beyond their words to find patterns, paradoxes, and even hidden catalysts to disease in their homes. Dead cats show the way to pesticide poisoning. Blind birds illuminate the path to Foreman's unknown disease. The contents of a refrigerator show why a girl's brain is dying as a pork-borne parasite eats her alive. Discovering that a patient drinks a normally harmless tea uncovers the cause of a deadly drug reaction.

House doesn't trust. He investigates. It's a good paradigm, one that works for us, making our purchases and watching the news, as much as it does for curing patients. If you look beyond the surface—cute TV ads that make us laugh, news headlines that infuriate and sicken, the names of cool designers on spiffy labels—you realize that the whole point behind it all is profit. When we are appalled at the company whose ads are better than their products (remember, everybody lies), we come to suspect that every service we interact with is hindered by the same demands of profit over honesty.

Which is why House is our hero. The truth comes from those who don't give a damn about the financial bottom line or the lawyers or the rules—renegades like House, who cut through the clutter regardless of the risks. House gets to the truth, even if the route he takes is a circuitous one through other lies—many of which are his own. "I lied to a patient," he says, as he admits his own fundamental truth to Cuddy. "I take risks. Sometimes patients die. But not taking risks causes more patients to die, so I guess my biggest problem is I've been cursed with the ability to do the math" ("Detox," 1-11).

The subtlety here is how that fundamental truth poses problems for Cuddy, who is charged with protecting the Establishment's interests.

When House lies about the size of a patient's tumor, for instance, Cuddy comes down hard:

> CUDDY: *Fraud!* Fraud was the only way?! There is a *reason*
> we have these guidelines. . . .
> HOUSE: I know—to save lives. Specifically doctors' lives, and
> not just their lives, but their *lifestyles*. Wouldn't wanna
> operate on anyone *really* sick—they might die and spoil
> our stats.
> CUDDY: Bergen has a right to know what he is operating on!
> HOUSE: True. I got all focused on her right to live, and forgot.

There are plenty of clashes between House and Cuddy. But what makes the series work is the layering of those conflicts. Instead of going over the top by making administrators the bad guys and doctors into saints, the series splits the tension, and that makes the tug of authority between House and Cuddy more interesting. Their tension is atypical because it operates on two distinct levels to generate its unique friction:

1. Diagnostic actions that risk the patient, the hospital, and/or its personnel, either legally or physically, on which Cuddy almost always backs House up.
2. Billing for clinical hours, which becomes the ongoing "war" between Cuddy and House.

When they interact in the first sense, Cuddy has learned that House is so often right that to thwart his progress puts patients at greater risk. It doesn't take long for her to realize that in every case where she has tried to step between House and a patient, if she had succeeded, the patient would have died.

In the episode "All In" (2-17), for instance, House connives with Wilson to keep Cuddy at a hospital benefit party while House himself takes over the diagnostics of one of Cuddy's very young patients. Given the symptoms of the boy's distress over the phone at the party, Cuddy diagnoses his bloody diarrhea as a simple gastrointestinal flare-up, orders fluids, and keeps on playing cards with Wilson. Hearing the same symptoms, House quietly folds his cards and goes to the hospital to diagnose the boy himself. After chasing one lead after another—Ahab pursuing his whale and nearly killing the boy in the process—House has to face an outraged Cuddy who, as an administrator, must intervene:

> I got called away by the angry parents of a patient. It's my case now. Go home, go ride your motorcycle, go brood in a dark room, just don't go near Ian again ("All In," 2-17).

Of course, Cuddy can't find out what's killing the child either. It's a mystery to everyone, a terrifying puzzle that just won't crack despite the skills of an entire team of doctors. Luckily, House refuses to give up. He doesn't go home, but instead secretly tests the remnants of tissue and cells he still has from the previous tests he performed on the boy. By not giving in, he finds what's killing the child. If he *had* given in, Cuddy knows too well that the child would have died.

That "savior" role is reversed (temporarily) in "Damned If You Do" (1-5), where House seems to be killing a nun in his search for a diagnosis. Cuddy tells him, "I am going to do you the biggest favor one doctor can do for another. I am going to stop you from killing your patient. You're off the case." Cuddy takes over, but despite her best efforts the nun continues to deteriorate. House, who has done some outside sleuthing, finds out that the nun drinks figwort tea—perfectly harmless in most cases, but deadly in combination with the epinephrine he had previously administered. Victorious in his find, House trumps Cuddy again, telling her, "I'm going to do you the biggest favor one doctor can do for another. I'm gonna stop you from killing your patient."

Perhaps the most dramatic and funniest moment of grace House encounters when defying Cuddy's direct orders comes in "Safe" (2-16). Here, House's usual method of narrowing down a diagnosis by trial and error results in the worsening of a young girl's condition to the point where Cuddy again intervenes, insisting on a trans-venous pacing wire to keep the patient's heart alive. House insists that what's really killing the girl is a tick, even though they've searched the patient's body and found no sign of one. This time, Cuddy forces House out of physical reach of the patient as well as out of the case, literally pushing him away from the girl's gurney, telling him, "Okay, magic tick hunt is over. Only real doctor stuff now."

Watching House hovering outside the treatment group, Wilson quietly suggests to Cuddy that the girl needs to get into the ICU for a stronger treatment than the ER has available. It's a ruse, of course; as Foreman wheels the gurney into the elevator, House steps in—before the entourage of doctors and parents can get into the elevator, blocking their path with his cane. Cuddy orders House out of the elevator. When he won't go, she entrusts the care of the unconscious girl on the gurney to Foreman. But once the elevator doors close, House pulls the emergency button—once again reversing roles with Cuddy by effectively locking her out of reach of the patient. In House's world, deviousness trumps authority every time.

Of course, Cuddy quickly finds out that the elevator's failure to move is no malfunction. As the patient circles cardiac arrest, Foreman berates House for being so stubborn: "We already kidnapped her, you want to add murder?! We've looked over every inch of skin on her body, House. It's over."

While Foreman releases the emergency stop button, House has his own epiphany. He shakes the teenage girl, asking if her pre-illness tryst with her boyfriend was the first time she'd had sex. As the girl faints again and Foreman grows more appalled, House lifts the patient's hospital gown, parts her legs, and begins rooting through her pubic hair. The elevator chimes and the door opens, revealing the scene to the girl's parents (who are waiting with Wilson and Cuddy). Believing House to be sexually molesting his daughter, the enraged father pushes House away, but not before we see that House has something in his hand. It's a tick—the same critter that House predicted was the source of the girl's affliction. No one believed him then. But with tick in hand, there's no way to refute the proof. House tells them, "Now *that* was dramatic. Push norepiniphrine, get her heart back to normal. She'll be completely cured by tomorrow."

And she is. Because often the only factors that save the patient (and thus the hospital) are House's manipulative cunning and his willingness to hijack authority at every level. When Cuddy takes cases out of House's hands, she's learned, bad things happen.

There are, however, times when having to follow the rules pits House and Cuddy into deeper conflict. When Foreman contracts a deadly illness that could be contagious, Cuddy insists on putting him in isolation and calling in the CDC. Her actions could mean death for Foreman and both she and House know it. "You're killing Foreman because of a *maybe*," House charges. He maneuvers to have Foreman's father brought in to meet Cuddy, to guilt her into doing a biopsy at the hospital instead of waiting for the CDC. But Cuddy doesn't give in, even when House says, "Oh, don't blame the rules. Don't hang this on policy and protocol." Cuddy's reply to Foreman's father is diplomatic, firm, and unswervingly administrative:

> I am well aware that it may cost your son his life, just as I am well aware that my decision has a devastating effect on family and friends without having them paraded in front of me. Your son has an unknown, contagious, and deadly infection. If we don't contain it here, even more people could be at risk. I am capable of empathizing with those people too—*without* having them paraded in front of me ("Euphoria, Part 2," 2-21).

Sticking to protocol at such a cost is not easy for Cuddy. This episode shows that while House will stoop to any level of cunning to get his answers, Cuddy herself is also capable of exercising administrative imperatives—even if she has to sacrifice others in order to do it. This is a mirror of House's own ability to orchestrate any situation and humiliate any person to achieve his goal. But while House embraces and even revels in that particular forte, Cuddy does not take any pleasure in it.

FOREMAN: Why are you here?
CUDDY: Because you're a friend. And I should be here.
FOREMAN: I'm sorry House used my dad to try and manipulate you. You've got integrity. You're not going to change your mind just because you're confronted by my father.

Just like I'm not going to forgive you just because you come by here and ask how I'm feeling.

CUDDY: You know I've had no choice.

FOREMAN: Of course you had a choice!

CUDDY: The regulations are clear. . . .

FOREMAN: And the punishment for violating those regulations? Is it death? Hmm? Because frankly, I'm okay if you get a fine, a suspension—hell, you can spend a couple of years in jail if it saves my life!

Without even realizing it, Foreman (who, ironically, doesn't appreciate House's outrageous tactics) is telling Cuddy that *she* should be more like House, that she should take the risk of punishment to save his life, that she is wrong to sacrifice that life to the cold abstraction of rules, regulations, and financial well-being. Still, Cuddy stands her ground, and while House connives a way to go around the rules once again to save the day, this episode shows that Cuddy is indeed willing to sacrifice, when necessary, to save the hospital instead of the patient.

While these conflicts provide the series with its unique gravitas, it's when House and Cuddy snipe at each other during their "clinic" war that they open the door to humor—the second layer to their fractious bond and a vital ingredient to the show's success. House and Cuddy's genders in particular provide an opportunity for interchanges that could never happen between two male characters positioned as constantly antagonistic polar opposites. Discussing a medical conundrum with Wilson, House catches sight of Cuddy coming within earshot and says loudly to Wilson:

HOUSE: The cutest little tennis outfit, my God, I thought I was going to have a heart attack. [acts like he's just noticed Cuddy's presence] Oh my, I didn't see you there, that is so embarrassing.

CUDDY: How's your hooker doing?

HOUSE: Oh, sweet of you to ask, funny story, she was going to be a hospital administrator, but hated having to screw people like that.

Scrimmage lines in the clinic wars can be devious, creative, and even shockingly funny. Entering a waiting room full of patients, Cuddy berates House for being half an hour late for clinic duty. Instead of sparring with her, he turns to the waiting room and addresses the patients:

> Hello, sick people. In the interests of saving time and avoiding a lot of boring chit-chat later, I'm Dr. Gregory House. I'm the only doctor employed at this clinic who is here against his will. But not to worry, because for most of you, this job could be done by a monkey with a bottle of Motrin. Speaking of which, if you're particularly annoying, you may see me reaching for this. This is Vicodin. . . . And no, I do not have a pain management problem. . . . But who knows? Maybe I'm wrong. Maybe I'm too stoned to tell. So—who wants me? ("Occam's Razor," 1-3).

To further discourage Cuddy from assigning him to clinic duty, House resorts to paging her for every ridiculously common ailment he encounters. Cuddy counters by telling House:

> It's not going to work. You know why? Because this is fun. You think of something to make me miserable, and I think of something to make you miserable. It's a game! And I'm going to win, because I have a head start. You are *already* miserable ("Occam's Razor," 1-3).

Sometimes, though, the game gets rough. In several episodes, House has to request donor organs to save his patients. More often than not, Cuddy finds a way to give House what he needs. But sometimes, the bottom line she's responsible for sinks deep.

For instance, when House discovers that a sixty-five-year-old patient's heart has been destroyed by bacteria he must make his case not only to Cuddy, but to the entire transplant committee. One of the executives, a doctor named Simpson, points out that even if the patient were given a heart, he would only have a few years of life left and thus wouldn't be a good candidate.

HOUSE: So you're saying that old people aren't as worth saving as young people?
CUDDY: He's saying that hearts are a scarce resource. We
obviously have to choose criteria—
SIMPSON: Your patient has already had a life. A family. We've
got eighteen-year-old kids who only—
HOUSE: How old are you, doctor? When do we get to toss
you on an ice floe? ("Sex Kills," 2-14).

When House is turned down, instead of fruitlessly raging against the
unfairness of the system, he goes around it. Ironically, he uses the much-
loathed clinic to do so. He finds a woman who is brain dead, and asks
for her heart—it can't go to anyone else, because it doesn't meet standard
transplant guidelines. The woman's husband protests, so House intro-
duces the husband to his elderly patient's daughter. Manipulated by the
girl's effusive thanks, the husband capitulates and gives House his dying
wife's heart.

To House, this is not an outrageous act, it's an economy of resources.
As he explains to a confounded Cuddy, "Committee says they won't take
her heart. Another committee says a guy can't have a heart. It's a marriage made in heaven" ("Sex Kills," 2-14).

The ultimate test of wills in the give-and-take between House and
Cuddy, however, comes in the form of an über-donor, Edward Vogler. As
the price of giving the hospital $100 million, Vogler becomes Chairman of
the Board—and immediately begins operating the hospital like a business.

Yes, it's the stereotypical administrator. Vogler is not a doctor, he's a
businessman—an entrepreneur who happens to have a stake in pharma-
ceuticals. He and House take an immediate dislike to one another. But
what takes their battle of wills beyond the pale is Vogler's insistence that
House abdicate free will entirely. This is his mistake. Vogler isn't engaging in the average administrative crackdown on waste; as Vogler
explains to House, he's demanding nothing less than complete control
over the doctor's actions: "This is not a negotiation. Never was. I need to
know that whatever I ask you to do, no matter how distasteful you find
it, you'll do it" ("Heavy," 1-16).

Vogler ups the ante by forcing House to choose between firing one of his staff or giving a dinner speech to hype Vogler's new medication, which House knows is bogus. Vogler rubs it in by telling House to "throw in a joke." By giving that little gem of advice, Vogler capstones his dominance over House and reveals his enjoyment of the doctor's capitulation.

Knowing he is under Vogler's thumb, hating what he has to do to save his team, House discovers from the courage of a patient that sometimes not winning a fight can make more of a difference than absolute victory.

At the dinner, House does indeed give a speech—and makes a mockery of what Vogler has told him to do. He gives an incredibly lackluster performance, reading a press release in a robotic monotone. When he sits back down, Vogler says to him, "That was not a speech. [Who goes?] Foreman or Cameron?"

House smiles, then goes back to the podium and reveals to Vogler that he can only be owned so much, can only be pushed so far. He tells the audience:

> You know how I know the new ACE inhibitor is good? Because the old one was good. The new one is really the same, it's just more expensive. A *lot* more expensive. See . . . whenever one of his drugs is about to lose its patent, Vogler has his boys and girls alter it just a tiny bit and patent it all over again. Making not just a pointless new pill, but millions and millions of dollars. Which is great for everybody, right? The patients, *pish*. Who cares? They're just so damned sick—God obviously never liked them anyway. [turning to Vogler, smirking] See? I threw in a joke ("Role Model," 1-17).

In retaliation, Vogler goes after House, Wilson, and Cuddy through the Board, lobbying to vote them out of their jobs and the hospital. Rattled, Cuddy tells House, "You are a great doctor, but you're not worth $100 million."

Ultimately, though, while House proves he can't be bought, Cuddy also proves that *good* administrators work to find that vital balance between profit and human loss in its many aspects. When Vogler calls the Board together, Cuddy tells the other members:

217

If you think House deserves to go, if you think I deserve to go, that Wilson deserved to go, then vote yes. But if you're doing this because you are afraid of losing his money, then he's right—he *does* own you. Now you have a choice. Maybe the last real choice you'll have here ("Babies and Bathwater," 1-18).

The Board decides to take back its authority *and* its people. House, Wilson, Chase, and Foreman celebrate in House's office with champagne. As Cuddy comes in, House is exuberant:

> HOUSE: Cuddy is a genius, convincing four people to give up a fortune to save our sorry asses. Dr. Cuddy! The man of the hour!
> CUDDY: What are you doing?
> HOUSE: We're drinking. I would have thought that was pretty obvious.
> CUDDY: [taking a glass] Well, here's to the great champion. [I] saved you, saved Wilson, saved the whole team. Of course, none of them would have needed saving if *you* could actually get along with another human being.
> HOUSE: Well, thank you, Miss Buzzkill.
> CUDDY: You only cost us $100 million. You should be in mourning. I know I am ("Babies and Bathwater," 1-18).

Here is where we sympathize with Cuddy, who becomes, in her role of administrator, the vicarious champion of our own vital interests. We understand that, costly as House can be, he is most often right to do what he does as he goes about diagnosing diseases that no one else in the hospital can fully grasp. But we also see that Cuddy can be a heroic figure herself, as she tries to find the right balance between giving House what he needs and keeping the hospital (and all the jobs it generates) alive and well.

The jobs Cuddy saves could be jobs like our own. The jobs she cuts could be those like ours. The reasons she does could either be as cold as a spreadsheet or as heartbreaking as a single doctor losing a donor's dollars. We love House for being the rebel with a cause. But we should also love Cuddy for knowing when to let the rebel protect a patient from death and when to protect the rest of us from the rebel himself.

Oddly, it is within this sometimes-precarious footing that the bond of trust between House and Cuddy is built. Both of them respect one another—not in spite of these conflicts, but because of them.

> HOUSE: Cuddy. Your guilt. It's perverse, and it makes you a crappy doctor. It also makes you okay at what you do.
> CUDDY: You figure a perverted sense of guilt makes me a good boss?
> HOUSE: Cuddy . . . you see the world as it is and you see the world as it could be. What you don't see is what everybody else sees—that giant, gaping chasm in between.
> CUDDY: House, I am not naïve. I realize—
> HOUSE: If you did, you never would have hired me. You're not happy unless things are just right. Which means two things. You're a good boss. And you'll never be happy ("Humpty Dumpty," 2-3).

As the series progresses, we begin to see House and Cuddy less as adversaries and more as one another's alter-conscience. Cuddy serves as the barrier between House and the financial disasters he incurs while he twists patients, colleagues, and institutions like a Rubik's Cube to figure out medical puzzles. And House serves as the ass that gets to the bottom of things, keeping score with God to "do the math" ("House vs. God," 2-19), and saving more lives with risk and abuse than he would with policy and *politesse*.

He pushes the boundaries and finds the answers. She deflects, protects, and gives him room to move. She sometimes draws the line herself. He often goes around it. And as long as their relationship works, and the patient lives, so does the balance.

Pardon the misleading title. (Everybody lies, remember?) There is no *versus* here. There is only the spin of opposition, in the differences that reveal two sides of the same coin and, with it, a similar sort of honor. Cuddy and House are a perfect team. Because even as House takes obvious risks with patients and staff and the hospital, Cuddy takes less showy risks that have just as much value—to cover House as he pursues whatever course he has to take to save a life even as she keeps the hospital itself alive and thriving. And that, apparently, *is* worth $100 million dollars—to both the doctor *and* the administrator.

VIRGINIA BAKER lives in Utah with a flock of large birds and the cats who fear them. She has a master's degree in English, but learned to write by reading really good books. A freelancer by day, she also writes award-winning fiction. Her first book, *Jack Knife*, published by Penguin, is a thriller revolving around Jack the Ripper. Whether she's creating or consuming them, she loves books like bon-bons—and believes that while reality may be the essential meat and potatoes of life, a good read is pure chocolate.

*If we've learned anything from House, it's that lying is a fact of life, not just medi-
cine. Lucky for us, lies reveal as much as they conceal. Donna Andrews analyzes
each of House's main characters to discover when and why they lie, and what that
tells us about who they really are.*

SEX, LIES, AND MRIs

DONNA ANDREWS

Patients lie. That's the gospel according to House—right?

Wrong. According to Dr. Gregory House, "Everybody lies."

Patients are only a subset of everybody. A particularly annoying subset, because their lies make it difficult for House to do his job. Actually,
first time around I typed "for House to do *their* job"; divulging every bit
of information that could possibly help with diagnosis is the patients'
job. How maddening it must be when they don't cough up the information and House has to extract it any way he can, with diagnostic tests,
interrogations, and . . . well, lying.

It all comes back to lying. As a mystery writer, I can relate to this.
Everybody lies about something, and that's what makes a mystery hard
to solve. If the culprit were the only liar around, few mysteries could last
more than a chapter or two. But it takes a lot longer to uncover the lethal
lies of a killer when they're camouflaged by all those other annoying lies
that are completely irrelevant to the crime but matter profoundly to the
liars.

So if anyone ever invents a really effective truth serum, the police will
rejoice, but criminals and mystery writers will both be out of a job. In

the meantime, mysteries are fun—and *House* is more a mystery than a medical show. The detectives wield stethoscopes instead of badges and guns, and the killers are often visible only under an electron microscope, but like in any mystery, you'll find the truth hiding behind the lies.

Because, as House said himself in the pilot episode, "Truth begins in lies." Which I take to mean that if you figure out why, and when, and how people lie, you're a lot closer to knowing who they really are.

> **DR. LISA CUDDY: When I hired you, I knew you were insane ("DNR," 1-9).**

As befits a hospital's chief administrator, Cuddy has a very corporate attitude toward lying. She strongly disapproves when her staff members lie to her—although years of trying to manage House have eroded her ability to feel outrage at his howlers, so half the time all she can muster toward him is mild irritation.

But she will lie, if necessary, to protect the hospital and its staff. As she told Edward Vogler, the billionaire who tried to control the hospital through his $100 million donation, "I protect people who are assets to this hospital" ("Mob Rules," 1-15). And despite all her exasperation with him, House is an asset. Sometimes protecting House means lying for him.

More often, it means lying to him. So far, two of Cuddy's biggest lies have been to House, both for his own good—as she sees it—and both with disastrous consequences.

Cuddy told her first big lie when House asked to be put into a medically induced coma so he could endure the pain of allowing his leg to heal. Cuddy knew that as soon as House was unconscious, Stacy would give permission to take out the dead muscle. It was a middle ground House didn't want, one that left him scarred, lamed, and in crippling pain. Not the intended result, of course, but that's what happened—and Cuddy has never forgotten it. She feels guilty. ("Because I'm a doctor. Because when we make mistakes people die" ["Pilot," 1-1].) Maybe that's another reason Cuddy is so willing to protect House and put up with his antics. Not just because he's a hospital asset, but because this particular damaged, drug-addicted asset is partly her creation.

Cuddy's other big lie, in "Meaning" (3-1), wasn't originally her idea. But she's the one who injected House's paralyzed patient with cortisol—and then, when the guy rose and walked in a fair imitation of Lazarus, cooperated with Dr. James Wilson's plan to hide this success from House. "Telling him 'no' is a good thing," according to Wilson. "Just because he was right doesn't mean he wasn't wrong." Cuddy and Wilson may have been lying for a good reason, in one more doomed attempt to curb House's self-destructive behavior, but the lie backfired, and sent House into the tailspin that landed him in Officer Tritter's clutches.

Of course, Cuddy's biggest lie of all came at House's trial, when she testified under oath that she had switched the pharmacy's painkillers with placebos. So far, it's been a fruitful lie—she's used it to wring many concessions out of House. But as the immediate fear of imprisonment fades and House begins to chafe under her orders again, isn't it likely that he'll threaten to expose her perjury?

And while Cuddy the administrator will lie like a trooper if necessary, Cuddy the woman seems far more susceptible to guilt. Perhaps, despite her obvious capabilities and her outward confidence, she suffers, like many strong women, from imposter syndrome—the irrational but inescapable fear that her success is a lie. In "Humpty Dumpty" (2-3), when she makes a mistake in treating a patient, she blurted out, "I was so anxious to get ahead, I haven't been a doctor in years." (Someone please remind Cuddy that House commits as many as half a dozen misdiagnoses on each case without letting it shake his self-confidence.)

So what else do Cuddy's lies tell us? That she's a woman torn between the demands of her job and those of friendship and loyalty, between the need to rein House in and the guilt that seduces her into going just a little easier on him—even though she knows that if she gives House an inch he will probably take over the entire hospital.

DR. JAMES WILSON: Beauty often seduces us on the road to truth ("Occam's Razor," 1-3).

Wilson's lies fall into two categories. There are his lies to his wives—they happen, presumably, though mostly offstage, because the show is *House*, not *Wilson*. And never mind that he claimed he "always told them" about his indiscretions in "Spin" (2-6)—cheating itself is a form of lying.

Then there are Wilson's lies to House, lies about House, and lies designed to help House, one way or another. The House lies probably started innocuously, as in the pilot episode where he pretended a patient was his cousin to trick House into taking her case. Or when he concealed the fact that it was his idea, not Cuddy's, to bet House four weeks' reprieve from clinic that he couldn't go a week without drugs in "Detox" (1-11). But eventually his lies built to the point where, in "Cane and Able" (3-2), he suggested hiding the success of the cortisol injection House recommended for a patient: "We tell him he was right, and we're feeding his addiction."

Sounds shaky as a reason for lying to his friend. Maybe Wilson realized that when he saw House skimping on his physical therapy and spiraling back into Vicodin addiction. Or maybe it was the strength of his friendship that caused Wilson to tell his own big lie, to Tritter, claiming that he signed the prescription on which House forged Wilson's name. Will House remember that initial, well-intentioned lie when he's living with the consequences of what he probably sees as Wilson's later betrayal?

Clearly Wilson's lies to and for House matter more, and have more effect on his life, than the lies to his various wives. Wives may come and go, but like it or not, Wilson's career and his friendship with House remain the twin pillars of his life. But if the lies he's forced to tell to protect his friend threaten his career, will the friendship survive? Since that storyline and the consequences of Wilson's big lie are still playing out as I write this, only time will tell. For the time being, however misguided his actions sometimes seem, Wilson remains the show's most altruistic liar.

> HOUSE: (to the Ducklings) I teach you to lie, cheat, and steal, and as soon as my back's turned you wait in line? ("Failure to Communicate," 2-10).

House probably didn't hire his three juniors because they were the best possible neurologist, immunologist, and intensivist available. They're very good, obviously, or House wouldn't put up with them for a second. But as we saw when Cameron temporarily quit, as soon as word gets out that House has a fellowship available, the halls of Princeton-Plainsboro Teaching Hospital swarm with highly qualified applicants. House could have his pick of doctors. Why Cameron, Chase, and Foreman? Could it be because they set off his internal polygraph most strongly? That he knew he'd have the most fun unraveling their various lies?

So what can we learn from the Ducklings' lies?

> **CHASE: You can trust me.**
> **HOUSE: Problem is, if I can't trust you, I can't trust your statement that I can trust you ("Mob Rules," 1-15).**

Trust is an ongoing issue between House and Chase, probably because Chase seems far more apt to lie than the other Ducklings. He lies because it's convenient . . . to protect his job . . . to look smarter. Having sex with a drug-addled Cameron wasn't a lie, but it certainly suggests that Chase is a bit of a lightweight in the scruples department. The same goes for ratting House out to Vogler.

But if you weigh Chase's many small lies against the huge one his father and House tell—concealing the senior Dr. Chase's impending death from lung cancer—Chase starts to look more lied to than liar. (And is it just a coincidence that House chose this issue for one of his rare and uncharacteristic attacks of discretion? No, but we'll get to House later.) Chase's father's behavior spoke volumes about their troubled, uncommunicative relationship. Dr. Rowan Chase came from Australia to see his son, probably for the last time, and perhaps to say a silent farewell. But he denied his son the chance for goodbyes and closure. After meeting the father, we can find Chase's poor little rich boy attitude and his cavalier approach to truth far more understandable.

And Rowan's lie led directly to Chase's mistake in, of course, "The Mistake" (2-8)—missing a key symptom and thus contributing to the death of his patient, Kayla—and to Chase's own big lie: that he had come to work hung over. Even when faced with a peer review (which, as Stacy told him, is "a misnomer. These are your bosses. This . . . could cost you your career"), the one thing Chase absolutely did not want to reveal was that he cared about his father—cared about him so much that news of his father's death could temporarily shake Chase's professional judgment. But however much he wanted to conceal the reason for his error, and however careless he is about the truth in minor matters, Chase couldn't bring himself to let Kayla's family go on thinking that he gave her the best possible care. So he claimed to have been hung over the day she came in, saving face at the expense of his reputation and very nearly his career.

But while Chase's mistake earned him a week's suspension and a letter in his permanent file, the fact that he insisted on taking credit for it also gained him some measure of respect from House. Pretending to have been hung over to cover up a genuine emotion was precisely the sort of lie House could understand, and one gets the idea that he likes Chase a little more after this experience. So perhaps Chase came out of "The Mistake" a winner after all. Especially if he can sort out the troublesome baggage he inherited from his father's life and death—the feelings of inadequacy and rebellion that seem to inspire his lies. A Chase at peace with his past could well turn out to be a Chase with less inclination to take liberties with the truth.

Assuming he can resist the temptation to identify a substitute father figure to do battle against. Let's see—Rowan Chase was a brilliant doctor, but an irascible, egotistical, and troubled human being. Who in Chase's immediate vicinity fits that profile?

> **DR. ALLISON CAMERON: (to House) I'm not expecting you to be someone you're not ("Love Hurts," 1-20).**

Except she is. Cameron wants to believe that House really cares about patients, and House keeps insisting all he cares about is the puzzle. She may have said, "I figured everything you do, you do it to help people. But I was wrong. You do it because it's right," in "Role Model" (1-17), but she still doesn't seem to believe it. Either her infatuation with House makes her see him as something he's not, or maybe, because of her infatuation, she has spotted something others miss: the occasional sign that House does care. After all, he never gives up until meeting an apparently insuperable obstacle. Cuddy issues an ultimatum. The patient refuses treatment. The disease proves incurable. Only then does he say, "I solved the case; my work is done," as he did in the pilot. Proof that he cares only about the puzzle, or a way of pretending he doesn't care? The flat, defeated tone of his voice suggested the latter.

If Cameron's deluding herself about House, it's typical of her approach to lying. She disapproves of it—witness her attempt to expose the cyclist's drug use in "Spin" (2-6)—and frequently protests House's unscrupulous tactics. But she lies, just the same—mainly to herself, about her own actions and motivations. House has her pegged: "You live under the delusion that you can fix everything that isn't perfect" ("Love Hurts").

A prime example was her inability to break bad news to a lung cancer patient for whom she felt considerable empathy in "Acceptance" (2-1). She procrastinated for several days, ordered test after pointless test, and basically lied to the patient, in the futile hope of finding a nonfatal diagnosis. She wasn't just trying to postpone telling the patient—she was lying to herself about her patient's prognosis, unable to accept her own inability to help.

As the series goes on, Cameron may be growing more of a spine, or perhaps just a better protective shell. In "Failure to Communicate" (2-10), she realized the patient was hiding something from his wife. ("Our little girl is growing up!" House exclaimed.) By season three, in "Que Será Será" (3-6), she had resorted to the Housian tactic of injecting a patient with something to keep him from leaving the hospital. And in "Informed Consent" (3-3), she, not House, punched the evil doctor's exit visa.

But still, it's all been about the patients. She hasn't yet lied for selfish purposes—unless you consider her all-consuming need to fix things selfish. And we've seen nothing to suggest that the new, tougher Cameron will learn to lead from her head instead of her heart. So maybe Cameron's not growing up after all. Maybe she's just been spending too much time around House.

DR. ERIC FOREMAN: Yeah, I'm just like him. Except for the angry, bitter, pompous, cripple part ("Poison," 1-8).

Cameron was accusing Foreman of being like House. An apt comparison in some ways—but where is House's penchant for playing fast and loose with facts? Foreman isn't as vocal as Cameron about House's deceptions, but he's clearly uncomfortable with them.

Yes, at first glance, Foreman looks like an exception to the rule that everybody lies. After all, Foreman's life is an open book. Especially now that House has outed him as a reformed juvenile delinquent, Foreman has nothing much to lie about, does he? And he obviously lies less than anyone else on the show.

That alone makes me want to keep an eye on him. He must be hiding something.

Foreman probably gave us the best clue to his relationship with the truth in the pilot episode: "You know what? After centuries of oppression, decades of civil rights marches, and more significantly living like a monk, never getting less then a 4.0 GPA, you don't think it's kind of disgusting I get one of the top jobs in the country because I'm a delinquent?"

Is that true, or has Foreman fallen for one of House's more outrageous lies? House seems to respect Foreman at least as much as the other juniors. For example, in "Autopsy" (2-2), when Foreman said that he saw the tumor they were all trying to find, House said, "That's good enough for me." House sets all the juniors off against one another, but he's slightly more apt to hold up Foreman as an example than Chase or Cameron. The evidence indicates that House hired Foreman because he was a highly competent neurologist.

But it doesn't matter whether or not House hired Foreman because of his juvenile record. As long as Foreman believes it (or at least can't completely talk himself out of it), he's allowing his life to be defined by someone else's opinion—or worse, someone else's mischievous lie.

And it's clearly bugging him.

Foreman presents the outward appearance of being cool, calm, and collected—at peace with his past, comfortable with his present, and confident of his future. But the façade of well-adjusted perfection is only that—a façade. Every so often, a crack appears, revealing all the baggage Foreman is carrying.

He may deny being as angry and bitter as House, but the denial rings false—he's clearly quite bitter about the difficult circumstances of his background. His bitterness is understandable—perhaps even justified—but it belies the image he tries so hard to project. He believes that he achieved his current status entirely through his own efforts. "Had to teach myself a lot of stuff," he said in "Needle in a Haystack" (3-13). "School sucked where I grew up." However, while his belief may, again, be justified, he has allowed it to make him intolerant of others' failure to achieve similar success. "My brother and I, we grew up in the same home. But I made something of myself. He didn't" ("Finding Judas," 3-9). And he resents his father's attitude toward his success: "He's not proud of me, he's proud of Jesus. Everything I do right is God's work; everything I do wrong is my own damn failing" ("Euphoria, Part 1," 2-20). In these moods, Foreman sounds uncomfortably like House—probably the reason that most of the time he tries to project his cool, rational persona.

But perhaps Foreman is beginning to realize that he's bought a little too heavily into the Horatio Alger myth. At the end of "Needle in a Haystack" (3-13), as he watched Stevie leave in the company of a troop of family members, and then again as he ate his solitary dinner, Foreman seemed more pensive than usual, as if he were thinking about what Stevie had said earlier: "You're a successful doctor. Your name is on journal articles. I would love that. It's just, I see you with doctors Chase and Cameron and you all got empty ring fingers. You're alone."

And one has to admire the way Foreman turned the tables on House in "Fools for Love" (3-5), when he bet that nurse Wendy was not dating Wilson—a bet he knew he would win because he was dating Wendy himself. A masterful scam, and he carried it off with a perfectly straight face, lying brilliantly without even saying a word.

Just the way House would have done it. We definitely need to keep an eye on Foreman.

HOUSE: Reality is almost always wrong ("Occam's Razor," 1-3).

Given the reality they live in, you can't really blame House's three harried juniors for lying. After all, they must have been lied to rather blatantly

229

before they took their current jobs. They're supposed to be fully qualified, board-certified doctors who have landed prestigious fellowships, and they spend an awful lot of time doing things that most hospitals delegate to the nurses, orderlies, and lab technicians.

In fact, with all due respect to the show's medical consultants, the picture *House* paints of the medical system is in many ways a reassuring lie. With limited exceptions, such as "Kids" (1-19), in which a possible meningitis epidemic swamps the ER, Princeton-Plainsboro Teaching Hospital is never overcrowded. It's an elegant, well-lit temple to the art and science of medicine, not a place designed to be regularly swabbed down and sterilized to prevent biohazards. And watching House's team at work creates the comforting illusion that if you ever come down with a really serious disease, you'll have an entire team of brilliant diagnosticians working day and night to solve your case.

Perhaps the most insidious lies on the show aren't told by the patients at all but by their bodies and diseases: The disease that presents with atypical, idiopathic symptoms, often because the patient is doing—and lying about—something that masks a key symptom (for example, the champion cyclist in "Spin" [2-6] with Pure Red Cell Aplasia that can't easily be diagnosed because of his blood doping and his hyperbaric sleeping chamber). The disease that hides behind another disease—preferably one whose standard treatment will make the hidden ailment that much worse (such as the kid in the aptly titled "Cursed" [1-13], who has both anthrax and leprosy). The tropical diseases not often seen in suburban New Jersey neighborhoods. The diseases so rare even House hasn't actually encountered them in real life. Not only can't you trust what the patients say, you can't trust their bodies to manifest the right symptoms for the diseases they've got. No wonder lying is so common in House's world. Everybody and everything lies.

Including, of course, House himself.

HOUSE: I NEVER lie! ("Pilot," 1-1).

But of course, he does. House doesn't lie less than most people. Maybe a little more. But he does spend a lot more time thinking about lies. This obsession probably dates from his childhood. As he confided to

Cameron after an awkward visit from his parents, "My dad's just like you. Not the caring 'til your eyes pop out part, just the insane moral compass that won't let you lie to anybody about anything. It's a great quality for Boy Scouts and police witnesses. Crappy quality for a dad" ("Daddy's Boy," 2-5).

House resents and rebels against his father's obsession with absolute truthfulness at all costs, and yet he has probably also internalized it. He doesn't shrug and say "everybody lies" with the casual disdain of a cynic—he thunders it with the passion of a true believer whose faith has been betrayed. So if House despises lying so utterly, why does he lie so much himself?

Well, it's more efficient. In "Skin Deep" (2-13), when House's leg pain had intensified, Foreman told him, ". . . you're going to want to rush everything; which is what you're doing. Don't." A keen insight, but has Foreman failed to notice that House has always rushed things? "Tests take time," House said in "Occam's Razor" (1-3). "Treatment's quicker." Just as telling the truth, following the rules and working within the system take time—lying's quicker. Cuts through all the nonsense. House will lie to the patients, to their families, to Cuddy, to other doctors, to the transplant board—to anyone, if he thinks it necessary to save a patient's life.

And while House might claim that it's not the patient's life but the puzzle that matters to him, the passion and desperation he feels about solving those puzzles contradicts his claim. How much House cares about the puzzle and how much about the patient is a riddle nobody, not even House—perhaps especially not House—can ultimately solve.

However much House may claim, out loud, that the end justifies the means, isn't it likely that he still measures himself against his father's standard and finds himself wanting? Lying's probably a major contributor to House's obvious self-loathing.

And since he's damned anyway by the lies he's told to save his patients, why not lie as much as he likes? To save himself trouble, to annoy Cuddy and Wilson, to play mind games on the Ducklings.

Or perhaps, considering his father's pathological addiction to truth, House finds lying a satisfying form of rebellion. Resentment of his father might also explain House's obsession with unmasking the lies of others:

if everybody lies, then his father's no exception. How much more comfortable must it be for House to believe that the stern taskmaster of his childhood is actually a hypocrite?

Is it any wonder that House felt conflicted about Chase's father's death and the events it triggered?

But at critical moments, House's ability to lie deserts him entirely. He wouldn't deliver the speech praising Vogler's underwhelming new drug, even though he knew not doing so would hurt him and his friends. He wouldn't apologize to Tritter because that would mean pretending to be sorry when he wasn't at all.

When, in "Honeymoon" (1-22), Cameron said, "I thought you were too screwed up to love anyone. I was wrong. You just couldn't love me," House stood mute. Since the storyline's still playing out, we won't know for a while—or may never know—if Cameron was right or wrong. Perhaps House doesn't know himself. But tellingly, he can't or won't provide a comforting lie.

When he finally won his months-long battle to take Stacy away from Mark, something—perhaps, again, that unwanted but inescapable moral compass—made him tell the truth: "I can't make you happy" ("Need to Know," 2-11). A hard truth—one that cost him the woman he loves. But not one he could hide.

Perhaps the most telling instance of House's inability to lie came in "Autopsy" (2-2), when the team was considering a dangerous diagnostic procedure on Andie, the nine-year-old who would still die of cancer in a year even if they cured the mysterious and more acute condition that brought her to House's team. Wilson obtained a consent form from Andie's mother, but it was House who insisted on telling Andie the truth about how dangerous the procedure was and giving her a choice whether or not to undergo it—a choice he wasn't given when they operated on his leg. House would have lied to her mother, if necessary, to give Andie the power to make her own decision. But he wouldn't—or couldn't—lie to Andie about her chances.

"It's a basic truth of the human condition that everybody lies," House said in "Three Stories" (1-21). "The only variable is about what." House can lie to anyone about anything—unless telling the truth is going to break his heart. Then, suddenly, he runs out of lies. Maybe it's only a symptom of his self-destructiveness, but maybe he has internalized some part of his father's attitude toward truth—the strong moral compass, minus any annoying self-righteous attitude.

Why does House lie? Because it works—except when it blows up in his face. Because he can—only sometimes, he can't. Because truth doesn't matter—except when it does. Deep down, I think House does care deeply about the truth. And maybe that's why Cameron, Wilson, Cuddy, and all the rest of us keep giving him one more chance.

The Penguin Who Knew Too Much (August 2007) is eighth in DONNA ANDREWS's Meg Langslow series from St. Martin's Press. She has also written the Turing Hopper series (Berkley Prime Crime), featuring an artificial intelligence as the sleuth. When not writing, Donna can be found puttering in her garden, making small inroads on her massive to-be-read collection, and playing with her computers. She's vice president of the Mid-Atlantic chapter of Mystery Writers of America, national chapter liaison for Sisters in Crime, the author liaison for Malice Domestic, and a member of the Private Investigators and Security Association. For more information visit http://donnaandrews.com.

Despite the name, House is a workplace show. With few exceptions, it takes place at the hospital—and the patients' homes are shown more often than the doctors' (usually as they're being broken into for clues). Jillian Hancock takes us through the characters' attitudes toward homes, their own and other people's, and what that says about them—particularly House himself.

HOUSE AND HOME

JILLIAN HANCOCK

There are few things as comforting as your home.

Stepping through the door is all it takes; you begin to relax before you even shrug off your coat. The color of the paint on the walls, the scent that lingers in the air, even the familiar way light floods in the window combine to result in a balm that goes far beyond the sum of its parts. Coming back home after a long absence completes a part of you.

So it must be unsettling to go to snip off your hospital bracelet only to find that the scissors aren't in that drawer where you've always left them. And the stained and moth-eaten sweatshirt you fold neatly under your pillow each morning is now wadded into a ball. By the time you get into the kitchen and discover that all of your sandwich ingredients have mysteriously vanished, you might wonder if you got your physical health back at the cost of your mind.

Having finally sawed through the plastic bracelet with a steak knife, you sit on the edge of your bed, uneasily twisting knots in the thin plastic strap, completely unaware that the explanation for your unease is literally at your fingertips:

ID: 58873
Adm: 12-31
Princeton-Plainsboro Teaching Hospital
Dr. Gregory House

"What sort of hospital has glass walls?"

Hypochondriacs must dream of getting admitted to a place like Princeton-Plainsboro; the hospital radiates a natural cleanliness through its architecture and design. The sign above the clinic glows a reassuringly antiseptic shade of neon blue; corridors gleam, enlarged by the light that pours through the atrium. Half of the walls in PPTH aren't proper walls at all but huge panes of glass split up into windows and sliding doors, creating long rows of human-sized terrariums containing all sorts of exotics: patients suffering severe allergic reactions, plague, bleeding eyeballs, lupus (. . . well, no, probably not lupus). Each and every specimen lies waiting for you behind a spotless pane of glass, ready to be poked and prodded and, just maybe, cured.

Luckily, Princeton-Plainsboro Teaching Hospital isn't all bleached coats and glass cleaner. What could seem like an alienating and sterile environment is warmed through by an insulating layer of wood paneling and moss-blue paint, and those giant panes of glass often offer a peek into spaces that are furnished more like libraries than offices. The elements of academia sprinkled around the set help to offset the more laboratory-like elements and make PPTH a soothing space for ill inhabitants. Just lie back in your private room, watch the spruces and evergreens waving in the wind. Enjoy a little *General Hospital*, even, because you're in capable hands.

Lulled into a sense of security yet? Good. Because right around now is when attractive doctors are breaking into your house, and they'd rather that you not freak out and interrupt them.

"A man's home is his castle," the saying goes. It's as true as ever—only now, instead of medieval fortifications of stone and iron, we surround ourselves with far more personalized barriers like furnishings and paintings, family photos, pets. A quick bout of channel-surfing will turn up a huge number of home design shows, all offering to help you project your inner personality onto your inner walls. While it's wrong to judge a book by its cover, we're told, it's perfectly reasonable to judge a person by their décor.

But a home isn't just about how we project our ideal selves onto our surroundings, it's also a history of what we're truly like, a trail of clues we unintentionally leave behind as a result of everyday living. Our natural instinct to tidy up when expecting a visitor is an impulse to hide behaviors or belongings that we don't want to display, and those are exactly the details of life that are most interesting to any investigator. The home of a patient with a sudden illness is ideal for forensic work, frozen precisely at the moment of illness with all possible sins laid bare. So, House wonders incredulously, why on earth would you want to make the detective work harder on yourself?

"Would the police call for permission before dropping by to check out a crime scene?" House exploded when Foreman initially suggested asking the patient for a set of keys. His phrasing wasn't accidental. Unlike most doctors who see their patients as unfortunate victims, House views all his patients as suspects, very possibly complicit in their own illness. And much like a rogue private eye, House will pursue any angle to solve his case. His shifty-at-best relationship with the law puts him in difficult situations at times, but his near-misses allow us a glimpse of how House views himself in relation to the laws that govern other people. Like detectives and FBI agents who find occasions when they're forced to act outside of the law, House sees his role as diagnostician to merely be the medical parallel. Sure, it hasn't got the legal framework to support it, but everyone else is just behind the times. With the noblest of all intentions, the saving of a life, House believes almost anything to be justifiable.

He can't do it alone, though. And as House's reluctant version of a S.W.A.T. team, Cameron, Foreman, and Chase are frequently deployed to do the dirty work.

House marks a first for hospital shows in the sheer number of questionable or flat-out illegal practices shown, and it's certainly unusual in that its protagonists seem to get away with their crimes scot-free. Whether this is a case of grateful patients glossing over the details or simply a matter of time is yet to be seen. To date, the young doctors at PPTH's diagnostics unit have smashed, stolen, and eaten their way through more residences than any show since *Law & Order*. And with two years of experience behind them, the House team shows no signs of stopping.

We were barely past the pilot's first commercial break before House asked his staff to commit a misdemeanor, establishing breaking and entering as a major theme of the series. Going from their shocked expressions, this was the first time House had made this particular request. The aversion didn't last long, though—House had his team so well trained by the end of season two that even the threat of divine retribution couldn't dissuade them. In the episode "House vs. God" (2-19), there were plenty of excellent reasons not to break into cancer patient Grace's home, including the pretty major hurdle that she wasn't actually House's patient. But not even the possibility of the direct gaze of the Almighty can break the B&E habit once it's ingrained. And considering how many lives have been saved since they started their white-coated crime spree, who could blame them?

Of course, you can't send out a totally green crew on such an important job; newbie criminals are going to need an old hand to show them the ropes. And if you're looking for someone to commit a crime, Foreman's your man—at least, according to House. He wasted no time in bringing up Foreman's criminal past, a juvenile record that included at least one prior conviction for B&E. He even pretended to be surprised that Foreman would have a problem with breaking a few windows to get what's needed. "Isn't that how you got into the Feltgers' home?" he goaded as Foreman seethed ("Pilot," 1-1). But in spite of the constant jibes House aims his way about his (supposedly sealed) juvenile record, Foreman still steps up to take on much of the house-casing duties his boss demands, showing that he does see the merit in bending the occasional rule to get results. Aside from the sporadic raiding of fridges, Foreman's excursions are professional ventures that bring back the necessary info no matter what his personal feelings are toward the patient involved. Even when entering the filthy home of a bent cop (and later contracting his deadly disease) in "Euphoria, Part 1" (2-20), Foreman remained level-headed and clinical, though not above editorializing as he meticulously sealed his evidence bags.

Chase, on the other hand, has a relatively bad run with his B&E

assignments— though you have to wonder how much of that has to do with luck and how much the boy brings upon himself. This is, after all, the same man who broke into a closet full of S&M gear in "Love Hurts" (1-20), knelt down and stared a bondage mask in the eye, and then promptly filched a handful of mints from the Pandora's Box below. While Chase seems to have a keen survival instinct when faced with the possibility of immediate career jeopardy or physical harm (such as wisely refusing to mingle with a prison's general population during "Acceptance" [2-1]), he also has some pretty incredible lapses of judgment when it comes to more subtle dangers.

Somehow, Chase always seems to be the one assigned to the least defensible break-ins, such as the empty house in "Cursed" (1-13) (when he ended up falling out of a tree to evade police) and more egregiously, the break-in during "House vs. God" (2-19), when Chase found himself without an excuse as keys rattled outside the apartment door. It was quickly revealed that there was nothing to fear, as Wilson was the live-in love and safely seated at House's table at the time, but it added up to a very tense few minutes for the cowering Chase (perhaps a sign of divine karma for the former seminary student). There's also the small matter of breaking into Stacy's home, where Chase and Foreman discovered a plate of cookies that literally had their name on it. Foreman, perhaps because he'd met House and was justifiably wary of the mind of a woman who could survive five years as his partner, didn't seem too interested in the snack, but Chase munched his way well into the next scene. It's amazing that the next episode didn't focus on the mysterious poisoning of a handsome blond Australian.

"When you break into someone's house, it's always better to have a white chick with you."

It's tough to say how far beyond Foreman's initial assessment of Cameron we should go; for someone known for getting over-involved with her patients, Cameron's remarkably cavalier about her role in their break-ins. It's not because she doesn't care—that's an impossibility with Cameron. But what fascinates her is the home's inhabitant, and with that person already a patient in the hospital, there's not much material for

Cameron to work with in an empty house. As far as she's concerned, she's already got everything she needs. As a result, her top priority during most field trips is typically the opportunity to work on her office gossip, often to the annoyance of her partner in crime.

Though a wash in the B&E stakes, Cameron is certainly the best example in the *House* universe of how we treat our homes as an extension of ourselves. Cameron's apartment (a bland, neutrally agreeable space) appears only fleetingly in the series, but its threshold features prominently in these scenes.

When Cameron demonstrated her propensity for self-sacrifice by resigning during Vogler's rule, House made the unusual move of actually going to her home. Ever the workaholic, Cameron was halfway through a treadmill routine and answered the door in her sweaty workout clothes. It was only natural to predict that she'd invite him in. Her history practically demands it, ticking off most of her requirements—she adores House as a person, and as a doctor she's inclined to cater to his disability. She also probably would have liked to change into something less sweaty before talking, and propriety generally requires that you invite a visitor into your home. But Cameron made a very different choice: she used her threshold as a bargaining chip, something that an astute observer of human behavior like House would instantly pick up on as unusual. The threshold became a figurative line in the sand for Cameron as she set her terms: either she got access to the welded-shut personal side of House (in the form of a date), or he didn't get any more access at all to Cameron.

The sanctity of Cameron's home was only reinforced in her later interactions with Chase. During the second season episode "Hunting" (2-7), after being goaded about her straight-laced personality by AIDS patient Calvin, she decided to experiment. Cameron's walk on the wild side was a rather contained trip. She palmed drugs only once they'd been cleared by the hospital's lab, and then carefully waited until her door was firmly closed to take them. It's unclear as to whether Cameron called Chase before or after she took the pills, but once he arrived on her doorstep she left no doubt as to why she'd invited him there. Apparently lured there by a last-minute acceptance of a drink, he found her wild-eyed and clearly high. Tellingly, it was only after she'd gotten him inside the door that she really went for it; only with four solid, familiar walls enclosing her could Cameron feel safe enough to indulge her impulses. It was a compromise for her, located somewhere between her goody-two-shoes image and the lifestyle her "party and play, drugs and sex" patient taunted her about. And for one night, she had decided that Chase could be trusted to help her keep those barriers up.

Maybe it's this fixation with her own boundaries that makes Cameron so hardheaded in trying to break down the walls of others. Because, more than anything else, Allison Cameron is devoted to getting into the guarded, ever-vigilant fortress that is House.

> CHASE: How'd you like it if I interfered in your personal life?
> HOUSE: I'd hate it. That's why, cleverly, I have no personal life ("Cursed," 1-13).

Breaking into House is no mean feat.

For a man who violates the privacy of others so casually, House is fiercely protective of his own space. He's learned lessons from the way he's treated his patients, and House's minions have already experienced the sort of emotional B&E which is his specialty. The death of Cameron's husband, Foreman's juvenile record, Chase's father's illness—House collects these details like a wicked magpie, dropping them into conversation as blackmail or when he's looking for a reaction. Cuddy got a taste of the more conventional form of B&E when House, Chase, and Foreman used her spare key to rampage through her thong drawer during "Humpty Dumpty" (2-3), but even then, part of his goal was to get a reaction. House knows all the tricks of the B&E trade and is well prepared to fend off all attempts to turn the techniques back on him.

It's useless to take House's physical surroundings as any indication of his character, other than to note the way both his home and office seem defiantly impersonal. House's office couldn't be picked out of a lineup without his trusty Magic 8 Ball or cane featured prominently, and Cameron once made the unpleasant observation that House's home décor seemed to mirror that of her obese shut-in patient. It's clear that House has not been surfing the cable home improvement shows, or if he has, he took them as a warning. To find out more about House, you have to go well beyond peeking into a few cupboards. You have to get a glimpse inside the man himself.

Casing House isn't a promising prospect for an interloper. He's made of solid brick, slightly scuffed and dilapidated, ringed with barbed wire and unkempt lawns. Even loitering on the outskirts of the property leaves you with the uncomfortable feeling that you're being watched. He's also a House with an unusual feature—where most houses mark their boundaries with white picket fences or stone walls, House has surrounded himself with formidable drifts of tiny, pebble-sized pills.

House's Vicodin habit is no secret; the muscle death in his thigh makes life without pain medication agony, or so he insists. But as Cuddy showed when she substituted his medication, House's reliance on the pills isn't so much a medical need as an emotional crutch. Though the Vicodin initially took the edge off of what we saw as excruciating physical pain, it's now taking the edge off all the other things that cause House discomfort. Like the man who walls or fences his property off from the rest of the world, House has laid foundations to keep the sharp edges of the world out—perhaps accidentally at first, but now deliberately, adding to the wall every time he dry-swallows another tablet.

For those brave or stupid enough to clamber over the Vicodin barrier, things only get more difficult. House's own parents never seem to get past the front door; most of the time, he just shuts off all the lights and pretends he's not home. Wilson discovered just how conflicted House is about Houseguests when he found himself trapped in what amounted to an emotional revolving door in season two. As House wavered wildly between jealously guarding his own space and enjoying the company of another human being, he put Wilson through hell. Given the reception House gives people who make it into his fortress, maybe the fact that he continually turns Cameron away is more an act of mercy than anything else.

House keeps his inner life like a series of locked rooms, all barely touching and never interacting. He keeps his parents from his coworkers, his card game from his friend, his emotions from his actions. It's hard to say whether House actually prefers his life to be so segmented; maybe he's just gotten used to it, and is too set in his ways to change them now. But even the steadiest traveler can be blown off-course by a chance wind. Unexpectedly, one person made it all the way to House's inner sanctum, so stealthily that he seemed shocked to turn and suddenly find her there. Of course, it helped that she had a map—she'd been there before.

House's pursuit of Stacy Warner started as just another con. He played his usual tricks: he sent his goons to her house, he spied, he rifled through her therapist's files and fashioned them into the perfect skeleton key. It's hard to tell exactly what House's goal was in all of this; it's possible not even he knew at the start. But that didn't stop House. In a more literal way than ever before, House established himself in her home, and then set about establishing himself in her heart, a more complete B&E operation than he'd ever attempted before.

But he missed a crucial detail in his mad pursuit. Stacy wasn't like his other pet projects. From the very first time we meet her, it was clear that House had found his match all those years ago. Sharp and witty and certainly on to him, Stacy was more clued in than anyone House had tried to hoodwink before. As he worked diligently on getting past her defenses, Stacy was just as effectively sneaking under House's guard. Where House might have expected to lure Stacy unwittingly into an affair, he seemed genuinely surprised to find her waiting for him, with all her wits firmly intact. Unfortunately, gaining entry isn't everything. Despite Stacy's familiarity with and acceptance of every shadowy corner House has, in the end he couldn't help himself and turned her away, returning to his shuttered emotional state, alone.

This combination of shut-in décor and emotional fortress would be suffocating, but House does have one last option in his search for a place to hang his hat: the place he loves to hate, the hospital.

The glassed corridors and soothing greens are unlikely to make much of an impression on House as he charges through the halls, cane thumping heavily on the tile. While his crew pry windows open and clamber through greenhouses, House traces the invisible patterns left by thought and behavior, assembling a picture based on the tiny clues that only he can see. The misanthropic behavior that gets him into trouble in every other segment of his life is a gift here, as he not only ignores personal boundaries, but is often commended for doing so. In the hospital, just being himself makes House a hero. In society, being himself makes

House a jerk.

To House, PPTH is an intellectual home like no other, a toy shop full of puzzles—and he has the key. With the pharmacy right down the hall and colleagues waiting for his word, the hospital provides House with the sort of structure the rest of his life lacks. For some people, it's a temporary refuge; for others, it's the last stop on the line. For House, it's home.

JILLIAN HANCOCK lives on the edge of the known world in Wellington, New Zealand. Information architect by day, writer by night, she spends her free time trapped in a complex barter cycle with ruthless pirates—but can't really talk about it. Whenever the pirate cartel gets her down she reminds herself that somewhere, someone is doing an interpretive dance, which cheers her right up. Like everyone else in NZ, she knows a Hobbit personally.

In the pilot episode, Drs. Cameron, Foreman, and Chase were preoccupied with figuring out why House hired them—or Cameron was, anyway. At the end of the episode, having gotten her answer, she still seemed dissatisfied. With good reason: it was House giving it to her, after all, and he's no exception to his own maxim, "Everybody lies." Cameron would have done better to ask Shanna Swendson.

BUILDING
FRANKENSTEIN'S DOCTOR

The Component Parts of Dr. House

SHANNA SWENDSON

d
r. Gregory House is one of the most complex and fascinating characters on network television today. He's equally brilliant, clever, creative, infuriating, stubborn, arrogant, witty, curious, and troubled. The creators of the series *House M.D.* gave themselves room to fully explore House by surrounding him with people who reflect various aspects of his character. Each of the three fellows working for House embodies a crucial element (or two) of House's character. Or, depending on how you look at it, House's team is a sort of Frankenstein's monster, another House built from component parts. This allows those key traits to be isolated and taken to extremes or inverted while being put in direct opposition with each other and with House himself.

House is arrogant and outspoken, with no respect for rank or position—a trait reflected in Dr. Eric Foreman, the team's neurologist. House is insatiably curious and won't quit until he finds the answer he needs—something we also see in Dr. Allison Cameron, the immunologist of the group. House is troubled, as well, with physical pain, a dependence on painkillers, and plenty of emotional baggage. Dr. Robert Chase, the intensive care specialist, is a lost soul who reflects some of House's baggage and his troubled past.

The pilot episode lays out these characterizations. In his very first appearance on the series, Foreman challenged House's approach to medicine and his insistence that there was something more unusual than a tumor affecting their patient. At that point, Foreman had only recently joined the team, but he was already arguing with House about the very basis of the Diagnostic Medicine department. In a department that's supposed to be about solving "zebra" cases, Foreman disputed House's interpretation of what the metaphorical hoofbeats meant.

Cameron likewise demonstrated her core characterization in this episode. Once she learned why House hired Foreman, she couldn't rest until she knew why he had hired her. She discussed it in-depth with Foreman, comparing the schools they went to, their grades, and their other credentials—even as they were supposed to be searching the patient's home for clues about her illness. When Cameron couldn't figure it out on her own, she went to demand an answer from House.

Although we didn't receive any information on Chase's back story in the pilot, we did see that he identified enough with the way their patient was essentially alone in the world that he arranged to have her students visit her. We also got a sense of separation and aloofness from the way he sometimes stood apart from the other fellows. He was often standing to the side instead of within the group, and he was the last one to speak in the scene that introduced the team.

As the series progressed, we saw these traits develop further, and we started to learn why each of these characters was this way, as well as how they mirrored House's core traits.

Foreman: House's Arrogant, Outspoken, Argumentative Side

"You're just as pompous and arrogant as he is."
— patient's mother to Dr. Eric Foreman ("Poison," 1-8)

Although there's a lot about House that's unhealthy—his leg, his love life, and very likely his liver (given the amount of acetaminophen in the

Vicodin pills he pops like Tic Tacs and washes down with plenty of alcohol)—you couldn't call his ego anything but healthy, and he has good reason. He's a brilliant enough doctor to have an entire department built around his unique abilities and interests. He gets to hand-pick his staff of specialists, come and go as he pleases, refuse to wear a lab coat, and take only the cases that interest him. In fact, he got to see just how much the hospital valued him when the board was willing to give up a $100 million donation rather than fire him. This is because he's almost always right, and he can solve cases nobody else can. If House weren't on the case, the kind of patients who are sent to him would almost surely die, and that gives him the leeway to say and do almost anything he wants.

In Foreman, House's traits of arrogance and outspokenness are isolated and magnified. He's still a fellow in a learning position, so he doesn't yet have the goods to back up his swagger. For now, he just has the swagger. Like House, he has to be right about everything. Unfortunately, he often isn't. That doesn't stop him from arguing his point until it's absolutely proven wrong—and even then, he'll claim that the test, not him, was wrong, and the doctor who conducted the test must have screwed up. When Foreman ended up as a patient with a mysterious illness himself, he continued arguing with House and insisting that House was wrong, even as he was blind, in terrible pain, and dying. He learned that Cameron was writing a paper on one of their cases and wrote his own on the same case, then got House to sign off on it and submit it to a journal while Cameron was still waiting on House's approval—and then showed no remorse for having done so. He seemed to think that she could have done the same thing, and that it wasn't his problem if she wasn't as smart as he was.

Foreman is the one of the three fellows most often compared to House, probably because arrogance is House's most obvious trait, one people notice even on short acquaintance. When House sent Foreman to cover his clinic hours for him and a patient complained about Foreman's attitude, it was House who got scolded—and the dean of medicine never knew that she and the patient were actually talking about two different men. Of course, the traits we possess are the ones that are most likely to annoy us in others, and Foreman is the fellow most likely to object to House's arrogance. He once remarked that it wouldn't hurt House to learn a little humility, and he relished the opportunity to take over the department when House was suspended.

While the writers may have developed Foreman's character as a way of exploring this particular facet of House, within the world of the series it appears that House himself chose Foreman for this quality. When Foreman returned from his serious illness and near-death experience with a changed attitude, House missed the arguing, even demanding that Foreman please start arguing with him again. House wanted the challenge Foreman presented; the constant arguing was an important part of House's thinking process. When House had to deal with a case while away from his team and created a substitute team to help him work, the role he assigned to the Foreman substitute was disagreeing with everything he said.

Foreman is also an essential part of the team because of his ability to say no to House. He's a balance to House, and his stubborn insistence that House is always wrong is part of what forces House to ultimately be right. House said he hired Foreman in part because of his juvenile criminal record—he saw Foreman as someone who was street smart enough that he couldn't be conned, and it turns out that even House can't usually get away with conning him. If House's reaction to Foreman's arrogance reflects how House sees it in himself, this could be a sign that House prizes his own arrogance and outspokenness—that it's something he feels no need to change. As House says, humility is an important quality for someone who is wrong a lot. If you're right, there's no need to be humble.

But Foreman takes the trait of arrogance one step further than House does. House may believe that he's right and everyone else around him is an idiot, but he doesn't pass moral judgment on people. He doesn't care enough to think about whether someone is good or bad, right or wrong (except in the medical sense). Foreman, however, is keen to pass judgment on others. He judges patients he feels don't deserve to be treated, such as the homeless woman he thought was working the system in "Histories" (1-10), the murderer in "Acceptance" (2-1) who he felt deserved to die because of his crimes, or the HIV-positive patient in "Hunting" (2-7) who Foreman believed could have avoided a lot of problems for himself and his family if he'd just had safe sex. He also judges his colleagues, seeing House as a junkie, Cameron as overly soft-hearted, and Chase as a spoiled rich kid who doesn't care about his job. He's unable to separate the person from the symptoms, and because of this, it often affects his medical judgment.

As Foreman grows as both a doctor and as a character by working with House, he's gradually learning some humility. Being in House's shoes as head of the department made him realize the pressure of having the final call with no one to fall back on, and his experience as a patient has made him slightly more tolerant of patients, their fears, and their foibles, even as he remains arrogant with his colleagues. By the time House is through with him, he may even have the skills to justify that arrogance.

Cameron: House's Curious and Persistent Sides

> "It's not a power play. Doing a differential in the clinic makes sense—piss Cuddy off. Same thing with Wilson's office—works indirectly. But now we are in office space because you don't want to be in your own office, which means this has nothing to do with Cuddy. You really are obsessed with your carpet, which means—"
> —Cameron to House ("Lines in the Sand," 3-4)

One of the traits that helps make House so successful as a diagnostician is his curiosity. He can't let a puzzle go unsolved, whether medical or personal—and often the personal puzzle is key to the medical puzzle. He won't let any question go unanswered. The surest way to pique his interest in a case is to show him an anomaly, something that doesn't fit or make sense, and he won't stop searching for the answer until he's sure he's found it—even if it's more than a decade after the patient's death. He's equally nosy about the lives of the people around him. He's snooped, broken into lockers, stolen confidential files, accessed medical records, dug through trash cans, and confronted people to demand information when he's been curious about his employees or colleagues. His friend Dr. James Wilson couldn't wear a new tie to work without House investigating whether or not he was cheating on his wife with someone at the hospital, and Wilson couldn't talk to a new nurse in the hallway without House looking for evidence to prove that Wilson was dating her. House stole notes from his ex-girlfriend's therapy sessions so he could find out what was going on in her marriage. He read Cameron's medical records to understand why she reacted the way she did to a case in which infants were critically ill. Because House tracked down clues after seeing things that made him curious, he knew that Chase's father was dying of cancer long before Chase did, and he's about the only person who has managed to actually get personal information out of the intensely private Chase.

Cameron is the team member who reflects this trait. She makes it her business to know things about the people around her, whether patients or colleagues, and she's as persistent as House in tracking down any information that interests her. Because of this, she's been known to go overboard in obtaining patient histories. She doesn't just get medical details, she delves into family and personal lives. This has been beneficial at times, such as the case in which her knowing that a female teenage athlete had been feeling depressed eventually led to a diagnosis of cancer that otherwise might not have been discovered until it was too late, but at other times her emotional involvement has distracted her from the case.

The topic that Cameron is most persistently curious about is House himself. She asked him outright how he felt about her and later demanded that he take her out on a date so she could learn more about him. She's asked just about anyone who knew House before she met him about their history with him, she arranged things so that House would have to have dinner with his visiting parents—so she could meet them—and was as obsessed with finding out why House was obsessed with having his office carpet replaced as House was obsessed with the carpet, to the point that she had to be reminded about the case they were working on. She's even become curious about a patient and tried to understand the patient's life largely because there were aspects of the patient that reminded her of House.

Cameron takes this curiosity and persistence even further than House does because she actually cares about the people involved. He just sees puzzles, with behavior as clues to solving the puzzle, and once the puzzle's solved, he moves on to the next one. But she gets more personally and emotionally involved the more she knows about a person—a trait that sometimes affects her medical judgment. When House suggested that a patient was about to leave her girlfriend, Cameron got nosy and started asking questions to find out what really was going on in the patient's life. That led to a moral dilemma when the girlfriend was willing to donate part of her liver to the patient, and Cameron felt the girlfriend deserved to know the true status of the relationship—even though the girlfriend might then not donate the liver, and the patient might die. Her caring can also lead her to be persistent in the opposite direction, as when she bonded with a lonely patient who very likely had cancer and then insisted on doing every test but the one that would definitively prove cancer. Her extreme caring, which came from knowing more about the patient than was medically relevant, made her incapable of accepting the truth.

While her curiosity and her persistence in obtaining information may be annoying to House and her colleagues at times, it's a trait they do sometimes value. House spotlighted her caring and devotion to personal detail (and mocked it some, too) when he lectured medical students about diagnostics. Foreman made her his medical proxy when he was critically ill because he knew she'd care enough to want to do the right thing for him and would be persistent enough to carry it through. House accepts her curiosity and persistence as long as it's not directed at him, even if he doesn't respect the way her collection of personal knowledge about others makes her care more about them. Her persistence is one of the reasons he hired her. He told her he hired her because she was pretty, but went on to explain that, because she was pretty, she'd worked harder than she needed to. She could have gotten by on her looks alone, but she went through all the hard work of medical school, internship, residency, and now a challenging fellowship. Presumably, he expects her to apply this persistence to the work of treating patients. Even if he's not around, he can count on her to keep prodding the others into finding answers.

Chase: House's Troubled and Clever Sides

"I tell you my dad left, my mum drank herself to death, you gonna care about me more?"

—Chase to House ("Cursed," 1-13)

House's arrogance and often obnoxious behavior is somewhat explained by the fact that he's physically and emotionally wounded. An undiagnosed infarction left dead muscle in his leg that causes him constant pain, requires painkillers for him to function, and forces him to use a cane to walk. Emotional fallout from his leg led to the dissolution of a long-term relationship and left him reluctant to even try to love again. He frequently wears his pain and disability on his sleeve, flaunting it to get sympathy or forgiveness; it's the trump card he plays when he wants to get out of something or wants to make someone feel guilty. Emotionally, he tries to drive people away or keeps them at a distance. He constantly tests his best friend's loyalty by making it almost impossible to remain friends with him. Although we don't yet know House's entire back story, the indications are that he chose his emotional isolation. He didn't have a good relationship with his father and had mentioned that his father was such a stern disciplinarian that his actions could have been called abuse, but his parents are still alive, and he says that his mother loves him unconditionally—yet he only consents to see either of them when he can't lie or trick his way out of it. His long-term friends say that he was the same way before his leg was damaged, and even he admits that he's been alienating people since childhood.

Frequently in fiction (and sometimes in real life), a troubled back story in a character is paired with certain creative or intellectual gifts. Appropriately, House's main strength as a diagnostician is his creative thinking. He makes unexpected logical leaps, coming to solutions due to inspiration from entirely unrelated things (a teenage girl's red thong underwear, for instance, which led him to run a test involving red dye). Sometimes even he can't show the scientific proof that leads to his conclusions, but his conclusions are still right. He figured out what was wrong with a paralyzed patient, but couldn't come up with enough proof to convince his boss to authorize the treatment—and then turned out to be right when she tried the treatment just on the basis of his track record.

Chase is the fellow that represents this "tortured genius" side of House. His back story sounds almost like something out of Dickens, and is enough to make House look like a whiner in comparison. Chase's father, a renowned rheumatologist, never made time for his son, and then left entirely when he couldn't take living with his alcoholic wife anymore. In doing so, he left his teenage son alone to care for his mother while she drank herself to death. Chase entered the seminary with the intention of becoming a Catholic priest, but left to become a doctor—according to House's theory (which Chase never confirmed or denied), at his father's insistence. Chase's father never told him he was dying of cancer, and Chase was so blindsided by the news of his father's death that he made a critical error that led to a patient's death. Then he learned that his father cut him out of his will.

Unlike House, Chase doesn't wear his pain on his sleeve. He's reluctant to let anyone know what he's been through, and he doesn't want pity. He's romantically interested in Cameron, but although, as House pointed out to him, she'd likely care more for him if she knew about his past, he's never told her anything and even rudely brushed her off when she tried to ask questions about his strained relationship with his father. We haven't seen enough of him away from work to know whether he's as bad about keeping people at bay emotionally as House is in his personal life, but he does keep his colleagues at a distance. He allows them to think the worst of him, that he's a slacker who doesn't care about his job or that he's a spoiled rich kid who only got his position because his father pulled some strings, rather than admit to what his life has really been like.

But he also shares House's positive trait of out-of-the-box thinking. He's come up with creative solutions like using an x-ray instead of an invasive test to convince a reluctant patient of the ultimate diagnosis, finding a way to save a patient's eye from a blood clot without interfering with other treatment, and using transcranial ultrasound when the MRI machine wasn't available. He often is the one to initially suggest the diagnosis that ultimately proves to be right, but lacks the proof to justify tests or treatments at that point. He's the one fellow who has even beaten House at his own game, coming up with the correct diagnosis when House got it wrong—and he did it in a very House-like way, inspired by a laser pointer to guess that light was what affected the patient.

Chase's traumatic past and resulting emotional issues hold him back from really benefiting from his cleverness. He avoids conflict when at all possible and will back down when challenged unless he's truly and completely convinced he's right. He's more likely to shut down and put up emotional barriers than to defend himself when he's attacked. When his position is threatened, instead of fighting for it openly he maneuvers behind the scenes, as in the case when House was told he'd have to fire a member of his team. Chase gathered incriminating evidence about some of House's misdeeds and fed it to the hospital chairman in return for his job being protected. It may have been lack of confidence that he would be chosen to stay or an inability to believe that he could count on anyone else looking out for his interests—which would be understandable, given his parents—that led him to fight for his job that way rather than trying to prove that he was an asset to the team.

We don't know exactly why House hired Chase. He mentioned off-hand that it was because Chase's father made a phone call, but that doesn't fit with what we know of either House or Chase. House has never been one to bow to authority or influence, or to do anyone a personal favor, so it's unlikely that he'd have hired Chase because his famous father pulled some strings. Meanwhile, Chase's strained relationship with his father and resentment of him make it unlikely that he'd be willing to ask for his father's assistance in getting ahead. Chances are that just as there was a deeper explanation behind House hiring Cameron for her looks, there was more to House hiring Chase than Chase's father making a phone call.

Looking at the way House treats Chase, we can see that House seems to recognize his potential and his failings, for he constantly prods Chase and tries to goad him into doing more and better. He issues challenges and attempts reverse psychology, calling Chase an idiot on a regular basis, possibly because he recognizes the seeds of his own brand of cleverness and is frustrated when Chase doesn't follow through in pursuing his better ideas. But when things are really tough for Chase, such as with his father's death, House can show a rare sensitive side in dealing with his fellow. House may play up his own woes to his advantage, but perhaps he does it because it's a pre-emptive strike against true pity, and he seems to respect that Chase wants no pity, either.

The Team: Frankenstein's Doctor

"Okay, I'll be you guys. [bad Australian accent] No way, mate, too much blood to be just a vein. ["Homeboy" accent] No way, Hizzy. If it were an artery, he'd still be bleeding. [in falsetto] Actually, he'd be dead."
                              —House to his team ("No Reason," 2-24)

In spite of—or perhaps because of—his flaws, House is one of the best doctors around, and examining his traits as they're embodied in his fellows shows why. Individually, the young doctors can't accomplish much. Chase may have the bright ideas, but without Foreman's arrogance or Cameron's persistence, he doesn't fight for them, which means he seldom gets credit for the correct diagnosis even if he's the one who came up with it during early discussions. Foreman may be arrogant and outspoken enough to press his own views, but his views are often wrong because he lacks Chase's creativity and Cameron's curiosity. Cameron may care until her eyes pop out, as House accused her, but not having been through the kind of childhood trauma Chase faced, she struggles when the real world doesn't match her idealistic view, and she isn't bold enough to be like Foreman and push things through even in situations where life really isn't fair.

But because House has all of these traits, he's able to solve the case and help people (although he claims he doesn't care about them as people). As brilliant as House is, he may even have deliberately hired a team that reflected himself. He certainly works to stir up conflict within the team so that these traits are put into opposition and tested against each other. If the fellows really worked as a team, cooperating instead of opposing each other at every turn, chances are they'd be more successful and possibly even beat House from time to time. Instead, House keeps them at odds so that he can use their arguments to test and stimulate his own thinking. That way, he gets to be the one to solve the puzzle.

After all, he's the one whose name is the show's title. The fellows can win when they get their own series.

SHANNA SWENDSON's first job out of college was in the public information office at a medical school, and while she didn't know a real Dr. House, she did have to work with the personifications of a few of his more interesting traits (to put it nicely). Now she's primarily a novelist, the author of *Enchanted, Inc.*, *Once Upon Stilettos*, and *Damsel Under Stress*. She's also contributed to *Flirting with Pride and Prejudice*, *Welcome to Wisteria Lane*, *So Say We All*, and *Perfectly Plum*, and she still does the occasional bit of medical writing. Visit her Web site at www.shannaswendson.com.